Wittgenstein and the End of Philosophy

Wittgenstein and the End of Philosophy

Neither Theory nor Therapy

Daniel D. Hutto
Professor of Philosophical Psychology
University of Hertfordshire

First published 2003 by
PALGRAVE MACMILLAN
Houndmills, Basingstoke, Hampshire RG21 6XS and 175 Fifth Avenue, New York, N.Y. 10010
Companies and representatives throughout the world

PALGRAVE MACMILLAN is the global academic imprint of the Palgrave Macmillan division of St. Martin's Press, LLC and of Palgrave Macmillan Ltd. Macmillan® is a registered trademark in the United States, United Kingdom and other countries. Palgrave is a registered trademark in the European Union and other countries.

ISBN 0–333–91880–0 hardback

This book is printed on paper suitable for recycling and made from fully managed and sustained forest sources.

A catalogue record for this book is available from the British Library.

Library of Congress Cataloging-in-Publication Data

Hutto, Daniel D.
    Wittgenstein and the end of philosophy : neither theory nor therapy / Daniel D. Hutto.
        p. cm.
    Includes bibliographical references (p.) and index.
    ISBN 0–333–91880–0
    1. Wittgenstein, Ludwig, 1889–1951. Tractatus logico-philosophicus.
    2. Logic, Symbolic and mathematical. 3. Language and languages – Philosophy. I. Title.

    B3376.W563 T73353
    192–dc21
                                                                2003049807

10   9   8   7   6   5   4   3   2   1
12 11 10 09 08 07 06 05 04 03

Printed and bound in Great Britain by
Antony Rowe Ltd, Chippenham and Eastbourne

For my son, Alexander,
Non nova sed nove

Contents

Acknowledgements

I don't believe I have ever invented a line of thinking, I have
always taken one over from someone else.

Wittgenstein 1980, CV, p. 19e

As an undergraduate at St. Andrews, one of my first impressions of
philosophy was that it seemed only to encourage interminable disputes
that permitted no resolution. However, I had been attending lectures on
practical ethics in the Moral Philosophy department. When I made my
complaint to the then Chairman of Philosophy in the hope of changing
subjects altogether he advised a more moderate course, switching to the
study of Logic and Metaphysics. Although this made me much happier,
it is not until writing this book that I have had the opportunity to return
to the question of why certain fundamental issues in philosophy have to
be approached in a particular way, giving the issue the proper and
detailed attention it deserves. Ironically, as the final chapter of this book
suggests, I now understand that seeing this in the right light should cause
one to re-evaluate what is going on, and what role philosophers might
play, in debates on important matters such as ethics.

My greatest debt of thanks is owed to my to wife Farah and boys,
Alex, Rais and Emerson, who have been unfairly robbed of my time
while I have been writing this book. It has interrupted weekends and
encroached on family holidays for far too long. I am grateful to all of
the following philosophers, whose comments have helped to refine my
thinking on many important issues: Gary Banham, Ignar Brinck, Paul
Coates, Dan Fitzpatrick, Phil Hutchinson, Brendan Larvor, John Lippitt,
Richard Menary, Peter and Daniele Moyal-Sharrock, Rupert Read,
Anthony Rudd, Jane Singleton, David Simpson, Barry Stocker, Karsten
Stueber, Jamie Turnbull, and those students who took my *Language,
Thought and Reality* course in 2002–2003. Special thanks goes to Barry
Curtis for his insightful and speedy comments on every chapter during
the final stages.

I am grateful to the audiences and organisers of the International
Wittgenstein Symposium, Kirchberg, 2001, for feedback on material
that has become part of Chapter 6. I am similarly grateful for the invi-
tations to present material relating to this project at the University of
Wales, Swansea in 1998 and University of Wales, Lampeter in 2001.

I would also like to express my gratitude to various editors and publishers for allowing me to re-use, rework and expand some of my previously published material in the composition of some of the chapters of this book. Chapter 3 makes use of, and builds on, the basic argument from my section of the paper, written jointly with John Lippitt, 'Making Sense of Nonsense: Kierkegaard and Wittgenstein', *Proceedings of the Aristotelian Society* Vol. XCVIII, Part III, 265–86. This material is reprinted by courtesy of the Editor of the Aristotelian Society © 1998. Chapter 4 incorporates material from 'Consciousness Demystified: A Wittgensteinian Critique of Dennett's Project', *The Monist*, 78 (4) © 1995. Chapter 5 is a slightly revised version of my paper 'Was the Later Wittgenstein a Transcendental Idealist?', in *Current Issues in Idealism* (eds. P. Coates and D. Hutto) Bristol: Thoemmes Press © 1996.

Finally, I give thanks to the University of Hertfordshire for its enduring support and encouragement in my research projects. Thanks too to Jen Nelson of Palgrave Macmillan, who, in taking over at the just the right time, helped to see this project to its conclusion.

Abbreviations

G. Frege

BLA	*The Basic Laws of Arithmetic*
FA	*Foundations of Arithmetic*
PW	*Posthumous Writings*
T	'The Thought: A Logical Inquiry'

G.W.F. Hegel

EL	*The Encyclopaedia Logic*
SL	*Science of Logic*

I. Kant

CPR	*The Critique of Pure Reason*

G.E. Moore

ROI	'Refutation of Idealism'

B. Russell

A	*Autobiography*
LA	'Logical Atomism'
MPD	*My Philosophical Development*
OD	'On Denoting'
OKEW	*Our Knowledge of the External World*
PLA	'The Philosophy of Logical Atomism'
POM	*Principles of Mathematics*
POP	*The Problems of Philosophy*
TOK	*Theory of Knowledge: The 1913 Manuscript*

L. Wittgenstein

NB	*Notebooks, 1914–1916*
TLP	*Tractatus Logico-Philosophicus*

WVC	*Wittgenstein and the Vienna Circle: Conversations Recorded by Friedrich Waismann*
BBB	*The Blue and Brown Books*
LFM	*Lectures on the Foundations of Mathematics*
RFM	*Remarks on the Foundations of Mathematics*
PI	*Philosophical Investigations*
RPP I	*Remarks on the Philosophy of Psychology*, Volume 1
RPP II	*Remarks on the Philosophy of Psychology*, Volume 2
LWPP I	*Last Writings on the Philosophy of Psychology*, Volume 1
LWPP II	*Last Writings on the Philosophy of Psychology*, Volume 2
Z	*Zettel*
OC	*On Certainty*
C&V	*Culture and Value*

Introduction

> When I was in Norway during the year 1913–1914 I had some
> thoughts of my own, or so at least it seems to me now. I mean
> I have the impression that at the time I brought to life new
> movements in thinking (but perhaps I am mistaken). Whereas
> now I seem just to apply old ones.
>
> Wittgenstein, 1980, *Culture and Value*, p. 20e

There are a number of fundamental topics, including 'reality', 'meaning'
and 'logic', that cannot be dealt with properly without an appropriate understanding of the end and limits of philosophy. I draw on
Wittgenstein's insights concerning how we must approach these topics
to challenge the idea that we face a simple, methodological choice in
philosophy: to advance theory or to attempt therapy. Consideration of
these matters tells against the prevalent opinion that philosophy is a
kind of theorising, scientific or otherwise. Yet, this should not lead us
to think that its business is *purely* therapeutic, designed only to help rid
us of such ambitions and attendant confusions. It is possible to deny
that philosophy is progressive, according to the standard conception,
while also denying that it is wholly negative and deflationary. I will
explore this third way by expounding, explicating and defending
Wittgenstein's claim that philosophy clarifies our understanding of
important philosophical matters.

I claim that we can see what is distinctive about Wittgenstein's
approach, throughout his entire career, in his early treatment of logic,
which helps to illustrate his views concerning the nature and limits of
philosophy. Despite other important developments, such as his famous
change of mind concerning the function and scope of language, essentially the method employed in that domain was retained and, indeed,

honed in his later writings. For this reason, we gain a powerful grasp of Wittgenstein's later philosophy by seeing how his *approach* to logic in the *Tractatus* was developed and expanded. In the end, this allows one to make sense of his take on the nature of language, realism and anti-realism, forms of life and the nature and source of philosophical confusion.

To make a plausible case for this it is necessary to situate and defend my reading against certain popular alternatives that dominate the lively debate about how to read Wittgenstein. But, although I do not shirk interpretative responsibility, it should be clear that my primary interest in this is not straightforwardly exegetical. That is to say, I am less concerned to establish that my interpretation is *the* correct one, as to show that it is a plausible reading, having the merit of enabling us to articulate a different vision of what philosophy can do, thereby allowing us to re-evaluate its real importance. Ultimately, I would be satisfied even if I failed to provide a convincing reading of Wittgenstein's actual views as long as I have succeeded in unearthing important insights from his work that give aid to my stated purpose. However, I hope to have achieved the former as well.

Although the structure and argument of the book are best reflected in its divisions into chapters, I must warn the reader of particular features of my argument and the way it unfolds in stages in order to prevent misunderstandings and to forestall the drawing of any hasty conclusions about its direction.

Chapter 1 attempts to identify the ideological context in which Wittgenstein's views about how we must understand and approach logic took root. Although I pay attention to a number of other thinkers, my aim is *not* to determine what influence, if any, they had on him. Rather it is to situate his thought with respect to theirs. For example, I plot Wittgenstein's views on logic along a Kantian/Hegelian axis in order to see where they sit with respect to what might be broadly termed idealist views of logic. This is an important prelude to the question of whether or not Wittgenstein endorsed transcendental idealism, which will be addressed directly in Chapter 5. Nevertheless, I also contrast his treatment of logic with the realist approaches of Russell and Frege. In this, I give particular attention to the pride of place that is given to what he identifies as the 'fundamental thought' (*Grundgedanke*) of the *Tractatus*: the idea that there are no 'logical objects'. I argue that his use of truth-tables was designed to serve, apart from revealing the nature of logical connectives, as an alternative to Russellian logical notation that would free us from the mistake of thinking of logic as a representational discourse. In so doing, he was focusing on the way we *use* logical symbols as opposed to what they putatively stand for. It is just here we find the seeds of his mature method for doing philosophy.

Chapter 2 seeks to explicate further his understanding of logic, while revealing its central importance, by considering how it connects with his views on the nature of 'objects', 'pictures' and 'analysis'. I hope to make clear that his view of logic is that it pervades the world and the pictures we make of it. In particular, I emphasise that, despite adhering to the idea that all propositions share a common representational function, he held that we must make intelligible particular acts of sense-making, occasion by occasion. This attention to the particular contexts and uses we make of our words is what sets the stage for his later, more liberal understanding of the nature of language. Yet while this idea is already present in the *Tractatus* in a limited way, it is seriously under-developed. I provide further evidence for this view in Chapter 3, where the contrasts between the early and later views are put into direct contrast to show how his thought developed. Crucially, in the process of making these connections, I argue against those who hold that Wittgenstein was trying to espouse a philosophical theory or theories in his early work. I maintain that his remarks on these topics were never offered as explanations of this sort and that it is therefore a mistake to criticise the *Tractatus* for any perceived explanatory shortcomings. Of course, to say that Wittgenstein was *not trying* to offer a theory is not to say that his work was entirely free from theorising. Discussion of these issues lays the ground for a proper investigation into how we should understand the seemingly paradoxical status of the *Tractatus'* propositions, given its own apparent account of sense.

In Chapter 3, I argue against traditional doctrinal readings that suggest that Wittgenstein understood himself to be advancing a series of meta-physical truths in the *Tractatus*. Yet, I also reject extreme therapeutic readings, arguing that they are flawed in the *way* they understand the *Tractatus* to be nonsensical, as they do when they attempt resolutely to give Wittgenstein the final word. By my lights, such readings prevent us from making best sense of the development of Wittgenstein's views and style. In contrast to both these readings, I argue that although Wittgenstein hoped to offer elucidations in his early work, by the end of it he was awkwardly groping for a way to characterise what these were. He was prevented from doing so *precisely because* he was at the time hampered by an overly restrictive view of the nature of language. In the light of this tension, something had to give. I believe it was, eventually, the idea that the singular function of language is representational. Consequently, what appears to be a radical conflict between his earlier and later views of language is best explained, on closer examination, not as a shift from one 'theory' of language to another but as the result of a wider application of the very same method that was initially employed in dealing with logical symbols, only now applied to *all* forms of symbolism. This explains certain illuminating parallels between aspects of the early and late work, such as Wittgenstein's use of truth-tables in the *Tractatus* and his use of imaginary language games in his later writings. From this, we can see how the transition in his understanding of symbolism enabled him to correct some residual errors in his early understanding of logic. Moreover, seeing his work in this light reveals why he was not advancing a philosophical theory in his later writings.

In Chapter 4, I hope to show how his understanding of the limits of philosophical explanation manifests itself in his later work. While repudiating certain popular misreadings of his views on philosophical psychology, I argue that there is a common agenda behind his rejection of mental objects and logical objects. Similarly, there are unmistakeable echoes of his early remarks on the explanatory impotence of logic in what he says about rule-following. Yet, I also attempt to put to bed the mistaken view that in being a theoretical or explanatory quietist on these topics Wittgenstein was thereby committed to philosophical quietism *simpliciter*.

In Chapter 5, picking up on a theme I left trailing in Chapter 1, I give reasons why we should deny that Wittgenstein sponsored a form of transcendental idealism in either his early or later writings. Although he replaces his early static notion of logical form with the more plastic notion of forms of life, there is ample evidence that his position concerning realism and idealism (transcendental or otherwise) remained constant throughout his writings. That is to say, he repudiated both in both periods.

In the final chapter I hope to remedy certain common misunderstandings concerning the import of and message behind Wittgenstein's famous remark that 'we must do away with all explanation, and description alone must take its place' (*PI* §109). In particular, it is neither 'passive' nor 'negative' in the sense of being deflationary with respect to task of philosophy. For example, although I do not deny that his method can be regarded as therapeutic, his purpose was not simply to provide relief from philosophical problems. Rather, it was to clear the way for seeing certain fundamental matters aright, which involves recognising that there are limits to philosophical explanation. To make this clear, I contrast Wittgenstein's understanding of the method of clarification with the proposals concerning the nature and methods of philosophy that dominate contemporary analytic philosophy: the positions advanced by descriptive conceptual analysts and progressive revisionists, of both the naturalistic and non-naturalistic bent. I argue that when we take stock of the primary commitments of such philosophers, it becomes clear why the slide towards scientific naturalism is so hard to resist, for it alone appears to offer the genuine assurance of real philosophical progress. Although there is not enough space to give a refined argument against such approaches in a single concluding chapter, I am comforted by the fact that this is something I have begun to provide in much more detail in my other books, *The Presence of Mind* and *Beyond Physicalism*. I will be content if in this book I manage to get clearer about what is valuable in Wittgenstein's approach, hopefully putting paid to some standard misunderstandings about its nature and scope. For, if I am successful only in this, then the battle-lines in the debate about the end of philosophy will have been drawn more sharply.

1
A Focus on Logic

The answer to the request for an explanation of negation is really: don't you understand it? Well, if you understand it, what is there left to explain, what business is there left for an explanation?

Wittgenstein, *Philosophical Occasions*, p. 177

Introduction

I contend that what is characteristic of Wittgenstein's method throughout his writings finds early clear expression in the approach to logic espoused in the *Tractatus*. In support of this claim, this chapter makes a start on identifying what made his approach unique and how it relates to his overall philosophical end: a task that will be pursued in greater detail in subsequent chapters. Rather than simply outlining its internal features, I believe the best way to achieve this is to lay his understanding of logic against that of certain other major thinkers, thereby bringing its distinct aspects into sharp relief. My aim is, therefore, to locate it ideologically. This is possible precisely because Wittgenstein was far from the first to realise that how one understands logic ought to determine the very character of one's philosophy. Recognising the centrality of logic to philosophical inquiry brings together such otherwise strange bedfellows as Kant, Hegel, Russell and to a lesser extent Frege.

In what follows, I give a rough sketch of how each of them understood logic and of how this resulted, in some cases, in quite different visions of the nature, end and method of philosophy. A key related theme is how this manifested itself in the various forms of idealism or realism they supported. The danger with any such survey, of course, is that it must ignore a great many important and interesting questions relating to the surrounding issues, origins and motive factors spurring on these developments. Although I will at times touch on these, I wish to state that attempting to establish or chart these connections is not my concern here. To do so would require traversing far too vast a literature and dealing with too many controversies. My purpose is the relatively more modest one of sketching a logical geography of their approaches to logic in the hope of bringing to the fore certain issues. This exposition will pay dividends in the final section by allowing the reader to see better the contours of Wittgenstein's early thought and by staving off certain misidentifications. Apart from serving this express purpose, mapping this terrain will also prove to be a useful platform for assessing his mature descriptive method against some prominent contemporary offerings in the final chapter. For, as we shall see, some of today's popular 'live options' not only strongly resemble the philosophies described here, they in some cases directly inherit their basic characteristics. Thus, they continue to grapple with the same difficult questions.

From transcendental to dialectical logic

It is well known that Kant's Copernican revolution turned the tables on the age-old question of how our conceptions conform to objects by getting us to ask instead about the *a priori* necessary, formal and material conditions that make *any* objective representation possible. This resulted in his stated concern to establish the legitimacy of synthetic *a priori* knowledge by appealing only to what is given by our intuitions of space and time and by the deduction of the pure categories of the understanding. In attempting this, he hoped to stake out, once and for all, the proper bounds and form of philosophical inquiry. Unlike the previous offerings of unconstrained metaphysical speculation, Kant hoped to instil a proper philosophical discipline by focusing only on what is necessary for things to appear to us; that which makes any experience possible. The conditions of possibility for the representation of objects of experience can only be securely known by focusing solely on what is required for rational cognition about the objects of our experience (*CPR* A 47–8).

These considerations are enough to remind us why Kant thought that a general logic – the principles of which are *a priori* necessary conditions for the possibility of *any* judgement – was purely formal. He writes:

> A general but pure logic therefore has to do with strictly *a priori* principles, and is a canon of the understanding and reason, but only

in regard to what is formal in their use, be the content what it
may (empirical or transcendental) . . .

(CPR A53/B77; cf. also A54/B78)

For example, the law of non-contradiction must be in operation if representations are to be harmoniously and rationally unified in sponta-
neous judgements of the various kinds he goes on to identify by appeal
to their distinctive logical functions and forms, such as affirmation,
negation, categorical, hypothetical, and so on.[1] An immediate consequence of regarding pure reason in this way is that it makes clear why
it could not be a source of substantive metaphysical deliverances,
thereby frustrating the hopes of rationalists and their ilk. Unchecked,
the free play of reason permits too many possibilities and leaves the way
open for insufficiently grounded speculation. In Kant's view, it was precisely the failure to see this that was responsible for some of the worst
flights of philosophical fantasy and it was against this misuse, or abuse,
of reason that, as its title announces, his *Critique* was directed. For pure
reason is not an *organon* – not a body of substantial knowledge.[2] As we
shall see, Wittgenstein's understanding of logic can also be broadly classified as formalist, but this manifests itself in an importantly different
way from the form it takes in Kant's thought. Yet to understand fully
the contrast it is vital to chart some of the intervening post-Kantian
developments in the understanding of the nature of logic.

Before we consider these it is important to get clear about the Kantian
distinction between empirical realism and transcendental idealism as it
applies to logic. In her recent Romanell Lecture, Maddy explains the
contrast in the following way:

> Speaking transcendentally . . . logic is . . . ideal; it is true of the world
> of experience because of the structure of the discursive understand-
> ing, not because of features of the world as it is itself. But logical
> truth is not dependent on the forms of intuition. So it is transcen-
> dentally ideal, but less of our cognitive structure is involved . . .
> Empirically, though, logical truth is as robustly objective as spatio-
> temporality and causality; logic is true of the world.
>
> (Maddy 2002, p. 67)

Still, there are different understandings of what Kantian transcendental idealism entails. According to traditional metaphysical readings,
as the categories are meant to derive from our most basic forms of
judgement about the empirical world, although they hold good for

objects of our experience they cannot shed light on the nature of super-sensible reality. To use modern vernacular, observing a dualism of organising scheme and content, to see the *a priori* principles that govern judgement as transcendentally ideal, is to place them at a remove from reality as it is in itself.[3] It follows that to explicate the necessary structure of our way of representing things is not to explicate the necessary structure of the world itself, if one postulates the existence of a noumenal reality over and above that of empirical reality. On this reading, the high price of guaranteeing the credentials of our knowledge of the empirical world is that it necessarily falls short of knowledge of ultimate reality. This sort of picture is often fostered by the causal-mechanical metaphors rife in today's cognitive science, with which Kant's philosophy is frequently associated. It encourages us to think of 'the mind' as something affected by the world beyond, pushing us to regard logic and the basic categories as something 'innate and inner'.[4]

However, some time ago Allison argued that 'the attribution of such a theory to Kant, with its postulation of two distinct yet parallel activities, one of which is in principle unknowable, renders absurd his claim to be offering a critical philosophy' (Allison 1983, p. 248). In its place Allison proposed a deflationary reading, according to which there are not two realities at play in Kant's thought, of which it makes sense to wonder how the more fundamental one might interact with the other. Rather, to talk of things in themselves is to move towards a transcendental perspective, as opposed to an everyday empirical one, on the one and only reality. Adopting such a perspective, to the extent that it is possible for us to do so, is nothing more than an exercise in abstraction (see Allison 1983, p. 241). Seeing things in this way promises to slay a host of dragons. As Langton says of Allison's reading, 'He thinks Kant's problems will go away only if we stop injecting him with the poison of metaphysics. Otherwise we are left with a philosophy that crudely divides the world into different entities, that supposes an incoherent double affection, that attempts to tell the untellable' (Langton 1998, p. 12).

None the less, there remains serious controversy amongst Kantian scholars over which of these readings is to be preferred. For example, despite noting its attractions, Langton finds the deflationary, or as she calls it the anodyne, reading to be a suspect rational reconstruction. This is because, she holds, 'When Kant tells us that we have no knowledge of things in themselves, he thinks he is telling us something new and important' (Langton 1998, p. 10). However, whichever reading one favours, we need some way of understanding the thought that logic, which is at work everywhere in *our* thinking, is transcendentally ideal. But perhaps this could be modestly accommodated by the simple fact that Kant is prepared to entertain the mere possibility of a different, non-logical, but still *intellectual*, vantage on reality – even if it is not one we can comprehend. For example, he says:

> Nevertheless the concept of a *noumenon*, taken merely problematically, remains not only admissible, but even unavoidable, as a concept setting limits to our sensibility. But in that case it is not a special intelligible object for our understanding; rather an understanding to which it would belong is itself a problem, namely, that of cognising its object not discursively through categories but intuitively in a non-sensible intuition, the possibility of which we cannot in the least represent. Now in this way our understanding acquires a negative expansion, i.e. it is not limited by sensibility, but rather limits it by calling things in themselves (not considered as appearances) *noumena*.
>
> (*CPR* A256/B312; see also Allison 1983, pp. 238–9)

The mere possibility that there could be such a perspective on reality – one involving a godly, purely intuitive, intellect, entails there are limits to our finite, discursive intellect; revealing that it is not the only valid mode of representation. The point is that allowing for this possibility, even though we cannot make it intelligible, marks a contrast with our own case and thus, in a sense, relativises our schema (see also *CPR* A251–2).[5] Acknowledging this is enough to explain why logic is transcendentally ideal as well as empirically real.

There is little prospect of deciding where Kant stood on these issues without a much more extensive investigation, but these considerations suffice to set the stage for understanding Hegel's objections to what he understood Kant's views of logic to be. Indeed, Hegel's philosophic method developed as a direct, critical response to the perceived shortcomings of what he saw as two unfortunate dualisms inherent in Kant's transcendental idealism. First and foremost, Hegel rejects the idea that reason is purely formal. That is to say, he does not think the principles of the pure, general and transcendental logic should be thought of as 'empty' until inflated by intuitions (or single representations). The extended quotation below epitomises his complaint:

> For the *thinking* that goes on in this way, even when it reaches its highest point, *determinacy* remains something *external*; what is still meant by 'reason' then is just a radically *abstract thinking*. It follows

as a result that this 'reason' provides nothing but the *formal unity* for the simplification and systematisation of experiences; it is a *canon*, not an *organon*, of *truth*; it cannot provide a *doctrine* of the Infinite, but only a *critique* of cognition . . . Kant did, of course, interpret reason as the faculty of the unconditioned; but his exclusive reduction of reason to abstract identity directly involves the renunciation of its unconditionedness, so that reason is in fact nothing but empty understanding . . . For Kant, however, the activity of reason expressly consists only in systematising the material furnished by perception, through the application of the categories, i.e., it consists in bringing that material into an external order, and hence its principle is merely that of non-contradiction.   (*EL* §52, p. 100)

Kant's 'formalism' is predicated on his central distinction between what is given, as passively received through intuition, and the *a priori* principles and categories that enable us spontaneously and actively to experience it at all. That Hegel regarded this distinction to be unsupported and unfounded is not in doubt; establishing his reasons for so thinking is more controversial. For example, Guyer claims that 'Hegel's critique of Kant reflects a profoundly different philosophical sensibility than Kant's, and it is by no means obvious that his work should be taken as addressing the same issues' (Guyer 1993, p. 172). But others see matters differently, for although it is true that Hegel is less than careful in spelling out the basis of his concerns, it is nevertheless possible to reconstruct what lies at their heart, as Pippin has attempted.[6] Indeed, Pippin rightly identifies the disagreement between Kant and Hegel as one concerning the distinction between concepts and intuitions and argues, convincingly, that in just this territory Kant is indeed vulnerable (Pippin 1989, p. 25).

Kant tried to effect a delicate balance by both acknowledging the formality of what is necessary in our scheme – which, *pace* Hegel, he regarded as a great asset – while at the same time holding that what is 'given' in intuition is properly subject to it. Here we can see the basis for Hegel's charge that the Kantian view of logic ultimately suffers from 'subjectivism'. For, even if we cleanly distinguish the role of intuition from judgement, it must be supposed that what is given, or received, is nevertheless amenable to rational judgement: that is to say, reality provides *possible* inputs for subsumption. This seems to imply that what is given is in some sense already appropriately structured for such reception. The corollary of this is that we must suppose that what anyone encounters in the world is somehow *always already* in line with logic.

Yet, if so, why should we regard logic as transcendentally ideal as opposed to transcendentally real?

Pippin argues plausibly that Kant's recognition of the need to address this very issue is what drove him to try to develop his Deduction further.[7] In places, Kant appears to want to establish the existence of a 'synthetic link', thereby allowing the possibility of knowing in advance that what is presented necessarily conforms to the rules by which discursive intellects understand and judge it.[8] Thus, in the relevant section of the B edition, he remarks that 'since experience, as empirical synthesis, is in its possibility the only kind of cognition that gives other synthesis reality, *as* a priori *cognition it also possesses truth* (agreement with the object) only insofar as it contains nothing more than what is necessary for the synthetic unity of experience in general' (*CPR* B 197; emphasis mine). But, even noting this last proviso, Kant's difficulty is to explain how we can make sense of such a necessary link without collapsing the distinction between 'receptivity' and 'spontaneity'.[9] The problem of having one's cake and eating it too with respect to this very issue is still played out in modern dress in McDowell's *Mind and World* and in the responses that have been made to it. The crux is that to maintain that we can be assured that reality, even transcendentally considered, will always be in harmony with logic appears to require letting go of the idea that it is transcendentally ideal (or for Hegel, subjective), in the sense that it can be known to apply only to *discursive* schemes of representation. To take this thought seriously requires abandoning *any* possible contrast between our way of representing the world and what might be afforded by a purely intuitive intellect. It is to surrender the idea of a non-logical intellect altogether. Hegel's solution is to insist on this by denying that there is any interesting distinction between concepts and intuitions, thereby relinquishing any possible distinction between scheme and content. In the wake of the removal of this distinction what Hegel saw as unwarranted Kantian formalism and subjectivism about logic, which offended him so greatly, fell too.

Seeing matters in this light is important because it makes clear in what way Hegel saw himself as extending and developing Kant's philosophy in a more thoroughgoing way than his master. In this, his approach was not a retrograde reversion to pre-critical metaphysics or simply the product of an entirely different philosophical temperament.[10] Another such example – his communing with the critical spirit – is Hegel's accusation that Kant was insufficiently circumspect in his Metaphysical Deduction of the Categories: the pure concepts of the understanding.

For although these were meant to be simply derived from the set of our most basic forms of judgement, in Hegel's eyes Kant had not done nearly enough to demonstrate that the judgement forms in his Aristotelian table really had the determinate functions ascribed to them, that they were ultimately logically distinct, that they were basic or that they were comprehensive.[11] Thus, despite admiring the general method, Hegel found Kant's critical philosophy was not nearly critical enough: it rested on too many ungrounded assumptions.

It is not necessary to settle whether or not Hegel's attributions or criticisms are fully warranted, for enough background has been sketched for the reader to get a general sense of the origins of his his understanding of logic developed and how it drove his entire philosophical approach. Just or not, his objections to Kant help us to understand precisely why he thought a properly critical philosophy must be uncompromisingly radical: involving neither prior judgements, nor assumptions, nor postulates of any sort. He proposed a very different means of demonstrating the objective validity of the categories or, rather, of *the* concept, hoping to proceed without presuppositions or assumptions and to be guided only by what is essential and necessary, as revealed by explicating what is inherent in our thinking. By first considering the single and most minimal concept, *pure being*, he moved slowly forward, then back and beyond. For in entertaining the idea of 'pure being', one is led to strip away all particular qualities. Following through on this thought leads to the conclusion that to be *simpliciter* is in fact to be *nothing* in particular. In this way, we naturally progress from our first thoughts about pure being to the idea that it is, in fact, its very opposite, nothingness. But matters cannot rest there for consideration of nothingness drives us to revise our understanding once again. Not enough will have been done to accommodate the idea that something, pure being, is nothing. In a bid to reconcile this new conflict, we are pushed to entertain the idea of *becoming*. Consideration of this notion will then take us still further down the road opening up before us as we attempt to draw out the full implications of the concept of pure being. Dialectical reasoning advances in this way, by both momentarily reconciling and yet also embracing the contradictions implicit in our thought, which arise due to the incompleteness of our ordinary concepts. In this way, Hegel's philosophical method was inextricably bound up with his logic. Having rejected the Kantian dualisms, logic itself cannot be distinguished from the development of *the* substantive concept itself. It is not merely the very engine of conceptual development; he identifies it as thought thinking itself, something that cannot be understood in the absence of an engagement with its dynamic nature. In a recent paper, Houlgate emphasises the importance of the connection between this view of logic and Hegel's method:

> It is this idea, that concepts transform themselves into further more complex conceptions of what there is, that constitutes logical or philosophical necessity for Hegel . . . for Hegel the concept of sub-stance turns out logically to be the concept of causality when it is properly understood . . . Hegel is led to his view by his distinctive *method* of philosophizing – a method that involves not regressing from one concept to its precondition or criticizing concepts by reference to some anticipated *terminus ad quem*, but rather allowing concepts to transform themselves into new concepts and so, as Alan White puts it, to 'make there own' way.
>
> (Houlgate 2000, pp. 246, 248; first emphasis mine)

The rational movement of thought involves continual attraction and repulsion – unveiling and internally negating specific renderings, a process required to make *the* concept determinate. In working out what is demanded by concepts we are forced to wrestle with paradoxes, requiring us equivocally, but harmoniously, to think both sides of contradictions. Yet the very attempt to do this spurs us on to make more complete determinations, and so thinking does not come to a rest. Thought proceeds and develops, as it were, under its own steam, through the necessary and reflective development of *the* concept. Hegel, as is well known, had high hopes for this process. He writes:

> The most important point for the nature of mind is not merely the relation of that which it is in itself, but furthermore of that as which it knows itself, to that which it is in actuality; this self-knowledge, because it is essentially consciousness, is the fundamental determination of the mind's actuality. These Categories function only instinctively and as impulses – they are at first introduced into consciousness piecemeal, and therefore are mutable and mutu-ally confusing, and thus yield to mind only a piecemeal and insecure actuality. To *purify these categories* and to raise the mind through them to Freedom and Truth, this it is which is the loftier task of Logic.
>
> (*SL*, p. 46; emphasis mine)[12]

There are several things that are important to note about Hegel's philosophy and its attendant understanding of logic. The first major consequence is that it represents a complete break with the tradition, it threatens to undermine our familiar understanding of logic altogether. As Bencivenga observes,

> Within Aristotelian, analytic logic – the logic of the understanding – we are stuck with thinking of things as either identical or distinct ... But within the new, dialectical logic Hegel is offering, that very distinction – the distinction between identity and distinctness – can be conquered.
>
> (Bencivenga 2000, p. 33)

Secondly, properly worked out, the logical development of thought leaves aside all that is arbitrary or speculative. The logical movement of thought involves only what is essential. Given that this activity is identical with doing philosophy itself, our philosophical pursuits turn out to be rationally progressive. Some Hegelians hold that the movement of thought will ultimately culminate in the development of 'the idea'. For others, more modestly, it is simply meant to get us to attend to the activity that is essential to our self-determination as we pursue this development. Without trying to settle the tricky question of the exact status of the Absolute in all this, we can see that on either view a proper working out of logic or philosophy is progressive. That is to say, Hegel and his followers were equally enamoured of the idea that logic was substantive, in this sense, and could yield results. I will revisit this facet of his philosophy in the final chapter when I consider the work of some of Hegel's current followers.

Finally, and in the chief place, he put logic back into the very fabric of the world in direct contrast to Kant. In the final analysis, he allowed no separation of thought and being: no division between thought and reality. Working out what is inherent in our concepts is understood as the dynamic engagement with what *must* be with reality *by itself* and *for itself*. This last point is important if only as a means of comparing how post-Hegelian thinkers variously understood logic to be 'in' the world, for it is the very key to understanding much of what Wittgenstein objected to in the accounts of Russell and Frege. As we shall see, in some important respects, Wittgenstein's position was closer to Hegel's in this regard.

Russell's factual logic

Hegel was not alone in his hostility to the limits of Kant's idealism. Early analytic philosophers equally hoped to escape the fetters its acceptance would place on philosophy, for to agree with Kant would be to dash the grander hopes that philosophy might achieve results on a par with science. Indeed, some have gone so far as to claim that the whole analytic tradition 'was born in the effort to avoid Kant's theory of the *a priori*' (Coffa 1991, p. 21; cf. also Hanna 2001, p. 5). It is interesting in this regard that the two most pivotal figures in the development of the British strain of analytic philosophy, G.E. Moore and Bertrand Russell, had been initially attracted to Hegelianism, before rejecting it in favour of uncompromising naïve realism.[13] Russell would later reminisce about this change, sometimes describing it in active terms, painting himself as a revolutionary with Moore in the vanguard, while at other times characterising it more passively, as if he were recovering from an ordeal, as when he speaks of 'emerging from the bath of German idealism' (*MPD*, p. 42; *A*, p. 134).

In his infamous and inadequate 'Refutation of Idealism', Moore makes clear that its counterintuitive holism was what he found most objectionable about the Hegelianism he had once embraced. Thus, he scathingly writes: 'The principle of organic unities . . . is mainly used to defend the practice of holding *both* of two contradictory propositions, wherever this may seem convenient. In this, as in other matters, Hegel's main service to philosophy has consisted in giving a name to and erecting into a principle, a type of fallacy to which experience had shown philosophers, along with the rest of mankind, to be addicted' (*ROI*, p. 24). Likewise, Russell objected to what he calls Hegel's 'main thesis', upon which the edifice of the whole Hegelian system allegedly rested. Russell clamed that Hegel's 'fundamental tenet' insisted 'that what is incomplete must not be self-subsistent, but must need the support of other things before it can exist' (*POP*, p. 83).

Yet, while Moore and Russell agreed in their distaste for such monism, neither of them can be said to have properly laid it to rest. For example, it is no use merely to point out that Hegel's philosophy is at odds with common sense and scientific thinking, since his followers were not interested in these ordinary forms of thought, only in the extraordinary one that lay behind them all. Moreover, given that they did not impugn the legitimacy or importance of such abstractions within their own restricted spheres, pointing out this contrast would not have embarrassed them. Equally unconvincing is Moore's attack on idealism, which relies on the law of non-contradiction (see *ROI*, pp. 22–3). For, as this law was precisely what Hegel's logic had put into the hazard, invoking it as the main tool in his argument against the Hegelians, with nothing more than a nod to the tradition, surely begs the question. Although as proper arguments these attempts are clearly lacking, it is instructive to note the way in which in the course of advancing them a standard view of logic – one concerned with identity and difference – was restored to good standing without further ado. This manoeuvre is of historical importance because it set the stage for Russell's more elaborate analysis and dismissal of what he took to be the very heart and soul of Absolute Idealism.

In his view, it jointly depended on an explicit commitment to the idea that the object of philosophy is complete, unqualified, non-relative truth complemented by the tacit assumption that all judgements have a subject–predicate form. These dual assumptions apparently breathed life into the idea that logic must develop dialectically, for this idea is allegedly the natural consequence of holding that the only truly adequate philosophical judgement is one that succeeds in being genuinely all-encompassing. For Russell, this is what gives the dialectic its structure. Thus, a philosopher attempts to advance a given thesis, in the form of a premise about the nature of everything, but which on closer inspection is shown, necessarily, to be lacking in some vital respect. This thesis is then countered by a corrective, its antithesis, which at first appears superior in that it is fashioned to avoid the limitations of the first. But on reflection, it is recognised that in some way both are needed to provide the correct account, so a compromise premise is proposed, which synthesises and unites the two opposing claims, thereby achieving greater completeness. To bring out this inevitable result he lampoons the process by considering what would follow if one advanced the ridiculous proposition, 'The Universe is an uncle' as a philosophical thesis. It would immediately be objected that the Universe cannot be an uncle because to be an uncle requires both a relation to and the existence of something else, specifically, a nephew. But if the universe *is* everything, then there would be no room in it for anything other than an uncle, thus no such relation is possible. To propose the antithesis that 'The Universe is a nephew' fares equally badly for the very same reasons. Hence, the tension begins to resolve itself only if we advance the seemingly nonsensical claim that in some way reality is both an uncle and a nephew, inseparably related.

Although silly, Russell's purpose in using this illustration is to highlight the crucial role subject–predicate logic plays in making monism plausible. For him, the decisive move is the limiting of metaphysical statements to the form 'A is x'. The general lesson, no matter what the content we give to our theses, is that any attempt to ascribe any single, sensible predicate to everything must result in it telling less than the whole story. It is nothing short of attempting to identify the whole with one of its parts, which is bound to generate paradoxes. But the underlying assumption that makes this inescapable is precisely the claim that no thesis is philosophically adequate unless it captures the whole, in its entirety. With this in play and a commitment to subject–predicate logic, we can know, in advance, that any thesis will stand in need of its antithesis and ultimate synthesis, ensuring an extreme holism that insists on the 'unreality of separateness'. Although the world appears to be made up of a plurality of things, it is, in fact, a single whole, the Absolute.

But in identifying the commitment to subject–predicate logic as a driving force behind Absolute Idealism, at the same time Russell thought he had spied its Achilles' heel. Indeed, he would later pin a great many errors in traditional metaphysics on the crippling effect of using the limited logical tools of subject–predicate logic. He claimed it was responsible for rendering, 'most philosophers . . . incapable of giving any account of the world of science and daily life' (*OKEW*, p. 55). Coming to recognise this was his official reason for thinking that absolute idealism met its ultimate defeat when the revolution came in the understanding of formal logic at the turn of the century. Prior to the development of the propositional calculus, all argument forms were held to be syllogistic and all premises thought to be nothing more than the ascription of a predicate to subject. Notoriously, this does not accommodate many everyday judgements, such as those involving relations and multiple generality. Using such resources alone it is not possible to express adequately even the simple relation of (1) or, worse still of (2).

(1) X is bigger than Y.
(2) Some Xs are bigger than all Ys.

As Russell puts it, 'If we say "this is bigger than that" we are not assigning a mere quality to "this" but a relation of "this" and "that" . . . Thus propositions stating that two things have a certain relation have a different form from subject predicate propositions' (*OKEW*, p. 54). These severe limitations of subject–predicate logic dissipated as the technical developments of the new logic became apparent. Thanks to its functional underpinning the propositional calculus permitted the proper treatment of many logical judgements for the very first time. It incorporated all the power of Aristotle's logic, but went beyond it. That this was an incredible advance could not be doubted. However, the legitimacy of the effects it wrought in philosophy more generally is indeed dubious. For example, Russell claims that the real catalyst for his change of metaphysical stripes was his realisation that subject–predicate logic, one of the fundamental pillars of Hegelianism, was severely limited. If his analysis was correct, then Hegelianism becomes unstable if one accepts the new logic, for it kicks away the idea that all judgements must have a subject–predicate form and thereby puts a spanner in the works of Hegel's dialectical engine.

Although compelling in some respects, this account of idealism badly misrepresents its basis. This should be evident even from the very brief discussion above. For, given his express ambition to pursue a presuppositionless philosophy, it would be deeply ironic if Hegel's method had been based on an initial commitment to the 'fundamental tenet' that Russell ascribes to him. Thus, as Houlgate stresses, the dialectic was not motivated 'by any desire on the part of the philosopher to reach some tacitly anticipated goal' (Houlgate 2000, p. 246). However, although Moore's 'refutation' was a failure and Russell's portrayal inaccurate, they do tell us a good deal about what they found important and persuasive. In particular, the very way they argued against and characterised the opposition cleared the air of certain controversies about the nature of logic and opened the way for the development of a thorough going logical realism. This explains, in part, why in neither case were they forced to retreat from their lofty philosophical ambitions when they made their rapid transition from idealism to realism. No doubt the overarching metaphysical concerns, common to neo-Hegelians and naïve realists, eased this process.

Not only did the new logic reveal the shortcomings of absolute idealism, it simultaneously set the stage for another way of pursuing the goal of absolute truth. It resurrected and secured a new, more secure platform for the traditional concern with deductive argument and truth-preserving inference. But it also focused on complete propositions, not their internal structure, and restored the idea that truth or falsity has to be ascertained individually and absolutely. This, of course, presupposes that it is possible to know the truth of a given proposition independently of knowing the truth of *any* other. This had a deep, liberating effect on the direction of Russell's thinking since, in his eyes, it undercut the other main pillar supporting monism. And, unless monism is abandoned, neither ordinary nor scientific propositions can be regarded as absolutely and individually true or false – as not admitting of degrees of truth. The very idea that absolute knowledge of reality is available in a piecemeal way is simply incompatible with the idea that reality is essentially monistic. Of course, to deny monism would mean endorsing the reality of relations, but the new logic also appeared to make this move possible since the judgement forms involving them had finally been made respectable.

We can see from this that Russell did not reject idealism because he felt its concerns were misdirected, but rather because he gradually came to believe that it was essentially incapable of adequately providing the kind of absolute philosophical knowledge that, by his lights, it expressly sought. It is not surprising, then, given his lifelong interest in mathematics, that he hoped to deliver the death blow to absolute idealism by showing that this most certain of sciences could be grounded in the new logic.[14] Success on this front would be conclusive vindication of the tools of the new logic and, equally, would serve as a demonstration that our ordinary ways of thinking can be both truth-yielding in an absolute sense, although specialised.

It is just here that Russell's unwavering realism about logic began to take root. To appreciate fully how his views on this topic matured it is important to chart the main stops on his journey of thought, from its humble (and inadequate) beginnings in the unpublished manuscript 'Analysis of Mathematical Reasoning' to its final destination in the works *Principia Mathematica*; *The Problems of Philosophy*; and his abandoned 1913 manuscript, 'Theory of Knowledge'. What remained constant throughout was his postulation of the independent existence of logical forms. The first step was an endorsement of a theory of terms very similar to the theory of concepts espoused by his ally, Moore. In its crude, nascent form the essence of their shared intellectualist vision can be captured in the following simple doctrines. Reality is entirely composed of terms and relations between them. All such terms (or concepts) are *distinct* and separate 'entities' or 'units', each having the same ontological status. This constitutes an excessively liberal metaphysics, because all terms are thought to partake equally of being in some sense. They are all *real*, even though not all of them *exist* spatio-temporally. Hence this form of realism, which, following Hylton, we can usefully label Platonic Atomism, was thereby committed to the reality of a host of non-existent and even fictitious entities including 'a man, a moment, a number, a class, a relation, a chimaera, or anything else that can be mentioned' (*POM* §47).

The relations holding between terms are not intrinsic to the terms themselves, having instead real, independent existence. It is by means of such relations that terms are united with their brethren to form special kinds of complex entities – propositions – which alone have the properties of being true or false. Thus, the objects of thought are 'certain complex' objects, literally composed of terms (or concepts) standing in certain relations to one another, as specified by the particular way individual propositions are constructed. But, as reality is exhausted by terms – the very constituents of propositions – the latter cannot be understood as standing in a relation to something else that they are about. Propositions cannot refer to something beyond themselves since they are the very bedrock of reality. Given the way Russell and Moore understood reality to be populated, there simply was no room for relations of reference or correspondence. Rather, in some strange fashion, any given proposition was meant to be identical with its subject matter. This is why it is necessary that we be *directly* related to the complex objects that comprise the world – facts – and why these were identified with the set of true propositions.[15] This position is, of course, deeply antipsychologistic. Propositions are not perceived by ordinary means; rather, we are directly, and non-sensuously, acquainted with them. Hence, these complex objects of thought are entirely objective, mind-independent entities. In this, Russell and Moore revived a strong distinction between objects of judgement and acts of judging, *contra* the Hegelians, but without beating a retreat to Kant. Although such Platonic Atomism has some quite strange features, it appears less obviously counterintuitive and seemingly more faithful to the world we occupy in everyday life than the picture of reality supplied by absolute idealists.

We can see from this why Russell was committed to his famous doctrine of acquaintance and why, for him, truth was treated as an inexplicable 'property'.[16] Moreover, in promoting the idea that reality is purely conceptual, we can see that, at this stage in his thinking, he thought attention to language unimportant. The reason his metaphysics was so indiscriminate was that he originally regarded words to be nothing other than the transparent method of labelling terms or concepts. The interesting quarry was always what lay behind them. Yet, with respect to logical realism, the most important feature of his early metaphysics was that he held logic itself to consist in nothing more or less than propositions as understood above. They were composed of elements of the very purest kind. Modelled on his picture of the nature of ordinary propositions, which are simply external facts or complex objects of judgement, logical propositions were thought not to be merely formally valid, but *true* (cf. Hylton 1990, pp. 199–200). That is to say, *contra* Kant, that they have their own worldly subject matter. For example, he contrasted the propositions of mathematics with those of logic in the following way:

Symbolic Logic is essentially concerned with inference in general, and is distinguished from various special branches of mathematics mainly by its generality . . . What symbolic logic does investigate [are] the general rules by which inferences are made, and it requires a classification of relations or propositions only insofar as these general rules introduce particular notions. The particular notions which appear in the propositions of symbolic logic, and all others are definable in terms of these notions, are the logical constants. The number of indefinable logical constants is not great: it appears, in fact, to be eight or nine.   (POM §12)[17]

It follows from this that any given ordinary judgement, therefore, requires being acquainted at one and the same time with both a specific non-logical subject matter as well as a logical subject matter of the most general sort.

Russell's account of the substantive nature of logical propositions is important because his atomism about the non-logical components naturally suggests a particular understanding of conceptual analysis, based on decomposition. For, given that ordinary propositions are nothing other than complex objects composed of terms (or concepts) standing in specific relations to one another, it is natural to suppose that one could gain a full and complete understanding of them by breaking them down into their component parts. Indeed, this amounts to analysing things in themselves. Thus, conceptual analysis was to be prosecuted in order to get clear about 'what there is', not merely to improve our ability to communicate such insights. Unfortunately, the very idea that analysis might take this form was confounded by the fact that in order to succeed, a proper account would have to be given of the relations holding between the constituent parts of any proposition. But there was no way to treat such relations as particular existents on a par with their *relata* without generating an endless series of further relations that would require similar explication. The problem, as Bradley had made clear, is that trying to get clear about the nature of relations will always require the invocation of more and more of them. Russell notes this when he writes: 'Against the notion of specific differences, it may be urged that if differences differ, their differences from each other must also differ, and thus we are lead to an endless process' (POM §55). But, even though he was driven to endorse the idea that 'relations do not have instances', he was also alive to the great problem this represents for analysis as he originally conceived it. Indeed, he openly acknowledged that 'the true solution lies in regarding every proposition as having a kind of unity which analysis cannot preserve ... [and that] every proposition has a unity which renders it distinct from the sum of its constituents. All these points lead to logical problems, which, in a treatise on logic, would deserve to be fully and thoroughly discussed' (*POM* §55).

Enough of the basic components of Russell's early metaphysics have now been introduced to enable us to see why its central tenets were too simple to stand. It should be clear that everything cannot be a term, and that all terms cannot have equal ontological status, without generating a catalogue of woes. For to take these two claims at face value makes it impossible to account for generality, deal with the existence of impossible objects or overcome the class paradox.

Consider generality or the general nature of logical propositions involving terms such as *a, some, all, every* or *any*. If we take both the above tenets seriously and without compromise, we are forced to treat the components of propositions (3) and (4) at face value, each being ontologically real entities:

(3) Alex is mortal.
(4) All humans are mortal.

That is to say, the term 'All' must be treated as a definite entity of essentially the same kind as the term 'John'. This should be transparent if we consider the fact that, if we regard (3) and (4) as having a common propositional form, then 'Alex' and 'All' appear to play the same logical role. This is to be subject to the same sort of confusion that afflicted Homer's Cyclops when he proclaimed, 'Noman is killing me by guile'. The problem is not just that the term 'All' must contain the term 'Alex', but also the terms for every human being so as make up the complete set of all the people who have ever been and will be. This being so, how can it be a term of the same type as the proper name Alex? How can it be merely a *single* entity while at the same time being a collection of *many* things?

Likewise, there is the infamous paradox that bears Russell's name. For if it is supposed that classes are themselves terms, each being a single, mentionable entity, then questions arise about the nature of the all-inclusive class, the class of all classes. For to be a class at all it would appear that it must be a member of itself. The paradox arises because being maximally inclusive it must contain all other classes, including itself. This is impossible. Yet, if it did not contain itself, then it could not be the class of all classes at all. There is no means of resolving this paradox if one clings to the idea that everything of which we speak is a term and that every term represents a unique, singular entity or unit. Although this version of the paradox is best known, it has equally virulent forms which draw on certain other predicates and propositional functions.

Finally, there is yet another serious problem in accepting that every term, being a proper part of a complex proposition, partakes of being equally (whether or not it exists). For, since it is possible to mention all sorts of things in coherent propositions, unless checked, this idea commits one to making ontological space for impossible objects even though these cannot partake of being at all, not even as subsisting things. How can this tension be accommodated? The paradox is most famously illustrated by the example of the round-square, which appears to be a genuine part of the true proposition: 'The round-square cannot be.' If true propositions are just facts that we judge, it seems we must admit that the primary constituent of this fact is an impossible object. If this result is simply left to stand, then the universe of Platonic Atomists is clearly shown to be seriously overpopulated, not just heavily so with otherwise dubious entities.

This series of insuperable difficulties was not overcome until the publication of 'On Denoting', which heralded a radical improvement in the prospects of Russellian realism. In that work, he deployed his newly fashioned theory of descriptions to show that putative denoting phrases were not reliable metaphysical indicators, but instead nothing but incomplete symbols. Hence, instead of treating (6) on the model of (5) and therefore implying the existence of some strange type of single entity that had the capacity to be about many others, under the theory of descriptions (6) was revealed as expressing something having the logical form of (6′).

(5) Socrates is ugly.
(6) Some man is ugly.
(6′) For some x, Mx & Ux.

The same trick works just as well with troublesome definite descriptions that seemingly pick out non-existent entities or impossible objects. These are logically analysed to reveal that although an entire proposition containing them may be true, they are not proper names but only non-referring elements. Hence, the true logical form of the proposition 'The round-square cannot be' is shown to be: 'There is no such unique entity x which has the properties of being both round and square' (*OD*, p. 54). Only what is asserted by an entire proposition has meaning. This is the basis for the famous distinction between what we seemingly say (grammar) and what we really assert (the underlying logic).

While there is no question that 'On Denoting' represents a landmark in Russell's own thinking and the development of analytic philosophy, there is controversy over the question of what truly motivated it. For example, the claim that he began to appreciate the dire ontological implications of his initial naïve realism late in the day is clearly incorrect. Even at the early stage he recognised the need to 'prune back the Meinongian jungle', for otherwise, as Griffin makes clear, he would have been unable to maintain consistently that logic is the most general science. For, unless impossible objects were dealt with, logic could not apply, quite generally, to the entire realm of being. Obviously, contradictory entities need to flout logical law, so to speak, in order to *be* at all. It was for this reason, not merely to secure ontological credibility, that he was first motivated to explore the notion of denotation that was to become so very important to him (see Griffin 1996, pp. 51–2; Noonan 1996, pp. 82–7). Hence, even in the *Principles of Mathematics*, he had already hoped to solve the above catalogue of problems by introducing a quick fix in his otherwise egalitarian metaphysics, that is, by postulating what he then called 'denoting concepts'. As Hylton neatly summarises, he held that 'a term is a denoting concept just in case the presence of that term in a proposition results in the proposition not being about that term, but rather about some other term (or collection of terms)' (Hylton 1991, p. 209). The point of doing this was to introduce a special class of terms that could *refer to* other terms, or a whole collection of terms, not themselves contained in the proposition in question. This was meant to remove the metaphysical awkwardness that attends the very idea of something being both one and many. The hope was that, for example, by treating 'All' as a denoting concept, the truth of 'All humans are mortal' would depend on the truth of many propositions containing a host of other terms such as, 'Rais is mortal', 'Emerson is mortal', and so on, not merely one proposition containing the single term 'All'.

Yet this move is clearly at odds with the simple realism expounded above in that a proposition containing a denoting concept could not just *be* as a part of an independently existing complex object of judgement: It had to *be about* objects that it did not contain. Given that the early Russellian metaphysics was not at all built for 'aboutness', denoting concepts generated a whole new problem. For how could a denoting concept refer to something beyond itself given a metaphysics according to which reality is something with which we are directly acquainted? There is no room in Russell's world for items of further reference. Put otherwise, the very idea of one term denoting another is quite antithetical to his single-level metaphysics. Attempting to make room for it put a terrible strain on his metaphysics, not less great than the problems they were meant to resolve.

Not only was this proposed solution at odds with the very nature of Russell's realism, his application of it was often decidedly messy. For example, it drove him to produce an unsystematic and inelegant treatment of the quantifiers. He recognised this by saying:

> There is then, a definite something different in each of the five cases, which must, in a sense, be an object, but is characterized as a set of terms combined in a certain way, which something is denoted by *all men, any man, every man, a man* or *some man*; and it is with this *very paradoxical object* [emphasis added] that propositions are concerned in which the corresponding concept is used as denoting.
>
> (*POM*, §62)

What the above makes clear is that it was only with the publication of 'On Denoting' that the very idea of *denotation* was properly handled, not introduced for the first time, in a way consistent with Russell's overall metaphysics. That paper is important because it marks the point at which Russell began to treat the notion of denoting concepts, understood as objects in their own right, with suspicion and scorn. The theory of descriptions allowed him to hold that what is denoted in such cases need not be a single entity since denoting phrases or descriptions have no life independent of the propositions in which they reside. Therefore, as such phrases do not name simples they cannot be regarded as objects. Put otherwise, the illusion that there are such things as 'Some' and 'All' or impossible objects, such as 'the round-square', were shown to be nothing but tricks of language.

Nevertheless, for our purposes, it will be prudent to keep two issues – one concerning the result of Russell's change of view, the other concerning its true catalyst – quite separate. For what we should not lose sight of is that his underlying motivation was always to derive his metaphysics from logic. Throughout his career his singular aim, and hope for philosophy, was to identify the basic constituents of reality. The main consequence of the transition for this project was that he gained an increased understanding and respect for the importance of language in mediating our access to reality. Indeed, he would later trace all the troubles which plagued his early, naïve atomism to this single source, claiming that they 'arose from the belief that, if a word means some-thing, there must be some thing that it means. The Theory of Descrip-tions . . . showed this was a mistake and swept away a host of otherwise insoluble problems' (*MPD*, p. 63).

Another way in which he later thought that language intrudes and obscures is by causing us to think that all *things* are of the same logical type because all *words* are of the same logical type. Thus, as it is easily possible to substitute any particular word for another, placing them any-where we like in sentences, we become prone to think that the things that make up reality are also interchangeable in this way. Of course, certain combinations are obvious nonsense, such as (8), which can appear to share the same logical form as (7):

(7) Athens killed Socrates.
(8) Killed killed Socrates.

Yet, if we accept Russell's early realism, there appears to be no reason why (8) should be a piece of nonsense. Or, at least, nothing explains why this should be so. If 'Athens' and 'Killed' were in fact of the same logical type it ought to be possible to swap the one for the other in significant propositions, without loss of sense. Only late in the day did Russell observe that this confusion is engendered by the misleading fact that while 'words' are all of same logical type, their meanings are not. A proper symbolism would distinguish the logical forms of (7) and (8) by indicat-ing the differences in meaning-type of their constituents. He held that this could be achieved only by developing a theory of types, to articulate these differences. Once in hand, this theory would provide the means to prevent nonsense combinations quite generally. For example, if we dis-tinguish between different types of 'meanings', we can insist on a rule against treating the class of classes in the same way as another type of class, given that ordinary classes do not have the feature of being inclu-sive of all others. In this way, Russell's paradox doesn't even get going. Importantly, he maintained that unless one subscribed to the theory of types, this 'solution [was] technically impossible' (*LA*, p. 334).

In all these respects there was a clear and definite evolution in Russell's views from his naïve realist days to his logical atomist period, tied to his having developed a newfound, albeit negative, respect for the need to attend to ordinary language. In his mature phase, it was no longer treated as a transparent medium or clear window that could be safely ignored when coming to understand how we encounter reality. Thus, he writes:

> There is a good deal of importance to philosophy in the theory of symbolism, a good deal more than at one time I thought. I think the importance is almost entirely negative, i.e., the importance lies in the fact that unless you are fairly self-conscious about symbols, unless you are fairly aware of the relation of the symbol to what it symbolises you will find yourself attributing properties to the thing which only belong to the symbol.   (*PLA*, p. 185)

Both these considerations, in line with his growing respect for the treachery of language, brought with them a new appreciation of the value of developing a perfectly logical language for philosophical purposes. Indeed, the logical language of *Principia Mathematica* was supposed to be the skeleton of just such a language. Of it he writes:

> The purpose of the foregoing discussion of an ideal logical language . . . is twofold, first, to prevent inferences from the nature of language to the nature of the world . . . secondly, to suggest by inquiring into what logic demands of a language . . . what sort of structure we may reasonably suppose the world to have.   (*LA*, p. 338)

In accordance with this philosophical ambition, his new order analysis was employed not only on the sorts of entities that had troubled his early metaphysics but also on ordinary names, such as 'Socrates' and 'Plato'. For upon rigorous analysis, he found that these too were merely putatively referring expressions, or dummy names. Even in such homely cases what appears grammatically simple turns out to be logically complex. With exemplary metaphysical parsimony, Russell was thus moved to endorse the view that only logical forms and non-logical sense data really exist. The corollary of this is that we can only be genuinely acquainted with these two kinds of simples. In taking this line, he saw himself as expressly following Ockham, cutting back on his ontological commitments. In Russell's hands, Ockham's maxim, normally interpreted as 'never multiply entities beyond necessity', became: 'Whenever possible substitute constructions out of known entities for inferences to unknown entities' (*LA*, p. 326).

As dramatic as these changes were, it is important to realise that they were spurred on by his steadfast commitment to the idea that ultimate reality is both atomistic and something with which we are directly acquainted. He never abandoned these ideas, even though it took him some time to realise that it is an illusion to think that we are directly acquainted with most of the things of which we seem to speak. This is why, despite the recognised need for a two-step treatment of the putative 'objects' known by description, in his late work these ideas find new expression in the thought that logical form *is* real form. Due to the misleading nature of grammar, only what is revealed by logical analysis has true existence. In the end, the real things with which we can be genuinely acquainted are logically simple: the residue of the process of analytic distillation. In this light, his mature conclusions about logic, language and reality were quite natural developments of his early naïve realism.

Most importantly, it is clear that although his metaphysics had become more discriminating, he never abandoned the realist view of logic it originally incorporated. He continued to postulate the existence of independent logical forms, which he thought were needed in order to account for the relations between objects and our capacity to make judgements at all. He maintained that the propositions of logic had to be intellectually grasped separately from the particular contents they related. As such they were vital components of genuine propositions, as revealed by analysis, having an independent metaphysical status. In this way the paradox of analysis, which haunted his early view, could finally be overcome. We are directly acquainted with logical forms, which are distinct objects grasped in judgement and which are responsible for establishing the unity of propositions by saying how the elements are ordered and arranged.

It follows from this that, metaphysically speaking, the subject matter of logic had to be purely factual. Logical forms and principles, despite being necessary and immutable, were just facts about the world, although quite general ones. He was unequivocal about this. Thus he says that the law of non-contradiction, the paramount *a priori* logico-mathematical principle, 'is . . . a fact concerning the things in the world' (*POP*, p. 50). Moreover, reviewing the passages in *The Problems of Philosophy* immediately preceding this claim reveals that it was provoked by his taking seriously the essence of Hegel's objection to Kant's 'subjectivism'; that is to say, he objected to the idea that logic is limited to our thinking as opposed to being a feature of reality itself. This point is worth attending to, given the concerns of this chapter. It is vital to observe that Russell responded to the matter in a quite different way from Hegel by insisting that the objects of judgement, including their logical frames, are completely worldly items.

A direct consequence of regarding logic to have a factual status is that the appropriate stance to take towards it is to treat it as a legitimate quarry for metaphysical theorising and speculation, like any other factual domain. For example, by these lights, the discovery, classification and cataloguing of various logical forms becomes a positive and important philosophical pursuit. Unsurprisingly, to take this thought seriously has an effect on one's whole understanding of philosophy's end and character. It is what brings Russell to hold that 'Philosophical knowledge ... does not differ essentially from scientific knowledge' (*POP*, p. 87).

Clearly, Russell's position on this score is not stable. For if logical forms are metaphysically factual, it implies not only that they have a distinct type of content, but that they are also contingent. But how can that be given that they are also meant to be necessary? Elsewhere, Russell himself recognised that *a priori* logical principles could not be equated with even the most general of empirical generalisations. In his own words, the latter always remained 'mere facts: we feel there might be a world in which they were false, though, in the actual world they happen to be true' (*POP*, p. 43). Nevertheless, apart form noting it, he was not sufficiently uneasy about it to offer anything that might seriously resolve this tension. Thus, as Coffa quips, 'an approach to logic had finally reduced itself to absurdity' (1991, p. 128).

Frege's laws of thought

Where does Frege stand on this issue? At first blush his position appears to be not dissimilar to Russell's in that he holds logic to be objective and independent, having a subject matter suitable to scientific study. Given this, some commentators declare him to be a straightforward realist. But getting to grips with Frege's view on this topic is a tricky business. For unlike Russell, who wears his philosophical orientation on his sleeve, 'One will search Frege's works in vain for a systematic discussion of the nature of philosophy. He was a mathematical logician whose primary interest was to "set mathematics upon secure logical foundations"' (Hacker 1986, p. 7). This suggests that the right question to ask is: What is the connection between Frege's alleged realism and his more practical concerns?

It must be remembered that his statements about the science of logic surface exclusively in his attack on the psychologism dominant during his time. His fellow logicians were threatening to bring confusion and disrepute to this domain by interpreting the laws of logic and mathematics as if they concerned nothing but the association of 'ideas' or 'representations', entailing that they could be investigated by uncovering the actual causes of such links by means familiar to the discipline of descriptive psychology. Frege, on the other hand, was steadfast in regarding thoughts and their laws as standing in need of a quite distinctive treatment, thus forming the subject matter of an entirely distinct science. This battle and theme are constants throughout his career, as revealed by work at both ends of it: *The Foundations of Arithmetic* (1884, 1980) and 'The Thought' (1918–19, 1988).

In the former work, his insistence on drawing a distinction between the subject matter of logic and psychology is immediately and expressly related to issues concerning the respective objectivity and subjectivity of their foci. Thus the first fundamental principle of the *Foundations* states: 'one has to separate sharply the psychological from the logical, the subjective from the objective' (*FA*, x). He saw these issues as connected because he held that, being a purely descriptive science, psychology is at most concerned to provide causal explanations of why we might 'take' something to be true, and thus with related subjective phenomena and processes. But to investigate this is not to be concerned with matters of justification and truth. These topics demand recognition of their universal objectivity given that their laws cannot be relative to different thinkers, or even different types of thinker, nor subject to any variation over time. He illustrates the kind of contrast between objectivity and subjectivity he has in mind when discussing the nature of spatial intuition. 'What is objective in it is what is subject to laws, what can be conceived and judged, what is expressible in words. What is merely intuitable is not communicable' (*FA* §26). These crucial insights are repeated and amplified in 'The Thought'.

A key feature that unites his early and late work is his continued emphasis on the role of his famous context principle in making the case against anti-psychologism. In the *Foundations* it appears as his second fundamental principle, which bids us 'never to ask for the meaning in isolation, but only in the context of a sentence' (*FA*, x). This is stressed because he recognises that psychologism follows quickly if we fail to observe that sub-sentential expressions have meaning only within the context of completed propositions. That such atomism is a mistake can be seen by considering the nature of judgement, because the thoughts that lie behind our judgements can be identified only with whole propositions. For example, merely imagining or speaking a name in isolation is not to express a judgement. To imagine 'The capital of Germany' is not as yet to think of something that might be potentially true or false. Greater determination is required to form a judgement such as 'The capital of Germany is in Italy'. For this reason, he objects to any attempt to identifying thoughts or judgements with 'ideas' (of the empiricist variety), pictures or mental images. Thoughts, which are expressed by sentences, are nothing like any of these purely subjective phenomena. In line with logic's special concern with truth, he is quite clear that he means, 'by "thought", something for which the question of truth can arise' (*T*, p. 36). This is why the cardinal sin in the study of logic is to conflate acts or processes of thinking with thoughts, for it is this that encourages the idea that a science of the laws of thought belongs to the study of psychology.

Once again, he illustrates the main point of this distinction by means of an example. He asks the reader to consider the difference between having thoughts as opposed to visual impressions of a tree. Imagine two people, each looking at the same tree from a different angle. Their impressions, conscious experiences and even physically discernible retinal images of it will differ uniquely. Hence, if we were to conflate any of these psychological or physiological happenings with their thoughts, on what basis could we say they were both thinking about the very same object? Why are they not, to use Frege's words, 'shut up in their own inner worlds' (*T*, p. 52)? The answer is that they, like us, are capable of agreeing in judgement, which is more than merely receiving and processing images. It requires 'grasping' the same thought. For as he says, 'I . . . acknowledge thoughts as independent of me; other men can grasp them as much as I' (*T*, p. 51). It is with this in mind that he held that thoughts inhabited a third realm, distinct from two other realms occupied by subjective ideas and physical objects. Thoughts cannot be identified with the latter because they are not perceptible by our ordinary senses. Grasping them requires a 'special mental capacity' (*T*, p. 51). Marks and sounds serve as their outer perceptible garb; various natural languages provide the necessary *means* of seeing and hearing them. Nevertheless, what is expressed must not be confused with the medium of expression. The sounds and marks that, in normal circumstances, constitute words and sentences would be meaningless without the thoughts behind them. It is only the *senses* of sentences that are true or false; these alone interest the logician.

This is not to ignore that there are many other aspects of language that can affect 'mood, atmosphere or illumination'. It is only to stress that these lack a special concern with truth. Thus, even while recognising the 'poetic' side of language, Frege is quick to remark that while such 'Transformations are not trivial in every respect . . . they do not touch the thought, they do not touch what is true or false' (*T*, p. 39).

On this basis he is further led to claim that 'What are called the human-ities are closer to poetry, and are therefore less scientific than the exact sciences . . . for exact science is directed toward truth and truth alone' (*T*, p. 39). Consequently, his understanding of the logical does more than reveal the limit of the legitimate scope of descriptive psychology; it also funds a divide between the arts and the sciences. Indeed, this has become entrenched in modern thinking, setting the stage for debates about the relative value and importance of these different spheres.

Early and late, the moral is the same: subjective psychological phe-nomena are the legitimate concern of psychologists, but these must not be confused with thoughts and their laws which, given their objectiv-ity and concern with truth, are the proper subject matter for logicians. Logic is set apart because it alone is charged with 'the task of discover-ing the laws of truth, not the laws of taking things to be true or of think-ing' (*T*, p. 34). He regarded the stakes of failing to recognise this as being extremely serious, as his rhetoric reveals.

> Would there be a science of history otherwise? Would not all moral theory, all law, and otherwise collapse? What would be left of reli-gion? The natural sciences too could only be assessed as fables like astrology and alchemy. (*T*, p. 50)

By way of response, he concludes:

> Not everything is an idea. Otherwise psychology would contain all the sciences within it, or at least it would be the supreme judge over all the sciences. Otherwise psychology would rule even over logic and mathematics. (*T*, p. 51)

His strongest reasons for maintaining that thoughts are objective derive from his views on what makes communication and the univer-sality of logic possible. For, in his view, when two (or more) people communicate they must grasp the very same thoughts, but this would be impossible if thoughts were subjective and private. Similarly, it is a requirement of valid reasoning that we can grasp the very same thoughts more than once in the course of a logical argument. Even if we locate thoughts in 'minds' or identify them with recurring mental 'tokens' as opposed to worldly items, as is the wont of today's classical cognitivists, they must remain independent and objective. For all this to be possible it must be that thoughts – the senses of sentences – 'can be true without being grasped by a thinker' (*T*, p. 50).[18] It is in just this sense that he regards them as paradigms of the publicly accessible and mind-independent. Even his use of the metaphor of 'mode of presentation' to describe them maintains their integrity in this regard. We can see from this that Burge is right to identify Frege's key reason for regarding thoughts and their laws to be objective as tied to his concern to secure 'the intersubjectivity and lawfulness of logic' (Burge 1997, p. 5).

It is in this context, and not due to any prior metaphysical commitments, that we should understand his metaphor of the third realm. This is also why he claims that the laws of logic are in one sense 'descriptive', in the way that the fundamental laws of physics are meant to be. Hence, as both are objective sciences, he favourably compares the logician's task to discover the laws of thought with the physicist's concern to establish the laws of heat. This analogy licenses his blatant proclamation that logicians make ontological discoveries on a par with those made by other scientists, such as chemists, and his claim that the discovery of the objects, the true and the false, is one such (see *PW*, p. 194). Likewise, he emphasises that the kind of truth with which logic is concerned is factual truth – or in his own words, 'the sort of truth which it is the aim of science to discern' (*T*, p. 34). However, although all sciences have this common target, logic is unique in being the science that seeks truly to discern the very laws of truth itself. For this reason its laws must hold universally, making it the most general science.

Observing these commitments, it is not uncommon to find interpreters concluding that Frege was committed to logical realism in the form of a realm of logical entities that can be read straight off the breaks in his extensional logic. Such readings often begin by focusing on the substance of his other writings and on what made this approach to logic genuinely revolutionary: the replacement of the categories of subject and predicate with those of function and argument, already familiar to mathematics. Thus, to take a simple expression like '$x^2 + 2$' it is easy to see that the variable x can be replaced by a variety of arguments (i.e. specific numbers or names). By replacing x with one of a range of appropriate arguments such as, 2, 4, 6 or 8, a result, or value, is yielded – in this case a number.[19] With but a slight twist, the same moves are famously re-employed with respect to Frege's account of the bivalency of whole expressions. As not all completed expressions yield values of the same sort, the assignment of an appropriate argument to a special class of functions determines the truth-value of whole propositions. Unlike the algebraic example just mentioned, in which the resulting value would be number, the function expressed by '$2^2 + 2 = 6 =$' can have only one of two results; it will designate either *the True* or *the False*, to use Frege's labels. He calls this special class of functions 'concepts' and finds them at work wherever the question of truth arises in any domain.

That this was the framework of Frege's logic is not in question. But we ought not to be misled into ascribing to him a straightforward logical realism on this basis, holding that the aforementioned logical entities – objects, functions, values and truth values – all have a separate, real existence. However, it is treacherously easy to make just this kind of attribution if one is already encouraged by the fact that he clearly endorsed the idea that logic is objective and independent, as noted above. For example, Burge and McCulloch both seem to be following just this train of thought when they conclude:

> Broadly speaking, Frege was a Platonist about logical objects (like numbers and truth values), functions, and thought contents.
>
> (Burge 1997, p. 2)[20]

> Now, just as Frege took it that numerals and complex arithmetical expressions represent real extralinguistic things – numbers – so he took the patterns also to represent something real (although abstract). These things he called functions, and he considered them to be complementary, but fundamentally different from, objects . . . .
>
> (McCulloch 1989, p. 8)

To take these claims seriously would seem to indicate that Frege sponsored roughly the same kind of atomistic realism as Russell. He would be committed to the existence of an independent framework of distinct entities with different kinds of combinatorial possibilities. Presumably, to follow through on this suggestion, these would unite to 'create' or 'produce' other sorts of objects. One attraction of this idea is that it might seem to hold out the promise of potentially explaining how and why whole expressions become meaningful by appeal to their parts.[21] But taking it seriously would also require, as McCulloch makes quite clear, that functions (and concepts) as well as objects have independent existence. This will encourage us to 'think of a function as a sort of abstract machine or processor which needs to be fed with certain things, like numbers, and which duly extrudes others' (McCulloch 1989, p. 8). But this is to model unsaturated expressions on physical devices, existing with their own integrity but unable to produce anything unless they are supplied with inputs of the appropriate kind, like open circuits – powerless until closed. Once so satisfied, they 'generate' something else equally real and distinct. But minimal reflection reveals that a host of nasty questions attends this picture. What kind of existent has this sort of individual integrity while being, by definition, incomplete? In absence of our contributions what 'in the world' supplies the inputs?

Putting aside these awkward puzzles it must be stressed that this kind of atomism positively militates against the context principle. With that principle in play it is simply not possible to marry a straightforward realism with his approach to logic. Luckily, there is no good exegetical reason to ascribe such an atomism to Frege in the first place. Unlike some of his readers, he does not crudely conflate the distinctions he drew in the course of his logical investigations with the nature of reality. He is explicit about the fact that all his so-called logical discoveries came from working backwards from complete expressions to their logical skeletons, as he clearly states:

> What is *distinctive about my conception of logic* is that I begin by giving pride of place to the content of the word 'true', and then immediately go on to introduce a thought as that to which the question 'Is it true?' is in principle applicable. So I do not begin with concepts and put them together to form a thought or judgement; I come to the parts of a thought by analysing the thought.
>
> (*PW*, p. 253; emphasis mine)

If we abandon the productive talk of 'yielding' and 'generating' results in previous paragraphs, and remind ourselves that Frege regarded complete functions as nothing other than *names* of the objects they designated, his approach can be understood without any particular metaphysical trappings. His talk of 'objects', 'values' and 'functions' is nothing more than fallout from the way he carved up extensional logic. Consider his distinction between the 'sign and thing signified', which he drew in his mature period. Thus, if we say '8 + 8' or '4^2', these are both signs referring to *the number 16*, just as the signs '16' and 'XVI' do. Other examples of proper names include definite expressions like 'the capital of England' and 'London'. The important thing for Frege was just that if names denote the same objects, then they must play exactly the same logical roles. Given that the identity sign indicates absolute logical equivalence, saying '2 + 2' is *just another way of saying* '4' and saying 'Frege revolutionised logic' is just another way of saying 'the True'. For, like all names, whole expressions that denote one or other truth-value designate one of other of these objects. As everyone knows, matters are not as simple as this since inferences are intensional. His full recognition of this was at least partly what led him to draw his famous distinction between sense and reference.

My point is just that by reminding ourselves of the context of his work we can see that his concerns were not metaphysical, but practical. His focus in all this was not on discovering the furniture of the universe, as it was for Russell, but on the fact that, clearly, having two different names for the same object can cause a variety of confusions and make us prone to cognitive errors, which we will wish to avoid if we are seeking truth. In particular, an inadequate symbolism hinders our ability to make inferences and thereby to provide proofs and demonstrations. Hence, unless I know that Margaret Thatcher and John Major's immediate predecessor are one and the same, I will not be able to infer anything about the one from the other or to show why any such transitions are valid. The moral applies not only to sub-propositional names that refer to the same object, but also to statements that name the same truth-value, as in (3) and (4) below:

(9) The Queen of Scotland rules Scotland.
(10) The Queen of Scotland rules Australia.

Although both statements have the same reference, in this case 'the True', only the first wears this fact on its sleeve. Proposition (3) allows us to immediately infer its truth, whereas (4) does not; we need mediating information in order to be able to see that it is true, even though they both designate the same object. It is easy to see from this why taking note of different modes of presentation is of paramount importance to any truth-seeking mode of inquiry, for failure to do so can hamper our ability to make valid inferences and show them to be such. Talking of *the true* and *the false* as objects is not to endorse a specific metaphysics *per se*, but simply to note their logical roles.

We have seen that Frege believed thoughts and logic to be objective but, unlike endorsing logical atomism, this is perfectly consistent with the fact that he should put the context principle in the forefront of his thinking. Great care must be taken, therefore, in understanding his brand of logical realism. In this regard, even to call him a realist about logic is strictly a misnomer since he carefully distinguishes that which is 'objective from what is handeable or spatial or real' (*FA* §26). For him, what is objective outstrips what is 'real'. What we might better say is that he subscribed to 'logical objectivism', in line with the fact that his primary distinction between logic and psychology rests on observing a dichotomy between objectivity and subjectivity.

Moreover, this logical objectivism had quite different roots from Russell's logical realism. This is evident if we consider that the latter expressly hoped to establish the truth of logicism, in part, to give advantage in the battle against idealism.[22] But as Frege had no such ulterior ambition for his project, we ought to be suspicious of any claim, such as Dummett's, that 'In a history of philosophy Frege would have to be classified as a member of the realist revolt against Hegelian idealism' (1978, p. 88). Nor should it surprise us that, 'apart from his assault on psychologism, Frege barely troubled to attack idealism at all: he simply passed it by' (Dummett 1978, p. 88). The plausible reason is that, given his hope to develop a *Begriffsschrift* capable of clearly demonstrating any truth-preserving valid inference in any scientific domain, Hegel's logic would hardly suit.

But if this is right, a serious question remains. For if Frege was not metaphysically motivated, how exactly should we understand his claim that logic is an objective science? Getting clear about his views on this requires situating them within the debate that raged amongst his contemporaries, who felt the pull of two quite different notions of the regulative. For example, Wundt saw logic as a normative science with prescriptive ambitions on a par with ethics, whereas Lipps regarded it as having only descriptive status, identifying it as the physics of thinking.[23] Frege sought to avoid choosing one or the other. He hoped to reconcile the descriptive and normative readings by restricting logic's concern to divining the 'correct' laws of thought or of valid inference, as opposed to mere laws of thinking or psychological processes. This implies that while non-logical judgements are possible, since it is possible to infer incorrectly, one can still insist that all *proper* judgements *must in fact* conform to the laws of valid inference. To identify the latter laws would be to describe how logic both *does* and *ought to* stand with respect to itself. To articulate the laws of thought that necessarily lead to the truth is at one and the same time to identify positively the laws that ought to govern all correct forms of thinking, universally and absolutely. In this way, logic could then be a potentially informative science, no different from any other. Properly characterised, its laws could play a practical role in guiding our thinking about any particular subject matter. Frege is explicit about this:

> In one sense a law asserts *what is*; in the other it *prescribes what ought to be*. Only in the latter sense can the laws of logic be called the 'laws

of thought': so far as they stipulate the way in which one ought to think. Any law asserting what is can be conceived as prescribing what one ought to think in conformity with it, and is thus in that sense a law of thought. This holds for laws of geometry and physics no less than for logic. The latter have a special title to the name 'laws of thought' only if we mean to assert that they are the most general laws, which prescribe universally.

> (*BLA*, §12; emphases mine)[24]

In this way it is at least possible for logic to be a science, the laws of which are simultaneously descriptive and prescriptive, but also objective in the sense that they exist in a way that is completely independent of our psychology and practices: they are unchanging and universal.[25] Nevertheless, this set of ideas rests on the fault-line of a serious and irreconcilable tension. For, as suggested above, the very idea that we can make logical discoveries about the *correct* form of thinking implies that it would still be possible to think and judge, even if such laws were violated. But there is simply no room for the idea that there could be an incorrect thought in the sense of an 'illogical thought', for nothing could be a thought at all if it did not already conform to the laws of logic. Not to obey such laws is not an option for thinkers, unless they have simply failed to judge, full stop. Frege appears to be aware of this, given what he writes elsewhere:

> But what if beings were ... found whose laws of thought flatly contradicted ours and therefore frequently led to contrary results even in practice? The psychological logician could only acknowledge the fact and say simply: those laws hold for them, these laws hold for us. I should say: we have here a hitherto unknown type of madness. (*BLA*, §14)

The point is that the very possibility of alien 'thinkers', in the sense described, is not intelligible. Logical laws clearly cannot be all-encompassing and yet allow for exceptions. As a consequence, the idea that the laws of logic hold in a maximally general, but objectively *independent*, way, ought to be viewed with suspicion. Rather, these laws hold without exception because they are *constitutive* of judgement itself. To break them is not to judge incorrectly, but to fail to judge at all. It is simply wrong to model them on independent physical laws, such as gravitation, which might fail to apply in special circumstances, such as in zero gravity, without thereby threatening their general truth (*pace* Cartwright). Logic laws cannot be of this sort.

Logic determines the limits of sense and nonsense, which are wider than the limits of truth. This being so, it is not possible to adopt a merely theoretical stance to logic. Misdescribing it is possible, but having a false *theory* of logic does not make sense. It is not possible to have a sensible disagreement about logical laws in the way we might disagree in our speculations about the contents of a closed box. The difference between writing a well-formed logical expression and writing something that is not a logical expression at all better captures the form of disagreements about logic. The important lesson, as Diamond puts it, is that:

> We cannot criticise a concept-script by *stepping outside* the business of making concept-scripts . . . To step outside would be to say: 'What we are expressing in a concept-script is *thoughts*. They have a logical structure, and once we find out what *that* is, we shall be able to see what logical structure to build into a concept-script to better reflect the structure that thoughts have.'
>
> (Diamond 1995, p. 121)[26]

In sum, it is not possible to unite the claim that the laws of logic are descriptive of something *independent* of us with the Kantian thought that they underwrite the very possibility of any rational thought at all, be it true or false. Frege, however, is, at different times, on both sides of this issue. Perhaps these tensions were not resolved in his thinking because they did not conflict with his ultimately practical concern to develop the new logic as an ideal logical language, a *characteristica universalis*, applicable to any scientific discourse concerned with truth and admitting of valid inference and proof. For whether or not such a symbolism is really possible, it would at best yield practical benefits in 'particular fields', just as he hoped. But, even if this were achieved, it would not establish the credentials of logic as an independent, general science with its own subject matter. This separatist dimension of Frege's thinking must be called into question for the reasons just stated. The inescapable conclusion is that – not being independent of thought – logic cannot have any substantial content of its own. Hence, apart from its use in specific sciences, this raises a serious question of how logic should be understood and used for philosophical purposes. It also suggests that the answer will not be straightforward. As I will argue, the *Tractatus* is marked out by its unique response to this very question.

Wittgenstein's insight

I claim that in Wittgenstein's early treatment of logic the seeds were sown for what distinguishes and is of lasting importance in his philosophy. It provides the best and clearest example of how philosophy can clarify matters and expose philosophical nonsense, without proceeding by means of theoretical speculation, which is the unifying thread in his philosophical method throughout his entire career. I will expound and develop this central theme throughout the following chapters of this book. However, I conclude this chapter by honouring my promise to illuminate his view of logic by viewing it in the light of the foregoing treatments. Drawing on that exposition, I want to bring out the distinctive features of the Tractarian view of logic with respect to three issues – realism, subjectivism and formalism.

His opposition to Russell's realism and Frege's objectivism about logic is well discussed because Wittgenstein openly identifies their views as his target. His self-avowed fundamental thought (*Grundgedanke*) that there are no logical objects lies at the very heart of the *Tractatus*.[27] To understand his crowning thought fully it is important to note his distinction between logical form and logical space, which will be elaborated upon more fully in the next chapter.[28]

Logical form is what is common to our pictures and what they depict: it is the very *form* of reality that reveals how the elements of facts and propositions might possibly be arranged. In the prelude to his attack on logical objects, Wittgenstein gives attention to the nature of formal concepts, found in logic, which he contrasts with proper concepts. He writes:

> 4.126 When something falls under a formal concept as one of its objects this cannot be expressed by means of a proposition.

The thought is that the nature of a formal concept can only be shown in the way that it is employed. It cannot be spoken of. For, taking his views about the general form of the proposition seriously, to be spoken of requires that objects be pictured in some possible state of affairs. But logic has no objects and thus none that can make such appearances. He writes:

> 4.1272 Thus the variable name 'x' is the proper sign for the pseudo-concept object.

There is no 'thing' that the apparent name 'object' (or variable, *x*) stands proxy for over and above the ordinary things of which we speak.

There is no super-object that answers to the name x, and so thinking it serves a representative function results in nonsense. Our understanding of the seemingly sensible, but general, term 'object' is something that has no *independent* life of its own. If we want to understand it, we can do no more than attend to how it manifests itself on particular occasions by considering what we say about ordinary objects and the specific situations in which they find themselves. Through talking sense about mundane objects, in this or that context, the character of logical variables is revealed. Logical form is immanent in the very structure of ordinary statements and facts, it is not something 'extra' that needs to be or could be added in or separately attached. To use a workaday analogy, it is akin to the way ingredients are blended together to make a cake. One does not add the eggs, flour, sugar and then add in 'the mixing'. Neither is related to objects in the sense of being *separate from*, or *additional to*, them. As logic is inherent in the very fabric of world and thought it cannot exist independently. Hence, if Russell is a Platonist about logic, then by contrast Wittgenstein is decidedly more Aristotelian.[29]

But focusing on logical form alone is not enough to feel the full impact of Wittgenstein's objection to logical realism. He introduces the metaphor of logical space in order to make clear that not only will seeking to articulate the internal structure of facts and propositions end in nonsense, but so will any attempt to describe logical relations that hold *between* facts and propositions.

He discourages this idea by getting us to think of logic not as representing a separate body of facts, but as revealing the necessary framework of possibilities that exists within an internally defined space. Thus, P leaves open: $P \lor Q$, $P \& Q$, but it necessarily closes off the possibility of $\sim P$. Thus, Wittgenstein turns the idea that these inter-relations are expressible on its head by saying:

> 5.535.1 The certainty, possibility, or impossibility of a situation is not expressed by a proposition but by an expression's being a tautology, a proposition with sense, or a contradiction.
>
> (cf. also 4.464)

Consequently, logic cannot inform us about the world. To say 'P $\rightarrow$ Q' is not to make a statement about how things happen to stand, but to offer a framework for seeing which facts would have to hold, if P and Q were so related. If one holds, as he did, that the general form of all propositions is simply to say how things happen to stand, then it is easy to see that, by definition, logic has no propositions. In revealing the necessary structure of possibilities that exists between propositions he is exposing the misnamed 'propositions' of logic to be without sense; they are not propositions at all. Therefore, they cannot be understood as expressing *necessary truths*, for that is an oxymoron. Yet to say they are senseless is not to say they are nonsensical, after the fashion of the confused products of trying to generate propositions by misusing formal concepts. For these reasons, great care must be taken even in saying that 'the truths' of logic are senseless in that they are empty tautologies. Like all logical possibilities (I do not say 'logical propositions', since this too is nonsense) tautologies do not represent any possible state of affairs. They occupy but one extreme in logical space, while contradictions lie at the opposite pole. Clearly contradictions do not occupy the same location in logical space even though, like tautologies, they are sense-less. Therefore, it makes no sense to identify the one with the other, or any other logical possibility with any other. In this regard, we understand them more clearly by looking at how they function.

Yet once again we must be careful in characterising these functions. Indeed, Wittgenstein bids us to think of these relations between facts and propositions operationally, as opposed to functionally, in order to show that we are dealing with internal relations only.[30] He marks this distinction precisely in order to distinguish his understanding of truth functions from Russell's productive characterisation, as Hylton has convincingly argued. For, in line with his views that logical forms have an independent status and that logical constants are genuine objects, Russell held that propositional functions were used to generate yet more complex representations from simple elements. This must be the case if logic represents a distinct subject matter. For example, according to Russell, 'the propositional function X is wise . . . share[s] a structure with the proposition that Socrates is wise: the propositional function is not a mere mapping of objects onto propositions' (Hylton 1997, p. 96; see also Coffa 1991, p. 90). But this idea was clearly anathema to Wittgenstein's understanding of logic, and his n-operator is designed to demonstrate that logical operations are indeed purely procedural, not productive. He uses it to show how complex propositions can be formed from elementary propositions without introducing or requiring any additional internal resources or thereby forming more internally complex representations.

Attending to expressions involving negation is the easiest means of showing why Russell's approach was hopeless. For to accept it would require saying that the expressions, ~P, ~~~P, ~P&~P, all exhibit distinct logical forms and, therefore, require different representational elements. But this is extravagant given that they all mean the same, despite employing different logical constants. Wittgenstein's insight was to reject this way of individuating logical forms in favour of noting that the above all occupy the same position in logical space, despite the difference in their outward expressions (see Friedlander 2001, pp. 79–86; Ostrow 2002, pp. 9–10). In making this move he effectively out 'Russell'ed Russell. In this connection, he writes:

> 4.0031 All philosophy is a 'critique of language' . . . It was Russell who performed the service of showing that the apparent logical form of a proposition need not be its real one.

Yet even in praising Russell's good work on this front, Wittgenstein was aware that his erstwhile mentor had not taken his own lessons to heart when it came to understanding logic itself. Part of the novelty and ingenuity of his early philosophy was to take Russell's method a step further by challenging the naïve representational view of logic.

Still, some of his remarks may appear to go against the idea that logic is not a separate domain of independent facts. For example, at one point he says:

> 5.552 Logic is prior to every experience – that something is so. It is prior to the question 'How'?, not prior to the question 'What'?

Confusion on what he is saying here comes from not attending carefully enough to the distinction between logical form and space. For what it means for logic to be *prior* to the question of *how* things are arranged is nothing other than a restatement of the idea that logic charts the logical space of what is necessary in the way facts or propositions can interrelate. It exposes the framework against which any possible judgement must be made. However, 5.552 is concerned also with logical form, which cannot be thought of as separable from its content. Logical form *is* the limit of all possible experiences, all the combinatory possibilities of things. It is revealed, shows itself, in the limits of how things *can be* possibly arranged. However, being so, it clearly cannot be prior to *what* there is to be arranged. Exactly how things can be arranged is determined by the nature of the things themselves – and this is built into the logic of those things, but only manifested by the existence of specific facts. In this way it constitutes the limits of what is possible, thinkable and sayable; the stopping point. As will be explained in more detail in the next chapter, logic is at one and the same time built into the nature of facts and propositions. This is the reason why logic is revealed simply by staking out what it is possible to say. Most importantly, it follows that this cannot be determined before making and evaluating an attempted judgement.

All this being so, there can be no science of logic, for it lacks a subject matter of its own that can be separately articulated. Nor, for this reason, can logic be the source of explanatory or governing laws of inference.[31] We are told that:

> 6.123 Clearly the laws of logic cannot in their turn be subject to the laws of logic.

Failure to accept this would in any case lead to an infinite regress. For if the propositions of logic did say something about the world, then they would not be the final basis for all making sense. They would have to be underwritten by a superior logic. If this superior logic were composed of genuine propositions, then it too would need to be underwritten by an even greater logic, and so on *ad infinitum*. We are brought to see that if logic is to underwrite all saying it must not say anything itself. Thus we are told:

> 5.551 Our fundamental principle is that whenever a question can be decided by logic at all it must be possible to·decide it without more ado.

> 5.473 Logic must look after itself.

As he also says, 'Absolutely necessary signs speak for themselves' (6.124). But in so doing, they say absolutely nothing.

Together, the above reflections on logical form and logical space constitute the basis for his observations that logical signs are not genuinely symbolic, that they have no corresponding objects; and that there are no logical facts or propositions. As he writes:

> 5.4 At this point it becomes manifest that there are no 'logical objects' (in Frege's and Russell's sense).

> 5.43.1 In fact all the propositions of logic say the same thing, to wit nothing.

To avoid misunderstanding these remarks, it will prove useful to consider how these views differ from Kant's, and how Wittgenstein would have responded to Hegel's charges of 'formalism' and 'subjectivism'. Where he stands on the first of these matters is tied to his thought that although logic has no objects of its own, it gets its life from the combinatorial possibilities and impossibilities thrown up by objects and facts. It is not just inherent in our thinking, but inherent in reality itself, comprising the limits of both. For example, even tautology and contradiction are limiting cases at the bounds of real possibility; they reflect what is always or never the case. Or again, our ability to distinguish strings of meaningless signs from well-formed expressions by appeal to their syntactical form alone depends on our having abstracted these 'forms' from the skeleton of meaningful expressions relating to genuine possibilities.[32] This is how a purely formal logic comes into being.

The point is that although logic takes care of itself, it does not stand by itself. In this light, unqualified talk of purely formal 'rules of logical syntax' or the 'rules of logic' is almost certain to mislead. Logic shows itself in the way things can be arranged and it reveals the limits of what is possible and not possible to say, but in doing so it says nothing itself. We are told:

> 6.13 Logic is not a body of doctrine, but a mirror image of the world. Logic is transcendental.

Thus, the sense in which he holds logic to be transcendental is not a sop to Kant. Although, *contra* Hegel, he regarded it as formal and empty he did not see it as 'subjective' as would be implied if he had been committed to Hegel's characterisation of Kantian transcendental idealism. Hence, when Friedlander asks of the opening lines of the *Tractatus*, 'How can one start with the world as such, after Kant?' (Friedlander 2001, p. 21): The reply must be: How could one not, after Hegel? For in seeing logic as being *in* the world, Wittgenstein was entirely in line with the post-Kantian tradition. Indeed given his critique of realism, as set out above, the way in which he held it to be 'in the world' is in one sense quite Hegelian. As he says:

> 5.61 Logic pervades the world: the limits of the world are also its limits.

Of course, these two would not have agreed on the issue of its formality nor, about its general character.

It is crucial to observe that these insights into the nature of logic do not merely constitute a unique position on an important topic, but they also entail that an entirely different approach to the subject is needed.

Establishing that Wittgenstein came to see that this same approach is the only one appropriate for philosophy quite generally is the primary concern of this book. It is therefore highly instructive to give serious attention to just *how* he attempted to free our thinking about logic. Although he does provide some arguments, he does not simply advance a counter-position to logical realism. Rather than offering a new theory, one of the things he does is to present us with an alternative notation, designed to discourage our tendency to treat Russellian notation as if its symbols for logical constants named objects.[33]

For example, he uses the truth-tables as a device for demonstrating that these signs do not correspond to anything. For instance, the so-called logical 'relation' embodied in the material conditional 'if p then q' can be represented by using the truth-table as an alternative symbolism. Representing P → Q in the form of a truth-table removes the temptation to think that there are logical objects in some nether realm that answer to the apparent name '→'. Consider the following:

P	Q	
T	T	T
F	T	T
T	F	F
F	F	T

This simple truth-table enables us to see the different possible ways in which facts would have to lie if the world was to be in accord with P → Q. But, so expressed, it is also clear that whether it does or not only depends on whether certain facts obtain or not, as indicated by each line of Ts and Fs. Seeing matters in this light ought to break the spell cast by Russellian notation since, written this way, the logical constant for the conditional does not appear at all. If we adopt Wittgenstein's convention of always writing the columns in the same order it is an easy matter to completely display the necessary framework of possible interrelations between facts and propositions (see *TLP*, 5.101). For by laying out the possible truth-values of all the elementary propositions we can, in principle, construct a complete truth-table showing all logical possibilities, framed by the two limiting cases. Crucially, to understand truth-tables we are forced to *use* them, not simply describe them. In so doing, the need and basis for positing the existence of logical objects is entirely undercut.

Once again, the point is that Wittgenstein not only argued that logical realism leads to paradoxes and nonsense, but by getting us to attend to the way logic operates through his use of the truth-tables he also removed one major temptation for thinking that there must be any-thing represented by the logical constants. Thus, the attractions of logical realism fade as we attend more carefully to the role of logic in our thinking and practices. The truth-tables operate in this respect as paradigms of perspicuous presentations. In elucidating and clarifying, they show what cannot be said. They tell us nothing new. Rather, they merely, and quite literally, re-*present* that which is already immanent in our use of logic. Used as demonstrations in this way they do not tell us anything about the state of the world, but they do succeed in getting us to realign our thinking. Given that logic lies at the heart of every-thing we think and say, they make evident something we must already, in a sense, implicitly understand, but which we tend to misrepresent in our reflective attempts to give expression to it. Yet none of this under-standing is imparted by merely advancing a superior theory or a more informed speculation about logic.

Conclusion

It should now be clear that it is not just the articulation of his fundamental thought and its consequences that makes the *Tractatus* treatment of logic ground-breaking. It was the inspiration for Wittgen-stein's view about the very end and limits of philosophy and about how it can achieve its end. As the bounds of sense are set internally, by the very topics about which we can think, philosophy can at best clarify and make perspicuous that which is already known to us. This is what it means to stake out the limits of thought from the inside. This is why philosophy must leave everything as it is even though it can alter our understanding. Consequently, although it would be correct to say that his view of logic distinguishes him from Kant, Hegel, Russell and Frege, this would be to vastly understate the importance of the related insights that followed from that understanding of this topic.

2
Just the Facts?

Language cannot express what belongs to the essence of the world. Therefore it cannot say that everything flows. Language can only say what we could also imagine differently.

Wittgenstein, *Philosophical Occasions*, p. 189

Introduction

I have argued that what is both important and distinctive in Wittgenstein's early view of and approach to philosophy is inseparably bound up with his treatment of logic in the *Tractatus*. Yet, apart from constituting the basis for his methodological innovation, his early approach to logic comes as part of a package, along with a host of other views on related matters concerning the nature of objects, facts, pictures, analysis, etc. As they are often misunderstood, these will need to be considered before I can make a proper case for recognising a methodological continuity between his early and later approach. I will prepare for that task by challenging the established view that the Tractarian 'metaphysics', 'semantics' and 'analysis' are *meant* to constitute a theory. This will be the main aim of this chapter. It will prove useful in any case since reviewing what Wittgenstein says about these topics is necessary in order to answer the vexed question of how we ought to understand his various remarks about the nature and function of the *Tractatus*' 'propositions'. Although this chapter makes a start on examining issues that will be relevant to this question, it will not be completely satisfactorily dealt with until the next chapter. Therefore I must beg the reader's indulgence and patience.

Theoretical readings of the *Tractatus*

There is a prominent school of interpretation according to which Wittgenstein's early work is best understood if we focus on the theory (or, indeed, theories) it putatively advances, such as its picture theory of language, its theory of logic, its theory of metaphysics, etc. Agreement about this, along with the recognition that his corpus splits into two main periods, fuels debates within this camp of readings about the nature of the change that took place between them that licenses talk of two Wittgensteins: the early and the late.

Hence, there are those who support the idea that the divide rests on his having espoused two radically different theories about the nature of language. By their lights, the sea-change in his views is thought to revolve around these – according to which he repudiates his initial representational, referential theory of sense and its attendant metaphysics, in favour of the a new, successor theory that 'meaning is use'. Kripke is perhaps the most prominent representative of this type of theoretical reading. As he describes it, the structure of the *Investigations'* opening passages are designed to refute the '*Tractatus* truth-conditional theory of language', according to which language is 'correspondence-to-facts'. This is followed by a statement of the sceptical problem of rule-following and its proposed solution, in the form of *a new theory* of language. However, the new theory is based on warranted assertibility, as determined by community standards. *Inter alia*, this understanding frequently partners the claim that his philosophy underwent an important shift from realism to anti-realism in the process.

For others, the change heralded the introduction of an anti-theoretical dimension to Wittgenstein's thinking for the first time, for good or ill. On this account, his theoretical ambitions were isolated to his early period. For example, Pears claims that the important thing to keep in mind, 'is that he is moving away from theorizing and towards plain description of the phenomenon of language' (Pears 1988, p. 218). This thought is echoed more recently by Gefwert, who notes that whereas theories must be systematic and general, it was Wittgenstein's later recognition that a theory of meaning cannot have such features that, 'led to an overall philosophical breakthrough in [his] own development – to the anti-mentalism and anti-essentialism characteristic of his post-1937 views. It is this that we mean by the title of this book: from theory to therapy' (Gefwert 2000, p. 5).

Despite the disagreement about status of the *Investigations*, these readings are united by the idea that his *early* approach to philosophy is defined by a single theory or an interrelated set of theories. At first blush, this suggests that it or they are open to confirmation or disconfirmation by evidence. Thus, Pears holds that the supporting evidence, which accounts for the 'explanatory power' of the Tractarian theory, is available only at 'a deep level of analysis'. But he also holds that this gives it 'a curiously ambiguous status' and places it in 'a quasi-scientific limbo' since it does not allow 'the careful deduction of testable consequences that is characteristic of science' (Pears 1988, pp. 26–7).[1]

But we need not go as far as this. Even if the *Tractatus* is seen as attempting to offer a powerful, comprehensive theory about the nature of logic, world and semantics its merits might not be 'tested against the evidence', but rather might simply shine through when compared with the inadequate theories of Russell and Frege. Goldstein sponsors this version of the theoretical reading when he remarks that 'Wittgenstein was dissatisfied with the various answers that his two distinguished predecessors had proposed, and he offered not piecemeal countersuggestions but an all-embracing theory which, so he says in the Preface, solves all the problems. That theory is known as the picture theory of language' (Goldstein 1999, p. 9). He expands on this shortly after, claiming that:

> This tradition is full of theories – the theory of sense and reference, the theory of definite descriptions, the theory of judgement etc. – so *in that tradition* a theory is required to solve its outstanding problems, and Wittgenstein accordingly constructs such theories, including a theory about the logical structure of the world, a theory of number and the picture theory of meaning. (Goldstein 1999, p. 26)[2]

Clearly, it is more plausible to stick to this relatively modest 'problem-solving' conception of theories. Nevertheless, if the Tractarian statements are advanced theoretically, this still implies that they must be in some sense speculative or hypothetical. Moreover, even if we do not judge them directly against the evidence we will do so against their rivals, evaluating their comparative virtues in terms of such things as overall explanatory power and general coherence.

Throughout the remainder of this chapter I will attempt to clarify the commitments of the *Tractatus*, while discrediting theoretical readings of it. This is vital because, if we cast Wittgenstein as advancing some form of theory, even modestly defined, it follows that he must have been offering proposals about how things stand independently of us. But if so, then we cannot take seriously some of his most important insights about how philosophy must be pursued, given our place in the world. It may have been that Wittgenstein was simply wrong or confused about what he was doing. I will consider this possibility more fully in the next chapter, but before so condemning him I want to explore the extent to which his remarks in the *Tractatus* might be in harmony with his understanding of logic and the approach to philosophy it dictates, as described in Chapter 1. This requires reviewing the nature and point of his remarks about the world and how we picture it by means of propositions. It also requires asking how such propositions are analysed and to what end.

Tractarian metaphysics

The ontological tone of the book's opening lines can encourage a theoretical reading. It can appear that Wittgenstein is making a series of basic ontological claims or posits, in the mould of a traditional metaphysician. He says:

1.1 The world is the totality of facts, not of things.
2 What is the case – a fact – is the existence of states of affairs.
2.01 A state of affairs (a state of things) is a combination of objects (things).

However, appearances can deceive. In order to understand the character of these remarks properly it is important to remind ourselves of the context in which they issue, for they are likely meant as a critique of Russell's ontology. As seen in Chapter 1, Russell claimed that we could 'get down in theory, if not in practice, to ultimate simples' (*PLA*, p. 270). These simples were regarded as the basic constituents of the world – its logical atoms. Moreover, they were the only objects that could be given true names. Of course, Russell realised this was not a satisfactory or complete inventory of the furniture of the world, recognising that 'the only other sort of object you come across in the world is what we call facts' (*PLA*, p. 270). Yet he swiftly qualified this by saying that facts 'are not properly entities at all in the same sense in which their constituents are. That is shown by the fact that you cannot name them' (*PLA*, p. 270). Facts are, therefore, 'made up' from things – i.e. things combined in specific ways. This kind of view is part and parcel of his constructive, compositional metaphysics, which starts with the basics and builds up from there. The upshot is that objects constitute our most basic ontological category.[3]

Wittgenstein's statement of 1.1 denies precisely this; things – understood in this way – do not comprise the world. For he notes that even if we accept that facts are in some sense nothing but particular arrangements of things, it does not follow that things comprise an independent ontological category. For we quickly are told that it would be impossible to imagine any 'thing' outside some possible situation (i.e. outside a given factual context).

> 2.011 It is essential to things that they should be possible constituents of states of affairs.

Consequently, things are not independent of facts, but nor are facts independent of things. Things are always in one situation or another and, being so, they constitute facts – which are nothing other than the way various things stand in relation to one another. Whenever we come to think or speak of an object it must be in the context of some possible state of affairs – we cannot even imagine what it would be for a thing to exist outside of any and all possible states of affairs. Thus:

> 2.123 If I know an object I also know all its possible occurrences in states of affairs (Every one of these possibilities must be part of the nature of the object).

It is natural, though ultimately misleading, to try to understand this point by means of a simple analogy. For example, if we consider an ordinary object such as a book, its very essence seems to depend upon the totality of possible situations it might (or might not) inhabit – i.e. it could be read, burned, dropped, dusty, open, closed, and so on. It cannot be drunk, driven, shattered like glass, etc. The list runs on indefinitely. Use of this sort of analogy might appear justified by Wittgenstein's talk of spatial objects – which, as he says, must exist in 'infinite space' (*TLP* 2.0131). What this means is that anything spatial in nature can be imagined as existing anywhere within space; that much is built into the very nature of spatial things. But, of course, objects can have many types of properties other than merely spatial ones and each of these comes with a spectrum of possibilities. For example, there are colour-spaces, acoustic-spaces, tactile-spaces, and so on.

> 2.0131 A speck in a visual field need not be red, but it must have a colour; it has so to speak a colour space around it.

It is an intrinsic, essential property of visual specks that they must have some colour or other, but it is not necessary that a speck has any particular colour. That specks must have some colour or other is part of the logical nature of such things: that they should have *this* or *that* colour is not. Recognising this, we can see that in alluding to the 'spaces' surrounding objects he is thereby also rejecting the idea that there is an *a priori* order to things.

However irresistible it may be to regard Wittgenstein's view of these matters in Leibnizian fashion, to do so completely misrepresents it. For this is to conflate his 'objects' with ordinary things by modelling the latter on the former: It is to think of them, wrongly, as postulated basic *constituents* of the world when they are really nothing more than place holders for various possibilities. Because they play this role they cannot have any determinable properties of their own. That is why he tells us that:

2.0232 In a manner of speaking: objects are colourless.

The remark that objects are colourless is designed to make a general point. It is because they must be identified with their space of possibilities that objects cannot be identified with any of the contingent properties that might be exhibited within that space. By their very nature they underwrite various empirical properties and therefore cannot be defined by appeal to such properties or sets of such. This is why coming to know differences in the external properties of a thing is not to understand its essence, its internal properties. This is how we should understand his remark that:

2.0233 If two objects have the same logical form, the only distinction between them, apart from their external properties, is that they are different.

Although it is in some ways close to the right reading, this remark does not say that two things are essentially tokens of the same type if they are qualitatively identical but numerically distinct, existing as it were in different circumstances – as a matter of chance. The danger in so understanding it is that we will be tempted to think of 'a type' as defined by a set of distinct properties. Yet, it simply does not follow that if objects have the same range of possibilities then what explains this, or makes *this* possible, is that they must share a set of determinate properties. Moreover, if we do say this, the yawning abyss of an infinite regress opens before us. Again, it must be underscored that Wittgenstein's 'objects' cannot be modelled on anything encountered in experience.

The logical form of objects is not any kind of metaphysical framework. It is not something independent of the things that explain why they interrelate as they do, for this would require that the logical forms have the status of a further set of facts with which we could be acquainted and which could be potentially described and catalogued. Of course, these extra items turn out, paradoxically, to be necessary facts, as we saw in the previous chapter. Again, this view was espoused most clearly by Russell in 1913 in his unfinished *Theory of Knowledge*, which he abandoned due to Wittgenstein's criticisms. Accordingly, logical forms, such as *aRb*, represented a kind of super-fact about the world that made it possible for us to assert that certain ordered relations exist. Russell writes:

> In order to understand 'A and B are similar', we must be acquainted with A and B, similarity, and with the *general form* of symmetrical dual complexes. (*TOK*, p. 112; emphasis mine)

In explicit opposition to the view that various logical forms are extra, discoverable items of the world, Wittgenstein's account is more subtle and sophisticated. He sees the logical form of the world as inherent in the very nature of objects themselves – and he rejects the idea that anything further explains how they interconnect. Thus we are told:

> 2.03 In a state of affairs objects fit into one another like the links of a chain.

Logical form is nothing over and above the combinatorial possibilities of objects: the totality of the various ways they can combine or fail to combine. It is immanent to objects themselves; it is the essence of the world. That nothing *extra* is required is made clear by the following remark.

> 2.0124 If all objects are given, then at the same time, all possible states of affairs are also given.

Moreover, in defining the full field of possibilities the logic of objects shows itself to be necessary. This is why:

2.012 In logic nothing is accidental: if a thing can occur in a state of affairs, the possibility of the state of affairs must be written into the thing itself.

Behind the contingent state of the world is its fixed, unchanging form: its unalterable bedrock (*TLP*, 2.026). He also calls this its 'substance' because it grounds the complete range of all subsisting possibilities. It is what the actual world and all possible worlds have in common (*TLP*, 2.022). He held that if there were nonesuch we would be unable to represent reality *at all*.

2.0211 If the world had no substance, then whether a proposition had sense would depend on whether another proposition was true.

2.0212 In that case we could not sketch any picture of the world (true or false).

To understand his position aright it is vital to keep in mind that the objects that make up the substance of the world are nothing like ordinary objects. They cannot be described or even imagined. Indeed, it is on this basis that he makes the crucial distinction between the world and its *essence* – that of which we can speak and that of which we cannot. That is to say, we can represent that state of the world, in its entirety, by saying how things actually stand. The realm of facts, inhabiting *logical space*, is the world, which is all that is the case (cf. *TLP*, 1.13). This is why the world can be completely described by the set of all the true propositions. Yet, it is only through the pictures we form of these facts, which are the world, that its *logical form* or essence is revealed.

How things happen to be arranged *de facto* at any given time is the world – this is nothing other than the totality of elementary states of affairs that happen to obtain, entailing that there is one, and *only* one, way the world can be, at any given time. As a consequence, Wittgenstein infamously held that each elementary state of affairs *must be* independent of every other.

1.21 Each item can be the case or not the case while everything else remains the same.

A given elementary proposition may be true or false without affecting the truth or falsity of any other elementary proposition. If any elementary states of affairs could possibly contradict one another, then the state of the world would be essentially indeterminate, such that we could not picture or talk about it at all. Since all genuine propositions are truth-functions of elementary ones, independence at the lowest rungs ensures determinacy throughout.

Bearing these points in mind puts us in a position to address the crucial question: What is he trying to achieve in saying all this? In one sense, it is clear that the *Tractatus* is offering a direct challenge to Russell. Yet there are two importantly different ways of understanding its nature. On the one hand, it might be seen as offering a straightforward theoretical adjustment to Russell's position, in the hope of simply 'building a better mousetrap'. Thus he may be thought to be attempting to improve on the theories of Russell and Frege. Read in this way, the opening remarks will, as we have seen, look like the preface to the development of the so-called picture theory. This too will also be seen as a corrective to his predecessor's theories of the proposition. The underlying assumption is that these theories are all advanced in the same philosophical spirit and with the same end in mind.

More radically, these remarks can be taken as revealing the bankruptcy of the very idea of philosophical theorising itself. That is to say, Wittgenstein can be seen as rejecting not only Russell's position but also, simultaneously, his whole approach and also his hopes for philosophy. On this anti-theoretical reading, his criticisms should not be understood as being advanced under the banner of a developing theory with its own set of new and improved posits. Instead of simply replacing Russell's ontology with his own, Wittgenstein revealed the deep logical confusions upon which the former, and *any of its kind*, rests. Read in this light, even 1.1 sets its face against all forms of philosophical theorising. Yet, in rejecting this whole style of metaphysical posturing, Wittgenstein was also trying to get us to see the nature of the world aright. In what remains of this chapter I will motivate further support for this reading by comparing it with others in light of his remarks concerning pictures and his understanding of and hopes for analysis.

The picture theory?

Many of Wittgenstein's opening remarks on metaphysics are mirrored in his discussion of pictures. He tells us that we make pictures of facts to ourselves by using pictorial elements arranged appropriately from within the range of possible ways they could be so ordered. To form pictures, the elements need to be arranged as they are in the state of affairs they depict. In so arranging these elements we present a specific scene or state of affairs by means of another medium. The pictorial elements act as 'proxies' for the elements they depict in the state of affairs in question (*TLP*, 2.131). In this way a picture 'is attached to reality; it reaches right out to it' (*TLP*, 2.1511). It is this feature that underwrites the possibility of representing the world accurately or inaccurately by means of a picture. For example, I could draw my hand as having only two fingers but since my hand has five, if I were to claim this was an accurate representation of how things stand, I would be wrong at best. Nevertheless, despite this, it could have been an accurate depiction. It is not a nonsense drawing, a scribble.

Moreover, just as their internal properties determine how objects might be possibly combined, so too if a picture presents a possible situation or state of affairs – never simply an object – its elements must share, or mirror, the internal properties of the objects they depict. This is why:

> 2.16 In order to be a picture a fact must have something in common with what it pictures.

More precisely, he tells us that they must share a common form, again understood in terms of the full range of combinatorial possibilities, for only in this way will the pictorial elements permit the same kinds of arrangements as the objects they depict. Thus, he writes:

> 2.171 A picture can depict any reality whose form it has. A spatial picture can depict anything spatial, a coloured one anything coloured, etc.

In other words, if we are primarily concerned with providing an accurate *visual* re-presentation, colours are the obvious choice since these can be used, in principle, to match those of the scene we wish to depict. In their proper arrangements, which would include shading, placement, hue, etc., they could unambiguously capture the visual dimension of a given scene without residue. The full limit of the possibilities for such arrangements is determined by the nature of colours themselves, seen or painted. Yet, this is entirely consistent with the fact that not every arrangement of colours on a canvas represents. This insight into the nature of depiction was inspired, at least in part, by the use of small-scale models in the Parisian law courts to indicate and debate the details of specific traffic accidents. For likewise, if our concern lies with the three-dimensional aspects of a car accident, then spatial models provide the ideal medium of re-presentation. Allowing for scale, they can depict the angle of collision, differences in speed, and so on. In the cases just described, what the pictorial elements and those depicted have in common is that they share the same space of possibilities for arrangement.

Although Wittgenstein initiates his remarks on picturing by discussing pictorial form, it is soon evident that this notion was introduced only to further explicate another, with which he had already made us familiar. For, he tells us, whatever the pictorial elements may have in common with the elements depicted (e.g. colour, space, etc.), to share the space of possibilities they must also share the logical form of what is depicted. Thus:

> 2.18 What every picture, of whatever form, must have in common with reality in order to be able to represent it at all – rightly or wrongly – is the logical form, that is, the form of reality.

What is essential in a picture is that elements are organised to depict some possible state of affairs, enabling it to agree or fail to agree with reality. This being so, it follows there is an asymmetric relationship holding between pictorial and logical form, the direction of which is made explicit by the following remark:

> 2.182 Every picture is at the same time a logical one. (On the other hand, not every picture is, for example, a spatial one.)

Every picture is also a logical picture because the range of possibilities for ordering elements, whatever form they exhibit, is the minimal requirement if a picture is to serve as a model of any state of affairs. It is the sharing of logical form that is absolutely necessary to allow depiction. Although all pictures must have some material properties or other, it is therefore also possible that a state of affairs could be pictured abstractly, even if it shared no particular material properties with what it depicted.

> 2.19 Logical pictures *can* depict the world.   (emphasis mine)

For example, it is easy enough to imagine a purely mathematical picture of the location and nature of the contents of a room, using a coordinate system and a special code. It is possible that if the elements were rightly ordered such a picture could accurately depict how things stood in the room. Propositions provide another excellent example of this for their correlations are not transparently shown by the nature of their signs (other than those formed in hieroglyphic script). However:

> 3.1431 The essence of a propositional sign is very clearly seen if we imagine one composed of spatial objects (such as table, chairs and books) instead of written signs. Then the spatial arrangement of these things will express the sense of the proposition.

Also, for this reason we must not confuse purely logical pictures with mere formal abstractions, for to be meaningful at all their elements must be correlated with objects. Failure to recognise this has encouraged some commentators to imagine wrongly that some kind of purely logical isomorphism between a picture and state of affairs is sufficient to establish a representational relation, whereas in speaking of logical pictures Wittgenstein was only pointing to what is necessary, not sufficient, for representation. What his remarks do make clear is that a picture need not have any particular set of material properties in order to perform its office.

Even more importantly, these considerations enable us to see why logical form is not something that can be represented by a picture. For the way things *might be* arranged is not some item or set of items that also needs representing. Unlike other elements it underscores possible arrangements, but is not open to them. Logical form, *pace* Russell, is not just how elements are related on a particular occasion – it is the whole necessary space of such possibilities. As this space of possibilities is not a possible state of affairs it cannot be depicted. Furthermore, as it is not an element within such it cannot be named. It is not a possible topic of any picture. Trying to make it so would be to attempt to capture what is necessary to the very space of all possibilities, as opposed to saying how things stand in a specific case which is the only viable sort of picture. All this is perfectly in line with his recognition that there are no logical objects and thus no *a priori* order of things.

We can see how his views on both these fronts unite by comparing his discussion of depiction and presentation, which is bound up with remarks on logical form, and those concerning representation proper, which is introduced alongside that of logical space. He writes:

2.202 The picture represents a possible situation in logical space.

3.42 A proposition can determine only one place in logical space: nevertheless the whole of logical space must already be given by it.

(Otherwise negation, logical sum, logical product, etc., would introduce more and more new elements – in co-ordination.)

(The logical scaffolding surrounding a picture determines logical space. The force of a proposition reaches through the whole logical space.)

Imagine again a simple depiction of a given state of affairs, say, my hand having just two fingers. Recalling Frege's observations about names and sub-propositional expressions, on its own this picture does not say anything unless I use it as the basis for claiming that *this is* or *this is not* how things stand in the world. A mere depiction is, strictly speaking, senseless until it is given a location in logical space. It becomes a representation proper only when we take it to say that *things stand this way* or *that*: when we use it to assert *p* or *not p*. This helps us to make sense of an otherwise cryptic remark.

2.221 What the picture represents is its sense.

3.13 ... A proposition contains the form, but not the content of its sense.

With the distinction between a mere depiction and a full-fledged representational picture in hand, we can regard the thought expressed in 2.221 as saying that when a depiction is used to make a claim it literally re-presents the sense, only this time in the form of an assertion.[4] The fact that all propositions share this same general form is what makes it possible for 'ordinary' propositions to be truth functions of elementary ones. For given that they all say 'things stand thus and so' they thereby rule in and rule out other possibilities. This is what is essential to something being a proposition. What is particular to individual propositions is the particular state of affairs they depict; from the perspective of logic this is accidental (*TLP*, 3.34).

Hence, when he alludes to the form as opposed to the content of representation, Wittgenstein is referring to this first aspect of depiction, as in the remark below.

> 2.22 The picture represents what it represents, independently of its truth or falsehood, through the form of representation.

Importantly, it is only at the non-propositional level that the elements of a depiction make contact with reality, the essential form of the world. Yet it is only when it is used to enable us to judge or claim that the world is one way or another, when we use it to say something, that a depiction becomes a picture and can be said to have representational content. For it is only in the context of such acts that:

> 2.21 The picture agrees with reality or not: it is right or wrong, true or false.

Specifically, he says:

> 4.24 To understand a proposition means to know what is the case, if it is true.

It follows from this that in representing the facts of the world we are not describing the internal, logical form of objects – but saying how things stand on specific occasions. However, what makes a representation unambiguous is that, at its core, its pictorial elements are internally tied to a specific, possible state of affairs: the elements of both sharing of a common form. Consequently, what it can depict, what it is *about*, is not arbitrary. It is here that we find the connection between logical form and logical space.

> 3.4 A proposition determines a place in logical space. The existence of this logical place is *guaranteed by the mere existence of the constituents*, by the existence of the proposition with sense.
>
> (emphasis mine)

A significant proposition represents unequivocally, therefore its particular logical form and its position in logical space are fixed. Of course, we cannot gather from pictures themselves whether or not they succeed in representing the facts correctly or not. Nothing internal to a picture gives us grounds for such an assessment. This requires a comparison between a picture and the state of the world. Hence, no picture can be true *a priori*.

With this exegesis in hand, we are in a position to address the question of whether his remarks were meant to constitute a theory. That this is the prevailing view is implied by the common use of the label, 'the picture theory' and by subscription to the idea that his account of picturing is just a further technical advance, albeit an ingenious one, on the work of his predecessors, Russell and Frege. Thus, it is common to treat Wittgenstein's achievement as another piece of the story of the rise and fall of the 'name-theory' of propositions; one bound up with a single metaphysical project. By such lights, the picture theory's virtues ought to be assessed in terms of results such as the way in which it deals with anomalies. For example, it might be praised for obviating the need to postulate negative facts that would otherwise bloat our ontology. Yet, if Wittgenstein's remarks are meant to constitute a theory, it hardly looks like a very adequate one, for too many important questions are still left hanging. The most prominent is: By what means do pictures gain their representational capacities? How do they link to the world? We are told that:

3.12 A proposition is a propositional sign in its projective relation to the world.

This remark is often read as echoing the Fregean observation that, understood as mere marks or sounds, words have no intrinsic representational capacity. If so, what is the projective relation of which Wittgenstein speaks and how is it established? It is a favourite pastime for philosophers to speculate about how names come to designate objects, especially since the correlation of any sign with an object appears to be achieved by means of non-natural conventions. For example, it is only an accident that the mark 'dog' designates instances of the species of animals we know to be man's best friend. The marks comprising the word 'cat' could just have easily served this role of naming dogs, chairs or whatever. Yet since the truth or falsity of our statements about cats, dogs and other sundries are not established by convention, some have supposed that beneath our naming practices there must be a more secure relation that *explains* how the first set of marks stand proxy for dogs, and only dogs. But these observations serve only to provoke the question: What elevates a mere series of marks into a full-fledged proposition? I intend to show that Wittgenstein never tried to answer this question, for good reasons. But this was not a failure on his part since, if I am right, providing such an answer was never his concern. Yet, those who regard him as advancing a theory must regard it as such or else find a substantial proposal about how our pictures do 'hook on' to reality in the *Tractatus*. There are three main proposals about what this might be, none of which turns out to be very plausible in the end.

The first is that Wittgenstein was implicitly advancing some form of resemblance theory. For it might be thought that in the case of ordinary pictures, photographs and portraits, it is their resemblance to their subjects that secures their representational properties. For example, what makes a photo a photo *of* X is the extent to which it resembles X. I will not give a detailed assessment of all the problems with this idea, which include the fact that resemblance could not provide a decisive link between pictures and the world since it is possible for a single picture to resemble more than one state of affairs. Recall the ambiguity in the Little Prince's drawing of a boa constrictor digesting an elephant, a picture which adults consistently take to be a hat. Wittgenstein uses a number of similar examples, such as the various ways we might interpret a picture of a 'cube' (cf. *PI* §139). Apart from this, it suffices to demonstrate that such a proposal flounders immediately as an exegesis of Wittgenstein's view if we consider that resemblance is a matter of degree, whereas in his view of representations are binary. Y can resemble X to a greater or lesser extent, but it makes no sense to think it represents X to a greater or less extent. These are not issues for Wittgenstein precisely because he sharply distinguishes depiction from representation. In light of this, it is not remotely plausible that he was advancing any kind of resemblance theory, certainly not one that was so poorly worked out.

The second, and *prima facie* more likely, proposal is that Wittgenstein had advanced a 'representationalist' understanding of the projective relationship, according to which propositional signs can be regarded as genuine bearers of meaning only if they are somehow imbued with thoughts and thereby given a sense. Thus it is a special feature of thoughts as paradigm logical pictures that they can provide otherwise syntactically well-formed propositional signs with their projective capacities. Putatively, if a thought-picture is formed everything else takes care of itself. Genova, like Malcolm before her, is a prominent defender of this view. Hence:

> In the later works, Wittgenstein stresses the dynamic activity of calculating with pictures, i.e. using them according to rules, rather than the static fact of having a picture. The *activity* of thinking rather than the *having* of thought takes center stage in the later works.
>
> (Genova 1995, p. 65; emphases original)

At first blush, the following remarks appear to provide strong evidence of his commitment to this idea.

> 3.11 The method of projection is to *think* of the sense of the proposition (emphasis mine).

Moreover, he also apparently identifies thoughts with logical pictures, the purest form of a picture.

> 3. A logical picture of facts is a thought.

Indeed propositions, or psychical facts, *contain* their own method of projection because there is a relationship between their elements and the elements of the pictured fact.

> 2.1512 So a picture, conceived in this way, also *includes* the pictorial relationship, which *makes* it into a picture.
>
> (emphases mine)

Thoughts *lend* propositional signs their content in this way. This interpretation, according to which language inherits its meaningful properties from thoughts, is further encouraged by the claim that propositions *express* thoughts.

> 3.1 In a proposition a thought finds an expression that can be perceived by the senses.

The upshot of all this seems to be that the projective link between language and the world might go via a waystation of thoughts. The link between words and world is therefore to be explained by a pre-existing *natural* projective relation holding between complete thoughts and specific possible states of affairs in the world. Accordingly, the objects of thoughts are intrinsically related to the objects of the world, and this link is transitively conferred onto natural language by conventional means. Hence, a proposition reaches right out to some possible state of affairs *because* of the mediating thought that stands behind it. Even if a proposition should miss its mark, if the world happens not to be as it says, this does not rob the proposition of its sense. Things might have been as the thought behind it says precisely because what is thinkable is also possible (*TLP* 3.02). Being logical pictures, thoughts can represent what is possibly as well as what is actually the case.

Obviously, such a view need not constitute a retreat to psychologism as the link between thoughts and reality is not achieved by means of any psychological processes that could be empirically investigated. It is simply that there is a natural relation between elements of thought and elements of the world. Wittgenstein's response to Russell's question about the nature of these thought-elements is evidence that he had no interest in these matters, which otherwise ought to loom large. For, in answer to the query 'Does a thought consist of words?' he replied:

> 'No, but of psychical constituents that have the same sort of relation to reality as words. What those constituents are I don't know'.
>
> (*NB*, p. 130)

Nor should this admission be surprising, since speculation on the nature of such constituents is not a proper topic for logic. At best the question about their nature would be one for empirical psychology or, one day, physics. That there *must* be such constituents can be asserted without further investigation into their nature. Like Frege before him, Wittgenstein recognises a clear distinction between the two approaches:

> 4.1121   Psychology is no more closely related to philosophy than any other natural science.
>
> Theory of knowledge is the philosophy of psychology.
>
> Does not my study of sign-language correspond to the study of thought-processes, which philosophers used to consider so essential to the philosophy of logic. Only in most cases they got entangled in unessential psychological investigations, and with my method too there is an analogous risk.

Hence, in holding that thoughts, language and the world have an internal correlation he is in no way making a claim in need of empirical support. He is stating what *must be* the case if language is to represent the world.

With the charge of psychologism quashed, there are some obvious attractions to this reading. Nevertheless, it suffers on at least two fronts. First, its explanatory credentials are, at best, weak and at worst, non-existent. For in postulating an intrinsic relation between thought elements and worldly objects to explain the projective link, it only postpones the original question by pushing it back a step. For if we were genuinely worried about this question such an explanation would only whet our appetite for a more robust one about how thought elements are intrinsically related to objects in the first place, and so on.

Second, it wrongly encourages us to imagine thoughts as reified entities in a way, *pace* Genova, that goes precisely against Wittgenstein's emphasis on the activity of making sense and applying signs. On this front, he unequivocally rejects the suspect notions of our being *acquainted* with propositions or *grasping* them as if they had an independent existence. In forming judgements we are not passively related to pre-formed external items in the mind or the world; rather, in the formation of thoughts the internal relation between our logical pictures and what they represent is forged. In this way, language becomes related to the world through being thought out. Thinking, in this sense, is judging, which is an active process.

> 3.262 What signs fail to express their *application* shows. What signs slur over, their *application* says clearly.   (emphases mine)

> 3.5   A propositional sign, *applied and thought out*, is a thought.
>   (emphasis mine)

> 3.326 In order to recognize a symbol by its sign we must observe how it is *used with sense*.   (emphasis mine)

The applications of which he speaks are bound up with particular acts of judgement, which involve the making of an assertion by assembling thought elements to *create* a psychical fact. As long as we are cautious and do not to try to picture 'objects', it may be useful to think of this activity by analogy to the putting together of Lego bricks – the physical shapes of these internally limit how they can go together. Our judgements are similarly limited by the very chemistry of thought, the possibilities of elemental combination. This is why sense is revealed through our successful applications, whereas nonsense is the product of malformed attempts at judgement.

Still, we might hope to articulate what determines the boundaries of sense and nonsense. This suggests a third possible explanation of the link between words and world. Perhaps the projective relation follows automatically once a designation of names has been made in accord with a rule which reflects what is required if a picture is to share a common logical form with what it pictures. Logical rules might be thought to determine which combinations are permissible and thus might be thought to underwrite our conventional use of terms. We find an early expression of this idea in Mounce's interpretation. He writes:

> In order to grasp the logical form of an expression one has to look at the rules for its use ... What is not a matter of convention, however, is how we can use this mark once we have fixed its meaning by a rule ... It is *only if a mark is applied according to a rule* which reflects logical form *that it has been given a meaning* in the first place.
>
> (Mounce 1981, pp. 29–30, emphases mine)

What is right about this is that it underscores Wittgenstein's insistence that:

> 3.141 A proposition is not a blend of words ... A proposition is articulate.

To represent a fact, a proposition cannot simply be a conglomerate of words. For an individual word to mean anything at all, all the components of a proposition must be so ordered that they can intelligibly mirror some possible state of affairs. They must be put together in the *right* way. Moreover, it is true that in this context Wittgenstein explicitly talks of the *rules* of logical syntax. For example, he tells us:

> 3.344 What signifies in the symbol is what is common to all those symbols by which it can be replaced according to the rules of logical syntax.

Of course, as Mounce is well aware, he is not conflating the rules of logical syntax with the rules of the conventional grammars of different natural languages. For, unless indefinitely supplemented, the latter always generate ambiguity and equivocation. Consider propositions (1) and (2) below.

(1) The dog chases the cat.
(2) The house chases the cat.

Although (1) and (2) both share the noun–verb–noun syntactic form, (2) is not an intelligible sentence because although 'house' is a noun, the sorts of thing that this noun designates are in no position to chase cats. This example is exceptionally crude, but it could easily be replaced with more sophisticated ones. Still, it is enough to show that what makes sense and what does not is not regulated by the surface syntax of natural language; rather it is written into the very nature of things. For Wittgenstein, the 'rules' of grammar and syntax run deep; they concern only essential possibilities that cannot be violated. Hence, they cannot be identified with the 'rules' in the ordinary sense at all and certainly not those relating to the various grammars of particular natural languages. This is why:

> 3.327 A sign does not determine a logical form unless it is taken together with its logico-syntactical employment.

However, it is also mistake to think that Wittgenstein's talk of rules reveals a commitment to something like the existence of a Chomskyian universal grammar or Fregean laws of thought. In speaking of rules he is not advancing any substantive conception of them. They are not something we can, to use Mounce's illocution, intelligibly 'grasp'. For this would require that we could give a positive characterisation of the logical form of the world, contravening what Wittgenstein expressly denied. Thus logico-syntactic rules for permissible combinations inherently mirror the logical form of the world and permit us to make sense of it, but they are revealed only retrospectively and on specific occasions of use. It is not possible to anticipate them or give them a general characterisation. In no way can they be specified or codified. These 'rules of use' neither exist as independent things-in-themselves nor do they occupy a distinct, internal or external, realm that can be separately investigated or discovered.

It should be recognised that Wittgenstein's talk of rules here is slippery and it must be compared with what he says elsewhere, such as:

> 3.334 The rules of logical syntax must *go without saying*, once we know how each individual sign signifies.
>
> (emphasis mine)

Indeed, it is on precisely these grounds that Wittgenstein revealed Russell's theory of types to be utterly superfluous. He realised that there is no point in charting the rules for how meanings may be grammatically employed if those rules must be derived from observing occasion by occasion whether sense has been made or not. At best, even if we could articulate them, such rules would need to be compiled antecedently to *all* particular acts of sense-making.

In the end, to understand Wittgenstein's position properly we must blend some aspects of the proposals of Malcolm and Mounce, while purging them of certain errors and abandoning any explanatory concerns. So edited, these readings can be synthesised to help us to see that his interest was in *particular* acts of judgement, which are governed not by an external set of rules, but only internally. This is why the limits of thought can only be revealed not stated. This is also why he sees individual acts of making sense along the lines of conducting an experiment.

> 4.031 In a proposition a situation is, as it were, constructed by way of experiment . . .

In the process, what works and what does not – what makes sense and what does not – is made manifest. We have no other means of determining this. Yet even without the existence of a separate set of rules, there are logical limits to thinking – we cannot think what is illogical (*TLP*, 3.03). That which is illogical is literally nonsense; it makes no sense.

Read in this light it is transparent that from the very beginning he regarded judgement not as something static but as an *activity*. Indeed, this was why philosophy itself was regarded as an activity. This undercuts any motivation for claiming that his early emphasis on thought stands over and against a very late focus on action in his final work. This reading is strengthened by paying attention to his understanding of the nature and purpose of analysis in a way that reveals his early commitment to the idea that there was an unsayable foundation to our particular acts of sense-making.

In light of this it becomes clear that the very idea of seeking an explanation of the link between language and the world is wrong-headed. Hence, although his remarks on picturing can appear as an elaborate but, ultimately, inadequate theory of the representational relationship, it is in fact meant to be nothing more, or less, than a non-explanatory working out of what is required if we are to represent the world to ourselves. The perspective adopted is not theoretical; it is meant to reveal what makes thinking and speaking about the world possible.[5] Indeed, he hopes to expose that it is a product of our imaginations to think there is any position from which we could offer theories on these matters. This warning is issued in the Preface, where he tells us that it is not possible to leave our side of the fence, as it were, so as to think both sides of the 'limits' of thought. As such, it is not possible even to begin to advance theories on such fundamental matters. We can neither ask *how* our pictures make sense, nor what, in general, enables them to agree (or disagree) with reality. These are the very conditions upon which our practice of picturing rests, and so are not open to intelligible characterisation. Although it is tempting to ask such questions, the *Tractatus* is designed to reveal their ultimate emptiness.

The aim of analysis

The above considerations put us in a position to understand better Wittgenstein's early view of the nature and purpose of analysis. This is important because, without such a context, some of the remarks he makes on this topic can mislead us about his understanding of the limits of and appropriate method in philosophy.

The primary thing to note is that he clearly held that in 'everyday language' the true form of our thoughts is 'obscured'. Nevertheless, determinate thoughts are there beneath this clothing, giving meaning to our expressions. We do not need to know how language works or indeed how our propositions picture reality in order to *use* them effectively. Ordinary communication is not hindered by this lack of knowledge, any more than it is by a general lack of understanding of phonology. Yet, it is because language obscures the true form of our thought, such that 'it is not humanly possible to gather immediately from it what the logic of language is', that its propositions apparently admit of analysis (*TLP*, 4.002). For he says:

> 4.024 [A proposition] is understood by anyone who understands its constituents.

But, as we shall see, to achieve this understanding would require making transparent the logical form of *specific* propositions. For it is only of individual judgements that it is supposedly possible to reveal which simple elements stand proxy, *in a particular case*, for simple objects of the states of affairs they depict. In principle, through analysis, the true meaning of our everyday propositions can be revealed, reflecting the true form of our thoughts. Thus:

> 3.2 In a proposition a thought can be expressed in such a way that elements of the propositional sign correspond to the objects of thought.
>
> 3.201 I call such elements 'simple signs', and such a proposition 'completely analysed'.
>
> 3.21 The configuration of the simple signs in the propositional sign corresponds to the configuration of the objects in the state of affairs.

It is worth considering just how Wittgenstein believed we might prosecute such a 'complete' analysis. At stage one we would need to decompose each seemingly complex proposition into the elementary ones that comprise it, for according to the *Tractatus*, ordinary propositions are in fact nothing but the truth-functional product of elementary propositions. Only through analysis could the elementary propositions that internally (and truth-functionally) constitute such complex propositions be revealed. Only at the end of such a process would we encounter elementary propositions, which constitute the true core of our thoughts. These each depict one, and only one, possible state of affairs in reality, which is why:

3.25   There is one and only one complete analysis of the proposition.

4.211 It is a sign of a proposition's being elementary that there can be no elementary proposition contradicting it.

Elementary propositions are in turn composed of the names of simple objects, bound together like links in a chain. They mirror basic states of affairs and constitute the point at which we reach bedrock, where analysis must come to an end. For:

3.261 Names cannot be taken to pieces by definition.

Once we have names that stand proxy for objects there is nothing left to analyse, for objects in elementary states of affairs are indescribably bound together. We cannot even begin to imagine what it would be to picture such 'objects' in isolation from some particular state of affairs or other. At best we could enumerate *all* the different states of affairs of which an object might possibly form part. This would be to picture that which is essential to the full range of possibilities of an object and which, apart from being a potentially endless task, could not be determined in advance. This is why a successful analysis of the particular use we make of everyday language would at best reveal the unspeakable essence of the world.

The parallel between his understanding of semantics and metaphysics is brought out most completely in this way. Just as the world is made up of facts, not things, language is made up of propositions, not names. It is important to note that for Wittgenstein these names are not ordinary names, because the latter are ambiguous and thus subject to further clarification. This is the basis of his distinction between the complex and the simple.

3.25 *A complex can only be given by its description*, and this will either be right or wrong. The proposition in which there is mention of a complex, if this does not exist, becomes not nonsense but simply false.

That a propositional *element signifies a complex can be seen from indeterminateness in the propositions in which it occurs*. We know that everything is not yet determined by this proposition . . .

The combination of the symbols of a complex in a simple symbol can be expressed by a definition.

(emphases mine)

3.23 The requirement that simple signs be possible is the requirement that sense be determinate.

That he understood the difference between what is simple and complex as inextricably tied to the question of determinacy is further confirmed by a passage early in the *Investigations*, in which he elaborates on this line of reasoning, which had initially led him to hold that there must be simple objects constituting the substance of the world.

A name ought really to signify a simple. And for this, one might perhaps give the following reasons: The word 'Excalibur', say, is a proper name in the ordinary sense. The sword consists of parts combined in a particular way. If they are combined differently Excalibur does not exist. But it is clear that the sentence 'Excalibur has a sharp blade' makes sense whether Excalibur is whole or broken up. But if 'Excalibur' is the name of an object, this object no longer exists when Excalibur is broken into pieces; and as no object would then correspond to the name it would have no meaning. But then the sentence 'Excalibur has a sharp blade' would contain a word that had no meaning, and hence the sentence would be nonsense. But it does make sense; *so there must always be something corresponding to the words of which it consists.* (*PI* §39; emphasis mine)

It is conditional on a proposition's having sense, whether it is true or false, that its most basic components name simple objects. Ordinary propositions and the names within them are clearly not elementary in this respect since the very existence of their component objects can be sensibly put into question without loss of sense. Real names, in contrast, stand directly for objects. For this reason they are indefinable. Nevertheless, they are the firm, fixed ground upon which language gets its feet. If it were possible to define them, if they could be further analysed, they would not be simple and language would have no secure basis. This is why he held that analysis must finish with indefinable simples, and not as Hamlyn proposed, that 'If Russell and Wittgenstein were asked why there must be simples their answer could only be that there must be simples if there is to be logical analysis; For here the complex presupposes the simple' (Hamlyn 1984, p. 123).[6]

Although his analytic *procedure* is clearly reminiscent of Russell's, it would be a mistake to think that their ambitions were alike, since Russell hoped to discover the basic metaphysical structure and components of the world as part of a general science, at least in theory. Yet Wittgenstein is frequently misattributed just this sort of project. For example, in line with the theoretical reading, Pears maintains:

> First, he had argued dogmatically and *a priori* that all language and thought must have an atomic structure imposed on it by the world. Then when he failed to find this structure on the surface or on any level of analysis that he actually explored, he still insisted that it must be discoverable on some deeper level of analysis. That gave his early theory of language a curiously ambiguous status.
>
> (Pears 1988, p. 206)

As he sees it Wittgenstein's 'whole way of doing philosophy is modeled on the methods of science' (Pears 1988, p. 203). Furthermore, in regarding him as engaged in pseudo-scientific theorising, Pears objects that it ought to have been an embarrassment to him that he never succeeded in providing any intelligible examples of elementary pro-positions and simple objects.

In contrast, on my reading, these were never going to be the result of analysis because objects cannot be understood apart from their appearances in particular situations. The full range of their possibilities of combination cannot be separately represented; hence it follows that the substance or essence of the world cannot be described. Given this, it is neither an accident nor a shortcoming that he provides no examples of elementary propositions. The focus of his concern, as I argued above, was rather to clarify propositions used on particular occasions. We can see this by considering the much discussed example of the watch lying on the table, which appears in the *Notebooks,* but not in the *Tractatus.* He employs it to show that in clarifying precisely what we mean on a given occasion we must unambiguously delineate what must be the case if the proposition were to be true. In this case it would entail stating countless facts about how things must stand with the watch, the table, their constituent parts, and their relation to all other things in space and time, etc. Thus:

> I tell someone 'The watch is lying on the table' and now he says: 'Yes, but if the watch were in such-and-such a position would you still say it was lying on the table'? And I should become uncertain. *This shows I did not know what I meant by 'lying' in general* . . . In order to show that I did know what I meant, I should say: 'I know what I mean, I mean just this' pointing to the appropriate complex with my finger. And in this complex I do actually have the two objects in a relation. (*NB*, §70; emphasis mine)

As I noted at the beginning of this section, although very determinate thoughts must lie beneath any such assertion (hence the long list of other things that would have to be the case), we neither need nor have access to the contents of such lists when we speak determinately in ordinary cases. For this very reason, if someone were to challenge me about what I meant on particular occasion I could do no better than give a *practical* demonstration: for example, by pointing to the very state of affairs that was the topic of the assertion. This kind of demonstration serves as a genuine substitute for a complete list of the indefinitely complex series of propositions that would determinately specify what I meant. Either one, the list or the demonstration, would ultimately clarify what is expressed by a given proposition *on a particular occasion* in such a way that no one could raise concerns on grounds of ambiguity (*NB*, 19.9.14; cf. Freidlander 2001, pp. 99–102; Ostrow 2002, p. 57). This is why his example of the use of models in the law courts is so apposite.

But we must bear in mind that the product of analysis will always be unanalysable propositions requiring demonstration, for the basic components of the last items on the list, the elementary propositions, cannot be spoken of in any *other* way. This is as it should be, for the general term 'object' does not name anything – as a formal concept we can understand it only by working back from particular sensible constructions concerning genuine things. Given his understanding of logical form as described in chapter 1, it is clear why he rejects the idea of a general catalogue of 'logical forms' detailing how things can be legitimately combined in states of affairs and why he remains silent on the question of what 'kind of things' there are.[7] It should be clear that Wittgenstein's insights about logic, 'objects' and 'pictures' are all of a piece with his views on the nature and purpose of analysis. He did not hold that stable and determinate 'things' ultimately fixed the meaning of every genuine proposition. Contact with the substance of the world is not like that. He did not think that that which underpinned the range of possibilities could be *described or pictured* as ordinary things are in our pictures of facts.

To understand his views on what we would find at the end of analysis we must strongly distinguish 'meanings' and 'names', which can only be disclosed, from what is ordinarily said and known. This is to distinguish what can be articulated from what cannot.

> 3.13   A proposition contains the form, *but not the content*, of its sense.   (emphasis mine)

> 3.144 Situations can be described but not *given names*.
>   (emphasis mine)

Although objects can be known in just the way we regularly speak of them, their essential nature is not open to characterisation or determination.

> 3.221 Objects can only be *named*. Signs are their representatives. I can only speak *about* them: I cannot *put them into words*. Propositions can only say *how* things are, not *what* they are.

> 4.002 Man possesses the ability to construct languages capable of expressing every sense, *without having any idea* how each word has meaning or *what its meaning is*.
>   (emphases mine)

For what they *are* – their form – is nothing other than their possibilities. Thus, going completely against the idea that analysis could determine a common set of essential but general properties that comprise the intrinsic nature of objects, he writes:

> 3.3411 So one could say that the real name of an object was what all symbols that signified it had in common. Thus, one by one, all kinds of composition would prove to be inessential to a name.

4.122 It is impossible, however, to assert by means of propositions that such internal properties and relations obtain: rather this makes itself manifest in the propositions that represent the relevant state of affairs and are concerned with the relevant objects.

His point is that as we can only make sense of individual propositions on specific occasions of use, it is not possible to capture what is essential to any and all such uses in a way that can be articulated. All such attempts to make such statements, which constitute the bulk of traditional metaphysics, are doomed to failure from the outset. In recognising this, he sees the implications for the ends, limits and method in philosophy completely otherwise.

3.3421 A particular mode of signifying may be unimportant but *it is always important that it is a possible mode of signifying*. And that is generally so in philosophy: again and again the individual case turns out to be unimportant, but the possibility of each individual case *discloses something about the essence of the world*.
(emphases mine)

Analysis is thus, in principle, nothing but clarification of our thoughts on particular occasions achieved by means of elucidation. It does not yield a set of intelligible propositions that describe the essence of the world. Thus:

3.263 The *meanings* of primitive signs can be explained by means of elucidations. Elucidations are propositions that contain the primitive signs. So they can only be understood if the meanings of those signs are *already known*.   (emphases mine)

Taking all this seriously must lead us to reject the idea that analysis would result in a general description of elementary propositions and simples. Therefore, it cannot be this kind of generality against which he later objects as hobbling his early writings. As we shall see in the next chapter, this repudiation was instead directed at the Tractarian claim that propositions have a general form, not the idea that analysis might articulate the general pattern of the meaning of words.

This is completely consistent with his remarks about the practical worth of operating with a superior sign language. Thus he writes:

> 3.323 In everyday language it very frequently happens that the same word has different modes of signification . . . or that two words that have different modes of signification are employed in propositions in what is superficially the same way.

This is nothing other than his making the familiar observations that in everyday parlance the same type of sign sometimes stands for two separate symbols, as in bear and bank, and that two different signs can misleadingly symbolise the same thing, as with the names, George Orwell and Eric Blair. This can, of course, cause confusion. Indeed, he recognises it as a primary source of philosophical nonsense. Thus in a fashion that is only *seemingly* similar to that of other early analytical philosophers, he tells us:

> 3.325 In order to avoid such errors we must make use of a sign language that excludes them . . . (The conceptual notation of Frege and Russell is such a language, though, it is true, it fails to exclude all mistakes).

Despite appearances, Wittgenstein does not say that it is the purpose of engaging in analysis to develop such a 'sign language'; only that one would be needed if we were to avoid all such errors. Nor does he advocate the active replacement of ordinary language with a perfectly logical one. Rather, making the observation is a sop to the Fregean idea that we might develop an ideal logical language to serve certain practical or scientific ends. Indeed, that this was Frege's purpose is made clear in the preface to his *Begriffsschrift* when he contrasts the 'flexibility and general applicability' of ordinary language with the 'sharpness' of scientific language by analogy with the different functions of the eye and microscope. All that separates Frege and Wittgenstein on this issue is that the former was concerned to aid the scientific enterprise, whereas the latter hoped to glean insights about the nature and limits of philosophical inquiry by considering the logical order he supposed underlay ordinary language. In this respect their projects differed in both spirit and end.

This raises the vital question: What use would a general 'sign language' serve in philosophical analysis?[8] Certainly, 'A concept-script is a mode of expression of thoughts so that what it is for them to be true is clear from how they are written' (Diamond 1995, p. 117). But this should not be confused with the idea that a concept-script would be able to show, in general and in advance, the logical structure of language, as opposed to showing it occasion by occasion. Indeed, wittgenstein dismisses Russell's theory of types because it has to mention 'the meaning of signs when establishing rules for them'. But in line with what was argued above, it is only in the specific instances of the *use* we make of symbols that we show what we mean by them. This is what is behind his talk of seeking a perspicuous notation; it is not the other way around. On this understanding the theory of types is shown to be a spare wheel, even for dealing with the paradox it is meant to overcome. He writes:

> 3.333 For let us suppose that a function $F(fx)$ could be its own argument: in that case there would be a proposition '$F(F(fx))$', in which the outer function F and the inner function F must have different meanings, since the inner one has the form $\phi(fx)$ and the outer one has the form $\psi(\phi(fx))$. Only the letter 'F' is common to the two functions, but the letter by itself signifies nothing.
>
> This immediately becomes clear if instead of '$F(Fu)$' we write '$(\exists\phi): F(\phi u).\phi u = Fu$'.
>
> That disposes of Russell's paradox.

Moreover, this also makes clear that the remark of 3.325 in no way signals a commitment to a scientistic metaphysics. Unlike Russell, in mentioning the value of such conceptual notion for everyday purposes, Wittgenstein was not proposing that it could be used to articulate the underlying nature of reality. There can be no doubt, in light of the above discussions, that he set his face squarely against the very idea of such a use. The activity of making sense (or failing to do so) and our evaluation of this cannot be settled in advance because there is no general schema that permits it. There is no *a priori* order of things upon which such determinations could be based. This is why, in line with his views on the nature of judgement, philosophy is necessarily an *activity*, and an ongoing one.

Bearing these points in mind, we can reassess Pears' best evidence for thinking that Wittgenstein was originally committed to a form of pseudo-scientific analysis. It stems from a conversation recorded by Waismann, in which Wittgenstein said of the *Tractatus*:

> There is another, much more dangerous error, that permeates my whole book – namely, that conception that there are questions for which answers would be discovered at a later date. Although one does not have an answer, one thinks that one has the method by which

an answer can be found. I for one thought that it was the task of logical analysis to discover the elementary propositions. I wrote that we are unable to specify the form of elementary propositions, and that was quite correct too. It was clear to me that there are no hypotheses here and that one cannot proceed with these questions the way Carnap did. But I did think that one would be able to specify the elementary propositions later.
(*WVC*, pp. 182–3)

Similarly, and by appeal to the very same evidence, Schulte maintains that, despite himself and what he wrote in *Tractatus*, Wittgenstein did not pay enough heed of his own methodological scruples and failed to distinguish sufficiently the nature of scientific and philosophical problems (Schulte 1992, pp. 41–2). But this would have been a quite incredible oversight given the amount of attention that he gives to contrasting the two domains.

Wittgenstein does make some seemingly positive remarks about the scope of science. For example, he tells us that it is the business of science to tell us which states of affairs do and do not obtain in the world. In this sense the state of the world is its exclusive concern. Consequently, he writes:

4.11 The totality of true propositions is the whole of natural science (or the whole corpus of the natural sciences).

This might appear to be an attitude of deference to science on matters of importance, yet Wittgenstein emphatically denied that philosophers ought to be interested in what merely *happens* to be the case. They ought to be concerned only with what underpins the world's being *one* way or *another*: that which is unsayable and prior to all discoveries. Logic alone, which says nothing, is the only genuinely *necessary* limit of possibility in both thought and reality. Hence, his remark:

6.3 The exploration of logic means the exploration of everything that is subject to law. And outside of logic everything is accidental.

In order to prevent confusion he sought to demonstrate that the general principles and laws associated with science are not necessary in anything like the way logic is. For to have this status they would have to be *a priori*, making them unfit to be expressed by substantive propositions. Thus, it must be a confusion to think that science can make such pronouncements. Again, there is one and only one kind of necessity – logical necessity (see *TLP*, 6.375). This is why Wittgenstein defends the view that so-called scientific principles and laws fall into one of two categories: either they ape the form of genuine logical laws or they are merely revisable systems for representing and organising other propositions.

For example, he sees the laws of causality and induction as members of the first class. He writes:

6.32 The Law of Causality is not a law but the form of a law.

By the law of causality he is referring to the claim that 'Everything must have a cause' – a deeply influential view in the history of thought. Indeed, reviewing just one of its more prominent appearances is enough to show why it cannot be a genuinely necessary but expressible law for it leads to paradox, as exhibited by the chain of reasoning common to St. Thomas Aquinas' 'cosmological argument' for the existence of God. Aquinas reasoned as follows:

> In the world of sensible things we find there is an order of efficient causes. There is no case known (neither is it, indeed, possible) in which a thing is found to be the efficient cause of itself; for so it would be prior to itself, which is impossible. Now in efficient causes it is not possible to go on to infinity ... Therefore if there be no first cause among efficient causes, there will be no ultimate, nor any intermediate cause ... Therefore it is necessary to admit a first efficient cause, to which everyone gives the name God.
>
> (*FPEG*, p. 548)

We need not take a view on the nature of this postulated 'uncaused cause' to see that such a thing would necessarily violate the so-called 'law of causality'. But, this being so, how can this be sensibly stated? For:

6.362 What can be described can happen too: and what the law of causality is meant to exclude *cannot even be described*.

Other so-called necessary principles, such as the law of induction, come in for similar treatment. It insists that 'Future happenings will conform to past ones', ensuring the general validity of inferences such as if *X* has always brought about *Y* in the past, it will (likely) continue to do so in the future. Many philosophers have long inveighed against the idea that this constitutes a strictly valid form of reasoning and Wittgenstein happily joined their ranks. Thus, several of his remarks echo the thoughts of David Hume and others. Of it, he writes:

> 6.3631   [The procedure of induction], however, has no logical justi-
> fication but only a psychological one.
>
> 6.36311 It is an hypothesis that the sun will rise tomorrow: and this
> means that we do not know whether it will rise.
>
> 6.7   There is no compulsion making one thing happen because
> another has happened. The only necessity that exists is
> logical necessity.

Yet, not all that passes for scientific laws are of this kind. For example, natural laws, such as Newton's laws of motion, are quite unlike the above principles, nor do they simply picture a given possible state of affairs. Recognising this, Wittgenstein suggests thinking of them along the lines of organising systems of representation. He imagines a 'fine mesh', which might be laid over a surface of irregular black dots to illustrate what such a system would be and how it might be used for certain practical purposes, such as distinguishing the location of the dots. The usefulness or otherwise of a net of a particular size and shape would then depend on the nature of the dots in question, even though it would not describe them. Thus:

> 6.342 The possibility of describing a picture like the one mentioned
> above with a net of a given form tells us nothing about the
> picture . . . But what does characterise the picture is that it can
> be described completely by a particular net with a particular
> size mesh.

We are then asked to think of the states of affairs that contingently hold in the world by analogy with the black dots, and natural laws by analogy with the net. Doing so reveals the sense in which Wittgenstein thinks scientific laws are contingent, for they still depend indirectly on how things happen to stand in the world. Thus, he writes:

> 6.3431 The laws of physics, with all their logical apparatus, still
> speak, however indirectly, about the objects of the world.

This is true even of the successes of great systems, like that of Newtonian mechanics, which attempt to provide a 'single, unified plan' with which we can construct 'all the true propositions we need for a description of the world'. The seemingly necessary elements of this system, like any other grand theory, are nothing more than '*a priori* insights about the forms in which the propositions of science can be cast' (*TLP*, 6.34). Moreover, being substantial, although these insights may serve us well they are, in the end, proper candidates for revision and development, as we discover more about how things do in fact stand with the world. Drawing on the net analogy, it is easy to imagine two different grids – with differently shaped figures – being laid over a series of black dots. Although neither alters the given pattern the usefulness of these might vary greatly for different purposes, such as cataloguing, classifying and even counting. Different scientific systems of representation might also be seen as different practical guides for engaging with the world in particular ways, more or less successfully. Hence, one system will be judged more useful than another against a specific range of criteria (cf. 6.342). In treating scientific laws in this way, Wittgenstein removes the temptation to think of them as genuinely necessary. In this sense the so-called fundamental laws of physics are not proper laws at all. Logic alone shows the limits of reality – not physics.[9] Only logic is truly necessary; it cannot be stated and is not open to revision.

This observation is the basis for his persistent, seemingly negative attitude towards the limited achievements of science and his distaste for the modern conception of the world, with its unrelenting demand for explanation. For:

> 6.371 The whole modern conception of the world is founded on the illusion that the so-called laws of nature are the explanations of natural phenomena.

This must be an illusion, for if the only necessity is in fact logical necessity then there can be no fundamental natural laws that *explain* what *must* be the case. In 1930 he remarks quite clearly on the difference between philosophy and science in a way that is completely in line with the views expressed in the *Tractatus*. He writes:

> It is all one to me whether or not the typical western scientist understands or appreciates my work, since he will not in any case understand the spirit in which I write. Our civilisation is characterised by

the word 'progress'. Progress is its form rather than making progress being one of its features. Typically it constructs. It is occupied with building an ever more complicated structure. I am not interested in constructing a building, so much as having a perspicuous view of the foundations of possible buildings. So I am not aiming at the same target as the scientists and my way of thinking is different from theirs.

(C&V, p. 7e)

In this respect, the modern attitude unfavourably compares to that of the ancients. We are told that:

6.372 People today stop at the laws of nature, treating them as some-thing inviolable, just as God and Fate were treated in past ages. And in fact both are right and both wrong: though the view of the ancients is clearer in so far as they have a clear and acknowledged terminus, while the modern system tries to make it look as if everything were explained.

By introducing God or fate as 'unexplained explainers', the Ancients were acknowledging that explanations only go so far, whereas the modern view sees no such limits. Its pretensions are much greater even though the limits remain just the same – certain things must be taken for granted. For example, we need not argue for the existence of a first mover by a crude appeal to the law of causality described earlier, nor posit its existence in an explanatory vein in just the way the 'Big Bang' is often postulated as the 'first event' that explains the origin of the universe. A more sophisticated move would be to regard it not as the primary event, on a par with any other in the world apart from its timing, but rather as the ground for the very possibility of all worldly events. This would be to think of the 'uncaused cause' in a non-linear way, as something akin to a formal as opposed to an efficient cause, which is less deceptive about the limits of explanation. This early concern with the proper scope and domain of explanation becomes a central theme throughout his writings and it figures prominently in the chapters to come.

Furthermore, Wittgenstein is well aware that his own philosophical remarks have a dubious status if treated as mere 'propositions' since they are specifically designed to contrast with the kind of factual statements that putatively typify the natural sciences. Although I will leave the question of how we are to understand these remarks until the next chapter, it is clear that even in recognising this contrast he was distinguishing his approach from both that of science and pseudo-science. Given all this, Pears and Schulte are wrong to think that the *Tractatus* modelled the business of solving philosophical problems on the way scientific ones are solved.

Nevertheless, Schulte is right to acknowledge that even though in the clarificatory aspect of the project we find the seeds of the descriptive approach that was to dominate the later writings, the sense in which 'elucidations' could serve as descriptions in the early work was quite different (Schulte 1992, p. 43). The elucidation of elementary propositions, at best, provides clarification of what is meant on particular occasions of use, even though no attempt is made to elucidate any general rules of linguistic usage – something he never went back on. But his early thinking about what there was to be elucidated was confounded by the idea that in making sense, even on particular occasions, we are always representing facts about how things stand in the world. It is this that drives his particular view of what it means to 'clarify' a proposition, and it is what lies behind his talk of an early commitment to the idea of a *postponed discovery*. The point is that this alone hardly constitutes a reason to think he was initially inclined to think of philosophy as having a Russellian scientific task. Indeed, even in the quoted fragment recorded by Waismann, he openly rejects the idea that his form of analysis would result in revealing some fixed form of such touchstone propositions. Rather, what he thought lay hidden within our ordinary propositions was the deep logical form that is the foundation of all sense-making; but although this could be revealed it could not be articulated.

But this being so, it ought to have raised questions in his mind about the need to engage in analysis with respect of ordinary propositions at all. For this is undermined if:

> 5.5562 In fact, all the propositions of our everyday language, just as they stand, are in perfect logical order.

I suggest that he later came to recognise that there was no *need* to elucidate what we mean in ordinary cases: those in which we are already making sense, in which language is functioning properly. This realisation is what provoked his rejection of the idea that there is anything at all to be discovered in philosophy. For in his discussion with Waismann he goes on to say, 'What I want to oppose here is the false idea that we could hit upon something that today we do not see, that we can *discover* something entirely new. That is a mistake. In truth, we already have everything; in fact it is *present*, so that we do not have to wait for anything. We move within the realm of something already there, the grammar of our accustomed language' (*WVC*, pp. 182–3). As he later sees, ordinary language shows itself to be vague in some respects without in any way compromising its usefulness; hence there is no need to postulate a more determinate substratum for it (see *PI* §§98–107). Ordinary language as it stands is just as determinate as it needs to be. That he could not see this at the time of writing the *Tractatus* I maintain was, in the main, because his vision was clouded by the idea that all language served a uniform representational function.

Conclusion

If this anti-theoretical reading is right, the need for analysis of everyday language is obviated because it is already in perfect logical order. If so, it seems that the point of clarifying our thoughts becomes simply to expose the fact that much of what passes for philosophy, where one is prone to certain kinds of metaphysical statements, is simply nonsense. This makes evident one vital connection between the early and late writings. Nevertheless, in the next chapter I want to explore the nature of the relation between the works of these two periods in more detail, distancing my reading of the *Tractatus* from the more extreme therapeutic interpretations in the process. For I maintain such readings are not plausible precisely because they fail to acknowledge some of the other important changes that occurred in this thinking between his early and late periods.

3
Seeking Clarity Throughout

> The aim of philosophy is to erect a wall at the point where language stops anyway. . . .
>
> Unrest in philosophy comes from philosophers looking at, seeing, philosophy all wrong . . . (Instead of turbulent conjectures and explanations, we want to give calm demonstrations . . . we want the calm noting of linguistic facts.)
>
> Wittgenstein, *Philosophical Occasions*, pp. 187 and 195

Introduction

In light of what has been argued in the preceding chapter it is incumbent on me to situate my understanding of the *Tractatus* with respect to other non-theoretical readings and make clear where I stand on the current debate raging over the status of book itself. This task will occupy the first section of this chapter and will serve as a necessary prelude to marking the continuities and differences that exist in his early and late understanding of, and approach to, philosophy.

Doctrinal truths

Although I have rejected theoretical readings on the grounds that Wittgenstein had set his face against philosophical speculation and explanation, this does not rule out the possibility that he was advancing doctrines, in the sense of stated principles or beliefs. Perhaps, his was simply an attempt to lay down a series of *a priori* truths. On the face of it, this is surely in line with the tone of the book – which is anything but tentative. For most readers confronted by the *Tractatus* for the first time it appears to be a strange, escalating series of philosophical pronouncements, issued almost as fiats or diktats. As Brockhaus suggests, it is not usual for it to be viewed as an undefended presentation of semi-independent metaphysical theses. He writes:

> Compressed, presented *ex cathedra* without argument and in a curious vatic voice, it offers an accelerating series of remarks on the world, logic, and the essence of language, suddenly and quite mysteriously blossoming into cryptic claims about the will, ethics, 'God' and 'The Mystical'.   (Brockhaus 1991, pp. 1–2)

It is therefore not entirely surprising to find frequent references to the *Tractatus'* 'doctrine of showing' and remarks such as the following, 'it seems necessary to find some other account of [elementary propositions] before we can grasp the *doctrines* of the book even in vague outline' (Anscombe 1959, p. 29; emphasis mine). Doubtless in some cases these are merely throw-away remarks, but even so, they serve to highlight the fact that for a long time inadequate attention has been paid to the relation between Wittgenstein's views and how they are expressed. But it is easy to find today's commentators making the same kind of attributions. Thus, despite reading the *Tractatus* by theoretical lights, Goldstein also claims its aim is to prosecute a traditional metaphysical end by 'deducing the general necessary features of the world and of language' (see Goldstein 1999, pp. 17, 19). However, to take this view seriously means that one has somehow to accommodate the fact that one of these central Tractarian 'truths' is that there cannot be any genuine necessary, *a priori* propositions. This can provoke the thought that although the book is indeed meant to convey such doctrinal truths, these cannot be straightforwardly stated. As a consequence, the more forthright defenders of the doctrinal reading are driven to support some awkward implications. Thus, in a revealingly entitled paper, 'Was He Trying to Whistle it?' Hacker tells us that 'there are, according to the author of the *Tractatus*, ineffable truths that can be apprehended' (Hacker 2000, p. 368).[1]

Following this line, Wittgenstein's understanding of these 'ineffable truths' is thought to be bound up with his distinction between saying and showing. Remarks concerning the latter spring up in various places throughout the *Tractatus*, but some of their most striking appearances are in the early 4s.

4.12   Propositions can represent the whole of reality, but they cannot represent what they must have in common with reality in order to be able to represent it – logical form.

4.121   What expresses itself in language we cannot express by means of language.

4.1211 What can be shown cannot be said.

Not being able to say anything about the logical form of elementary propositions is one example of the need to distinguish what can be said from what cannot. But if we were to accept a doctrinal reading, he must have been mistaken about the ineffability of the 'unassailable and definitive *truths*', which the Preface claims to be 'communicated' in the book. For if he did not successfully express something that is truly unsayable in everyday language, then he must have done so by means of some form of meta-language, one that functions unlike a purely fact-stating language. Paradoxically, then, to make the *Tractatus* consistent with its author's views about its achievements, it turns out that we ought to accept that Russell was right to reject Wittgenstein's central insight about what can and cannot be said (cf. Hacker 2000: 355). As Russell reminds us:

> In my introduction to the *Tractatus*, I suggested that, although in any given language there are things which that language cannot express, it is yet always possible to construct a language of a higher order in which these things can be said. (*MPD*, p. 114)

If so, straightaway, some of Wittgenstein's so-called 'necessary truths' – those concerning what cannot be said – turn out to be falsehoods. Either way, on this reading the *Tractatus* fails in one way or the other. The point is that, advanced innocently or not, talk of his having self-consciously advanced 'doctrines' is neither neutral nor without consequences. Certainly, it does not fit with Wittgenstein's own admission when describing the correct method of philosophy that it is not possible to go beyond what can be said. Of it we are told:

4.114 It must set limits to what can be thought; and in doing so, what cannot be thought.

It must set limits to what cannot be thought by working outwards from what can be thought.

Most obviously, doctrinal readings cannot accommodate the following remarks:

4.112 Philosophy aims at the logical clarification of thought.

Philosophy is not a body of doctrine but an activity.

A philosophical work consists essentially of elucidations.

As the only way to make sense of the doctrinal reading is to assume that he was committed to a metaphilosophy at odds with the central aspects of his stated project, such readings are unfaithful to some of his own remarks. Moreover, they suffer from a deep inconsistency in that they must characterise 'Wittgenstein as rejecting the idea of an external standpoint, [yet] offer interpretations of his thought which keep this idea in play' (Crary and Read 2000, p. 4).

Against the therapists

With the above concern in mind, James Conant and Cora Diamond have independently argued that straight doctrinal readings are wrong-headed because they fail 'to take seriously what Wittgenstein says about philosophy itself' (Diamond 1995, p. 18; cf. also Conant 1989, pp. 248, 266). As we have seen, the familiar labels 'picture theory of meaning' and the 'doctrine of showing' suggest that the book contains 'numerous doctrines which Wittgenstein holds cannot be put into words' (Diamond 1995, pp. 181–2; cf. p. 194).[2] Accordingly, as a work of philosophy, the *Tractatus* attempts to say what cannot be said – to express what cannot be stated factually, something than cannot be put into words. It appears to be a series of intelligible propositions that, unlike genuine propositions, employ pseudo-concepts, such as object, fact, and so on (cf. *PI* §134). It seemingly tells us things such as: the substance of the world resides in simple, indestructible objects; these objects combine to create states of affairs; the states of affairs that actually hold are the facts of the world, and so on. Yet if so, by its own scruples, the work must be condemned. For it requires us to treat its 'propositions' as meaningfully conveying something about the nature of the limits of language, but if it is correct about the limits of what can be said, then we must at the same time reject those very propositions as meaningless. They cannot *say* what they are seemingly trying to express, because there cannot be a possible world in which they do not hold true. Saying is restricted to the domain of stating something that might be otherwise for the book itself *seemingly tells* us that all propositions only serve to picture contingent facts and must be potentially true or false, depending on whether or not things happen to stand as they say. This condition of bivalency must hold in order for a proposition to have a sense. Yet, if this is the general form of all propositions, then no proposition can say anything *necessarily* true. The problem is that if we understand (and accept) what the *Tractatus* propositions seemingly 'express' by whatever means – especially those concerning the way propositions picture reality – we face paradox. It seems as if the entire book is an attempt somehow to express what cannot be said and yet it cannot even really advise us that this is so in any communicable way. Its propositions are strictly speaking, improper by its own *seeming* account.

The criticism levelled at doctrinal readings is that Wittgenstein is making a stronger claim than that suggested above when he identifies his propositions as nonsensical. If we stick with the ineffability reading, it would appear that if his propositions succeed in 'revealing' something it must be that they represent a kind of 'illuminating' nonsense that can be distinguished from the more workaday sort. This is the sticking point for it generates the tension just described. Diamond regards the easy acceptance that Wittgenstein would draw such a convenient distinction as a 'chickening out' response brought on by a failure of nerve, poor interpretation or both. She and Conant challenge the idea that he seriously wished us to recognise something that is 'nonsensical but significant'.[3] For them, from beginning to end, Wittgenstein regarded all nonsense as 'garden-variety' gibberish. Indeed, on these very grounds, they maintain not only that his aim to do away with philosophical nonsense remained constant throughout his philosophical career, but, more strongly, that his understanding of nonsense remained constant as well.

On this basis, they advocate a 'full-fledged' therapeutic reading of the *Tractatus* that bids us not only to recognise that his self-avowed method of clarification applies not only to topics discussed within the work but to the work itself and its mode of expression.[4] As Diamond puts it, 'We shall not understand Wittgenstein's critical response to metaphysical demands if we do not see the kind of criticism he makes of the *Tractatus*' (Diamond 1995, p. 20). Therefore fully to understand his project we must 'resolutely' or 'austerely' give up the idea that he was ever interested in advancing theories or doctrines of any sort at all. We must recognise instead that to the extent that any of the remarks in the *Tractatus* appear to gesture towards something metaphysically external to language they should be read ironically. Thus, in Diamond's view, 'the notion of something true to reality but not sayably true is to be used only with the awareness that it itself belongs to what has to be thrown away' (Diamond 1995, p. 182, cf. also pp. 19, 201). The greatest apparent virtue of such extreme therapeutic readings is that they provide the means of resolving the internal paradox described above and notoriously identified by Wittgenstein at the very close of the *Tractatus*, where he writes:

6.54 My propositions serve as elucidations in the following way: anyone who understands me eventually recognises them as nonsensical, when he has used them – as steps – to climb up beyond them. (He must, so to speak, throw away the ladder after he has climbed up it). He must transcend these propositions, and then he will see the world aright.

Such a reading allegedly provides the means of making sense of Wittgenstein's plea that not only must we overcome his propositions, but that we must *throw them away*. Only in this way can we avoid the conclusion that the work culminated in an insuperable contradiction. This can be achieved by focusing on how he self-consciously employed a 'strictly incorrect' method for therapeutic purposes. In this light, his penultimate recognition of the paradox is nothing but another means of getting his readers to see the impossibility of traditional philosophy.[5] Accordingly, the book works in something like the following way. First, it lets its readers imagine that they find sense in its pseudo-propositions but in the end it pulls the rug out by showing them that even to think this leads nowhere, or rather results in complete nonsense. Recognising the self-destructive aspect of the *Tractatus* would then be intended as part of the overall therapy. To effect the cure properly requires giving the patient enough rope to hang themselves.[6] Thus, Diamond sees the key to unlocking Wittgenstein's remarks of 6.54 in the sentence, 'anyone who understands *me* eventually recognises them as nonsensical' (emphasis mine). She makes great play of the fact that he asks his reader to understand *him* as opposed to understanding the propositions of the *Tractatus* itself, since if we take *him* seriously they are just nonsense (see Diamond 1991, pp. 55–7, 65). In line with this, the purpose of the *Tractatus* is to 'work on the reader' in much the way that some hold that after 1937 he thought 'a philosophical investigation is analogous to a Freudian psychotherapeutical session' (Gefwert 2000, p. 1). Thus *one* way of seeing a constant aim and purpose in Wittgenstein's work is to see it as always designed 'to take the reader from a piece of disguised nonsense to a piece of undisguised nonsense' (Conant 1995, p. 250; cf. *PI*, §§119, 464). As Conant insists, read in this light one can 'insist upon a greater continuity in his work than most previous commentators have allowed' (Conant 1989, p. 246). Yet even those who support this reading of the *Tractatus* do not deny that there is 'an equally significant discontinuity in the form of the investigation through which this aim is prosecuted' (Conant 1995, p. 249).

There is much to recommend this reading – both as a corrective and especially as a means of getting us to focus on otherwise relatively neglected issues in Wittgenstein scholarship, such as the style of his authorship (see Conant 1995, pp. 269–71). Moreover, it provides a clear rationale for treating the study of his early writings as being as important as his later ones in seeking to understand properly his views on the nature and end of philosophy. However, in its extreme form, therapeutic interpretations are not plausible. I will highlight two integral problems, one that raises logical conundrums and the other exegetical ones, but both reveal how such readings threaten to obscure some important aspects of the development of Wittgenstein's thought. Thus used as the sole means of reading the early Wittgenstein, these can be as distorting as the more traditional theoretical and doctrinal interpretations.

I begin with the logical worry. As noted above, on extreme therapeutic readings, 'the aim of Tractarian elucidation is to reveal (through the employment of mere nonsense) that what appears to be substantial nonsense is mere nonsense' (Conant 2000, p. 196). This way of putting things gives rise to a serious objection. For, given that it is integral to this reading that we cannot distinguish different classes of nonsense, its supporters are faced with the awkward question about how the *Tractatus* manages to get any 'message' across, therapeutic or otherwise. For example, what is the status of 6.54 itself? If it is really just a bit of nonsense, how can it offer serious guidance in our reading of the 'rest' of the text? By way of reply, it has been claimed that the remarks in the Preface and 6.54 comprise the book's frame and as such are not nonsense; therefore, they are neither to be overcome nor disposed of. The Preface tell us that the project is to set a limit to what can be said wholly from inside the bounds of sensible language and the closing remarks are just a final reminder of this vital message. But this will not do, since there are contentious remarks even in the Preface that flatly contradict these instructions, such as those emphasised by Hacker in which he talks of the book advancing 'truths'. Also, as we have seen, supporters of the extreme therapeutic reading draw on a selection of other internal quotations to make their case, such as 4.112 and 4.114.

Even if we tolerate such cherry-picking, there is an even more serious problem with this proposal. Diamond and her supporters cannot coherently maintain that Wittgenstein was never wedded to the idea that all language serves the singular representational function of picturing facts without also losing a sharp definition of nonsense as that which fails to fulfil that function. *A fortiori* without *this* understanding of nonsense in play the extreme therapeutic reading lacks motive force, since it would become unclear what drives the revocation itself. Against their own counsel supporters of this reading must not only recognise that his framing instructions make sense, they must also acknowledge that, at a minimum, the passages about picturing do so as well.[7] Of course, this requires us to read at least certain substantive sections of the *Tractatus* non-ironically.

Behind this lurks an even more general puzzle. How is it that the non-framing 'remarks' manage to have a systematic, dialectical effect on the book's readers? Although mere nonsense, if read correctly or in the right spirit, they reliably produce good results. The need to address this worry becomes urgent if we consider Diamond's characterisation of Wittgenstein's early treatment of ethics, the 'propositions' of which he also classes as nonsensical. She distinguishes the attractiveness of speaking ethical nonsense from speaking other forms of nonsense. In her view, he treats ethical cases as those in which we understand 'a person as saying in his heart something that makes no sense, [as] something which we have the imaginative resources to grasp as attractive where that imaginative capacity is tied to our own capacities as moral agents' (Diamond 1991, p. 84; cf. also p. 80). She writes: 'if we read the *Tractatus* right, the upshot of the book will be different in regard to the two sorts of utterers of nonsense. The attractiveness of philosophical sentences will disappear through the kind of self-understanding that the book aims to lead to in philosophers; the attractiveness of ethical sentences will not. But if we understand ourselves, ourselves the utterers of ethical nonsense, we shall not come out with ethical sentences under the illusion that we are talking sense' (Diamond 1991, p. 74). But if all nonsense is really on a par – if it is all like voicing 'piggly-wiggly', to use her own example – then how can uttering one bit of it be more attractive than uttering another. How can such noise-making be classed by type in this way? It might be thought that this can be achieved by considering effects rather than contents. But that simply resurrects the first question again. How can certain nonsense sounds predictably produce distinct effects on their hearers if they are all, in fact, equally meaningless? The problem is that some account is needed in order to make sense of what it is that those who misread the *Tractatus* think they understand when they claim to find sense in the book and how those who realise there is no sense in it achieve this by 'reading' it.

It may be that these observations are unfair to supporters of extreme therapeutic readings. Perhaps such technical objections miss the very spirit of their project. After all, Read and Deans claim it is 'a fairly loose programme for action . . . This ought to sound a note of caution to those critics who want to speak of "resolutism", or "the resolute reading", as expressing some fully defined and completed project" (Read and Deans, forthcoming). Moreover, there are other possible moves available to them in meeting the challenge of explaining, 'how the propositions of the *Tractatus* can elucidate something whilst being nonsensical' (Read and Deans, forthcoming). That is to say, the above objections all turn on the fact that those who support extreme therapeutic readings are committed to the idea that all nonsense is of the plain old garden-variety sort and that we must take Wittgenstein at his word when he designates the book as nonsensical. However, there is still room to say more about how we *determine* if some bit of noise and fury is nonsense or not and what it means to call it such. In particular, one need not take seriously the view seemingly stated in the *Tractatus* about the nature and scope of nonsense. On straight readings anything that is not representative of a fact would be nonsense. But presumably those who endorse extreme therapeutic readings are simply not bound by this definition.

Sticking with a resolute understanding of nonsense, one might hold that what is to *call* something nonsense is an occasion-sensitive business for which there is no general way of characterising how this is determined. On one occasion, say a first reading, we might *think* that the words of *Tractatus* make sense, but one later reflection we come to realise that they do not through the very process of trying to find a genuine application for them. Thus:

> The reader comes to see the world rightly through the unsuccessful attempt to try to make sense of the propositions of the *Tractatus* that attempts to express the philosophical concerns that apparently motivate the text. This leaves open rather than closes down the possibility that the text can be read dialectically, acknowledging the different levels at which the text operates and avoids the absurd belief that any line of the *Tractatus* is to be regarded as nonsensical as any line of *Jabberwocky*. (Read and Deans, forthcoming)

Supporters of this version of the extreme therapeutic reading hold 'that the text is so crafted that the reader can see-saw between sense and nonsense' (Read and Deans, forthcoming). If asked how this sort of to-ing and fro-ing is possible, we will be reminded that to see things aright is to have overcome any residual urge to explain our acts of sense-making in general terms. The ultimate irony is that this moral would also seem to apply equally to the attempt to identify resolutely all nonsense with garden-variety gibberish. For this too is to fall prey to the tendency to try to give a general characterisation of nonsense. Hence, this version of the extreme therapeutic reading risks implosion. Yet, perhaps such a destablising conclusion is simply a further lesson that needs to be learnt and embraced.

Another move is to adopt a more moderate conception of nonsense, such as the one that appears in Wittgenstien's later writings. For example, one could renounce resolutism and hold that, at least in some cases, when we designate something as nonsense we are not saying it is simply gibberish, but rather that it has no genuine application in our lives. Adopting this understanding would enable one to make sense of 'seeming sense' much more easily. For example, it is not that philosophers do not have systematic uses for their terms. Indeed, they deploy them in inferences and train others in their correct use. One can do something systematic with concepts such as 'object' and 'logical form' precisely because they have agreed uses that signs such as 'piggly-wiggly' do not. This is what creates the illusion that the former are significant, even though their uses lack any real point. The upshot is that when the later Wittgenstein exposes that a philosophical theory is nonsense, he does not show that what it seemingly says is a mere sign-salad that can do nothing. Instead, he shows that in an important sense it idles, failing to tie up with our lives. This would explain why rafts of commentators on the *Tractatus* have been able to engage in long-standing and systematic debates about what its terms *mean* and what its propositions *imply*, even if such debates are ultimately confused and misunderstand the point of the book. To accept this characterisation of nonsense would account for the capacity of the *Tractatus* to have systematic effects on *some* of its readers, explaining how they are able to draw limited inferences and conclusions from what it says, without committing one to the idea that significant forms of nonsense exist.

But to read either of these more liberal understandings back into the mind of the young Wittgenstein lacks exegetical plausibility. In assessing this, we must avoid conflating two quite distinct issues: what Wittgenstein thought about sense and its limits (whether or not he changed his mind about this) and what the actual character of sense and its limits really are. That is to say, one must keep separate the task of explaining the difference between 'seeming to make sense' and 'making sense' in his works from the exegetical tasking of deciding what his views on these matters were and whether they remained constant. It does nothing, of course, to address the question of whether or not Wittgenstein had such liberal understandings of nonsense at the time of writing the *Tractatus* to point out that he tells us that its propositions are nonsense in 6.54, since what is in question is precisely what that claim came to, at that time.

It is precisely on this score that extreme therapeutic readings are most implausible. For to take them seriously entails that Wittgenstien's views on the nature of sense and meaning did not evolve at all, since he never advanced any. But what, then, should we make of his confession in the Preface to the *Investigations*, in which he tells us that 'since beginning to occupy myself with philosophy again, sixteen years ago, I have been forced to recognise grave mistakes in what I wrote in that first book' (*PI*, p. viii)? If the book did not 'say' anything at all, then what *mistakes* could be present in what he had written in it? How also should we make sense of the following remarks, to select but a few instances in which he seemingly repudiates his early view (cf. also *PI* §§92, 46)?

> Thought is surrounded by a halo. – Its essence, logic, presents an order, in fact the *a priori* order of possibilities, which must be common to both world and thought. But this order, it seems, must be utterly simple ... It must rather be of the purest crystal. But this crystal does not appear as an abstraction; but something concrete, indeed, as the most concrete, as it were the hardest thing there is (*Tractatus Logico-Philosophicus* No. 5.5563). (*PI* §96)

> We see that what we call 'sentence' and 'language' not the formal unity *I imagined*, but is the family of structures more or less related to one another. (*PI* §108; emphasis mine)

> (*Tractatus Logico-Philosophicus*, 4.5): 'The general form of propositions is: This is how things are.' – That is the kind of proposition one repeats to oneself countless times. One thinks that one is tracing the outline of the thing's nature over and over again, and one is merely tracing around the frame through which we look at it.
> (*PI* §114)

Pretty clearly, he is selectively targeting certain claims of the *Tractatus* for criticism – specifically those tied to his early representational and referential view of language. Worse still, it is clear from their surroundings that *only later* he came to regard these views as confusions that needed to be overcome, suggesting that they could not have been something 'thrown away' from the start. For example, in what appears to be a continuation of the remark of section 114, he famously writes: 'A picture held us captive. And we could not get outside of it' (*PI* §115). Unless those who favour the extreme therapeutic reading can somehow explain away these later remarks, they will be unable to make sense of what it is that Wittgenstein is seemingly repudiating. For it rules out the very idea that his understanding of language could have developed, by not allowing that he ever made any claims about such things as the general form of propositions during his early period at all. It also follows that if no 'views' were ever espoused, there cannot have been a transitional phase between early and late approaches during which he developed his views on language.[8] This would make a mockery of the many scholarly attempts to identify the pivotal catalyst of this shift with such moments as his inability to deal adequately with the colour incompatibility problem that Ramsey first brought to his attention (see Jacquette 1990, p. 353; also Goldstein 1999, pp. 25–6).

But, apart from accommodating the explicit textual evidence cited above, accepting that there was such a change has other exegetical virtues. For example, it promises to help us to understand the dramatic changes in his writing style. From what we know of Wittgenstein, such changes would not be regarded as philosophically trivial. As McDonough notes, 'Wittgenstein regarded himself as an artist as well as a philosopher. [He] was obsessed with stylistic questions, as well as questions about the origin of his own style' (McDonough 1994, p. 42; cf. also M. McGinn 1997, pp. 2, 4, 9–10). Thus, it is natural to suppose that if he really did take seriously the idea that fact-stating propositions were only legitimate form for the expression of thoughts, it may be no accident that the remarks of *Tractatus* have the outward form of tightly compressed sentences, presented in strict sequence.[9] Nevertheless, given what he also knew about the status of propositions, he was equally self-conscious about the fact that in laying them out in this way his method was 'strictly' incorrect (*TLP*, 6.53). Also, the fact that his view of thought and language became more open in his later work might explain why his writing style followed suit, becoming more easy and free. For what we find there is no longer a numbered series of staccato propositions but a patchwork of aphorisms, conversational remarks, questions and observations.

Elucidating elucidations

Recognising these problems, Marie McGinn has offered an account of the status of the Tractarian remarks by defending the idea that there is an elucidatory core of the work, which is neither nonsense nor composed of statements of fact or metaphysical truth (McGinn 1999, p. 497). She writes:

> The principal application he makes of the concrete image of a world of facts which consists of objects in combination with one another is to use it as a means *to make clear* the distinction between content (objects), structure (the arrangement of objects in determinate relationships to one another in facts) and form (the possibility of objects entering into these determinate relationships).
>
> (McGinn 1999, p. 500; emphasis mine)

She holds that although he necessarily uses language to clarify these matters, his sentences 'are not putting forward a theory of the proposition or a speculative account of the relationship between language and the world' (McGinn 1999, p. 148). Despite having the outward form of ordinary propositions, his remarks do not 'say anything', but are merely pointers designed to remind us of what we ought already to know (cf. *PI* §§127, 89 and 90). They are supposed to get us to see what ought to be obvious to us all or what would be obvious to anyone not led astray by philosophical theorising. They offer no new information; rather they are 'an attempt to draw our attention to something that lies before our eyes' (McGinn 1999, p. 501). For example, we can say of the weather that 'It is raining' and seemingly we can say of the proposition 'It is raining' that it is a proposition. By the Tractarian criterion, there is no doubt that 'It is raining' *says* something, as it pictures a possible state of affairs in the world – a situation of which it makes sense to say 'Yes' or 'No'. But what exactly is being said that is of a merely factual nature when it is remarked that, ' "It is raining" is a proposition'? What merely possible state of affairs does this picture? What does it tell our audience about the state of the world? Anyone who understands it learns nothing new from it, but would simply assent to it.

Armed with the idea that the apparent philosophical statements of the *Tractatus* are elucidations, we can allegedly approach the work differently. By rejecting the idea that propositions and elucidations have the same status or can be understood on the same model, this proposal allows us to reject the idea that Wittgenstein would have required a 'higher-order language' in order to express himself, or that he was implicitly committed to the existence of such a thing. Yet, even if we allow this, it raises puzzles about how we are to understand the tension he acknowledges as present in the work. For to the extent that his remarks can be *understood at all*, the bulk of his elucidations, with perhaps the exception of his use of truth-tables, must convey *something* to the reader – even if what is conveyed should not be modelled on instances of purely factual discourse. If we accept the elucidatory reading, Wittgenstein seems to share Frege's predicament of 'being irresistibly compelled' to use language in a self-consciously inappropriate way in order to get his message across. Frege acknowledges this difficulty when making his famous reply to Benno Kerry. Kerry claims that the statement 'The concept *horse* is easily attained' shows that, paradoxically, concepts can be objects. Frege tells us that Kerry confuses matters by conflating the psychological and the logical. In this particular case, the expression 'The concept horse' plays the logical role of an object and therefore – whatever the appearances – it *cannot* designate a concept. For Frege and the early Wittgenstein, that an expression plays a particular logical role is something that must be shown in the way it functions in a specific proposition – it is not something that can be generally defined or stated. Thus, Frege admits that in using ordinary language to elucidate such matters he must – for instance, by talking of such things as the logical roles of 'concepts' – speak 'imprecisely'; indeed, he comes close to admitting that he is driven to utter contradictory nonsense (*PW*, pp. 119–20). Because of this, in explaining himself, he is forced to ask his readers to 'meet him halfway'; they must forgive and ignore these transgressions of sense if they are to grasp his 'underlying thought' (*PW*, pp. 177–8). The point is that, despite this, it is part and parcel of understanding his message about what can and cannot be said that one gains an insight of what is, 'deep in the nature of things' (*CP*, p. 156).

But if Wittgenstein is trying to instil something similar in his readers, asking them to do likewise, then his elucidations cannot be nonsense in the ordinary sense. But what, then, does he mean by explicitly calling them such? In the context of making this very objection to the elucidatory reading Conant is quick to remind us that, 'On the Tractarian conception, there is only one way a sentence can be *Unsinn*: by its failing to symbolize' (Conant 2000, p. 195). How, if at all, can Wittgenstein's remarks about his first book be accommodated?

Letting the tension stand

I have now considered four main proposals in the current literature about the status of remarks of the *Tractatus*. They are said to embody either:

A set of theoretical statements;
A set of ineffable, necessary truths;
Straightforward, but therapeutic nonsense;
A set of elucidations.

We have now reviewed reasons why none of these options is wholly acceptable. It seems that, on any reading that does not deny that the *Tractatus* makes sense, it turns out to be at odds with its own account of sense or its own characterisation of its remarks. But there is another way of regarding the status of the Tractarian remarks that makes sense of this tension and which is in line with Wittgenstein's claims about the book's purpose. The best way to smooth out these exegetical difficulties is to see his remarks as *attempts* at elucidation not theory, without suggesting that they succeeded in being such. Concentrating on the *actual* status of his remarks, the above interpretations fail to distinguish clearly what he was *trying* to achieve from the extent to which he was successful in achieving it. Clearly, he wished the *Tractatus* to be a work of clarification, yet in large part it failed this purpose, as he later realised. That this is so is entirely consistent with the fact that he made erroneous assumptions and that he failed to express himself in the correct way.

Furthermore, lacking a genuinely clear view of such important issues as the nature of language, it should not surprise us that he acknowledges that his attempted elucidations are *at best* ill-formed and that he is only able to characterise this deformity in limited terms. That is to say, apart from his *use* of the truth-tables to demonstrate the nature of logical possiblities, in telling us about 'objects' and 'pictures' he appears to be using ordinary propositions. But if, as he then thought, all such saying is merely an attempt to state facts, then his elucidations should not say anything at all. They ought to be like demonstrations in logic. Aware of this, he recognised his attempt to offer elucidations in the Tractarian form to be 'strictly incorrect'. The penultimate remark before the revocation repays attention. He says:

> 6.53 The correct method in philosophy would really be the following: to say nothing except what can be said, i.e. the propositions of natural science – i.e. something that has nothing to do with philosophy.

Contrasting logic, science and their respective spheres was his only way of pointing to the difference between the status of philosophical elucidations and ordinary propositions. It was because of his impoverished view of the function of language that the author of the *Tractatus* had limited means of characterising its remarks. They were *meant* to be elucidations, but he was pushed by his own understanding of sense to regard them either as statements of fact or as mere nonsense. This is the tension running throughout the *Tractatus* and my reading makes no attempt to resolve it, only to understand it. But this is no bad thing. The doctrinal reading denies its force only by allowing something the *Tractatus* explicitly wishes to deny, whereas extreme therapeutic and straight elucidatory readings go wrong by finding too much continuity with his more mature approach in the later writings already present in this early book. Diamond is therefore right to insist that the really 'dramatic' criticism that Wittgenstein's makes of his early work hangs on his later wholesale rejection of the 'laying down of philosophical requirements' (Diamond 1995, pp. 20, 32; Koethe 1996, pp. 20–1). As she put it, 'The philosophical theory lays down, without looking . . . while Wittgenstein's talk of what is possible is entirely different' (Diamond 1995, pp. 21, 32). Certainly, when approaching his *later* writings we must take very seriously his later claim that, ' "But it must be like this!" Is not a philosophical proposition' and his injunction, 'Don't think, but look' (*PI* §599, §66). Indeed, I will argue just this in the remaining chapters of this book, although we must be careful to understand what he means by these remarks, just as we must beware of seeing *too much* continuity, or continuity of the wrong sort, in his views from these different periods.

In this, resolute readings of the *Tractatus* make too much of remark 6.54 and the ladder metaphor. Emphasising this single remark, above all others, no more yields a coherent overall reading than does stressing Wittgenstein's avowal that he had advanced 'unassailable truths', in the way Hacker does. Moreover, that Wittgenstein should ask his readers to understand *him*, rather than what is written in the book, fits equally well with the reading I am proposing. Remember that even though we are instructed to throw away the ladder, the reader is also told that 'He must transcend these propositions, and then he will see the world aright' (*TLP*, 6.54). Rather than reading his remark at 6.54 as a note of straightforward guidance – marking an enlightened realisation on the part of its author – it is best seen as an awkward attempt to acknowledge a genuine tension in this thinking: an expression of the conflict between what he hoped to achieve and the way in which he proceeded, as provoked by the limited understanding of the function of language he had at the time.[10] For these reasons, I hold a superior reading allows the tension to stand, but accounts for it. It is not 'chickening out' to hold both that Wittgenstein had a firm, developing view about how philosophical problems *had* to be approached and that the *Tractatus* failed to approach them in a completely satisfactory way.

Furthermore, it is worth noting that even though this unresolved tension was in some sense manifest to him at the time of writing the book, it remained only a symptom of the underlying cause that had yet to be revealed. For Wittgenstein did not, at this point, recognise the real *reason* why the book failed its elucidatory task.[11] This was because some of the most central claims of the *Tractatus* are infected with assumptions about the nature of language and the limits of sense that are faulty. His commitment to what they said about language was not only a mistake in itself it also made it impossible for him to give a proper account of what he was trying to do. As we have seen, the major assumption which he subsequently recognised as unwarranted is that all propositions serve to represent facts and that all sensible language shares this uniform function. This thought permeates the book and has a derivative, negative effect on the majority of its remarks – including, as we shall see, some of those concerning the nature of logic – making them failed attempts at clarification. It is not possible to understand Wittgenstein's development properly without identifying this early mistake and its effects.

Still, we must carefully distinguish the claim that there are substantive assumptions about the nature of language in the *Tractatus* from the claim that these were *meant to* form part of a theory or statement of doctrine. To think the latter promotes a common misunderstanding of the nature of the change that took place in his thinking. He did not simply exchange one theory or doctrine for another. The fact that he was only ever *trying* to offer elucidations in both periods survives the observation that his early work was infected with mistaken assumptions, precisely because we need not suppose that he was always successful in achieving his aim. This, of course, requires a different account of the subtle ways his views on the function of language developed and matured, one that explains the important similarities and differences in a way that is in line with his early statement of method about how one ought to approach philosophy.

From logical form to forms of life

In the previous chapter I argued that even in the *Tractatus* there is an emphasis on application in Wittgenstein's understanding of picturing. If this is right, his focus on the contexts and function of instances of language use remained constant throughout his work. For example, compare these remarks about how signs get their life in and through the applications we make of them from the *Investigations* with the citations and discussions of Chapter 2. pp. 67, 58 respectively.

> How does it come about that this arrow → points? Doesn't it seem to carry in it something besides itself? – 'No, not the dead line on paper; only the psychical thing, the meaning, can do that.' – That is both true and false. The arrow points *only in the application* that a living being makes of it.   (*PI* §454)

> We want to say: 'When we mean something, it's like going up to someone, it's not having a dead picture (of any kind).' We go up to the thing we mean.   (*PI* §455)

Notice the strong resemblance of the metaphor of 'going up to the thing we mean' and his early figurative idea of a picture 'reaching right out to reality'. Also, in the quotation below there is a direct parallel with the idea that a practical demonstration is, in the end, an adequate substitute for a proposition, as previously suggested by his remarks about how we might ultimately make clear what we meant by saying 'The watch is lying on the table' in section 70 of the *Notebooks*.

> We say 'The order orders *this* –' and do it; but also 'The order orders this: I am to . . .' We translate it at one time into a proposition at another into a demonstration, and at another into an action.
>
>   (*PI* §459)

To note this degree of overlap should not lead us to overlook the important and well-known differences in his understanding of the nature of language that hold between the early and late periods. In the later works, he no longer regards the activity of making sense along a *purely* referential axis – no longer is it seen in terms of simply picturing the facts of the world. The crucial change was not that he swapped two quite different theories of language, but that in the course of developing his early ideas he rid himself of a mono-functional view of language in favour of recognising that it has a plurality of diverse uses (cf. *PI* §304).[12] Unsurprisingly, he directly cites this very aspect of the *Tractatus* as being the main target of revision.

But how many kinds of sentence are there? Say assertion, question, and command? – There are countless kinds: countless different kinds of use of what we call 'symbols', 'words', 'sentences'. And this multiplicity is not something fixed, given once and for all; but new types of language, new language-games, as we may say, come into existence, and others become obsolete and get forgotten (We can get a rough picture of this from the changes in mathematics).

Here the term 'language-game' is meant to bring into prominence the fact that the *speaking* of language is part of an activity, or of a form of life . . .

– It is interesting to compare the multiplicity of the tools in language and of the ways they are used, the multiplicity of kinds of word and sentence, with what logicians have said about the structure of language (Including the author of the *Tractatus Logico-Philosophicus*).

(*PI* §23)

Against many standard readings, this insight did not constitute a straightforward move from a 'theory of reference' to a 'theory of use' about meaning since even early on the referential aspect of *making* pictures to ourselves already presupposes that these were used for specific, if limited, purposes. Rather, Wittgenstein later came to see that in using language we do much more than represent facts or, more precisely, model possible states of affairs. It is with this in mind that we should understand his remarks about naming that appear at the beginning of the *Investigations*. There, in line with his own methodological proclamations, we find him trying to overcome the traps set by the misleading character of symbols by focusing on the many ways in which we use language. He writes:

It will prove useful in philosophy to say to ourselves: naming something is like attaching a label to a thing.   (*PI* §15)

I contend that his treatment of names in the remarks that surround the above quotation echoes his treatment of logical constants. Liberated from a quite narrow conception of the function of language, he comes to realise that ordinary names can mesmerise us in just the way logical symbols confused Russell. He wants to make us aware of just how much we presuppose when we employ the picture that language is a system of signs that stands for objects. It is with this in mind that he reminds us that:

> Naming is so far not a move in the language-game – any more than
> putting a piece in its place on the board is a move in chess. We may
> say: nothing has so far been done, when a thing has been named.
>
> (*PI* §49)

We are urged to think of words as akin to the handles and knobs in
locomotives. These all have many different jobs which must be understood in relation to one another. None of these moves is unfamiliar.
The 'fundamental thought' of the *Tractatus* is still driving the
later Wittgenstein only in a new context. In the *Investigations* what we
see is an extension of his early critique of logical symbolism; a more
thorough working through of the idea that remained at the very heart
of his philosophy from beginning to end; that signs can mislead by
obscuring the true *workings* of our language. In this regard, he was
not repudiating the direction of his early approach to philosophy
nor its central message; instead he was coming to recognise that it did
not go far enough. In developing his views about the function*s*, as
opposed to *the* function, of language Wittgenstein had not abandoned
the idea that if there is to be meaning at all, certain conditions must
hold and that these are revealed through our uses of symbols. It is
simply that, freed of his uni-functional vision of language, he was
required to give more careful attention to its rich variety of uses. Consequently, in adopting a more liberal view that acknowledged a variety
of linguistic practices, he began to examine closely specific uses of language (cf. *PI* §134–7). This realisation paved the way for the kind of case-
by-case analyses that populate the later writings.

Concomitantly, his understanding of nonsense was correspondingly
widened, as he makes clear in the following passage.

> To say 'This combination of words makes no sense' excludes it from
> the sphere of language and thereby bounds the domain of language.
> But when one draws a boundary it may be for various kinds of reason.
> If I surround an area with a fence or a line or otherwise, the purpose
> may be to prevent someone from getting in or out; it may also be
> part of a game and the players are supposed, say, to jump over the
> boundary; or it may be to shew where the property of one man ends
> and that of another begins; and so on. So if I draw a boundary line
> that is not yet to say what I am drawing it for.   (*PI* §499)

We are given, as Reid puts it, 'a strong warning from the perspective of his later thought that the frame of the *Tractatus* is not the expression of a clear grasp on the part of the author of the *Tractatus* of what it is to label some use of language "nonsense"' (Reid 1998, p. 146). Given that sense and nonsense were initially and straightforwardly defined against the binary criterion of being something that pictures a possible state of affairs or not, it becomes easy to explain why Wittgenstein thought philosophy, logic, ethics and aesthetics all 'say nothing'. For example, framed by his early account of sense, Wittgenstein had little option but to regard ethical remarks as strictly nonsensical but none the less important. This was a vital insight into the essence and function of ethical language, albeit a negative one. Even early on he realised that ethical remarks are not designed to represent independent, contingent facts.[13]

At the time of writing the *Tractatus*, he lacked the resources to say positively in what important respects they differed, even though to an extent he clearly recognised that they did. Being told that ethics is like logic in being transcendental and in lacking genuine propositions is not enough to distinguish clearly the different roles they play in our lives. None the less he attempts a more positive characterisation of the latter when he locates the transcendent nature of our ethical attitude at the limit of the world, whereas logic is regarded as internal to its facts and their interrelations.[14] This is his way of acknowledging that although ethics says nothing, its silence is pregnant in a way that the silence of logic is not. In this he struggled to maintain that ethics had a profound status, despite being 'nonsensical'. Indeed, his *emphasis* throughout was on its profundity. The difficulty he had in making these observations and giving such distinct treatments had its source in his being compelled to classify both ethics and logic as simply falling within the domain of the unsayable. Yet, if we allow ourselves to read the *Tractatus* with the insight of the later work in play, specifically the idea that the function of language is *not only* to represent, then it becomes easy to see how he might have expanded and developed these early insights. Restricted by his general and clear-cut account of sense and nonsense, he did not have the resources at the time of writing the *Tractatus* to ·develop properly what was latent in his more positive understanding of the nature of ethical remarks and the nature of logic. Only as his views on the essence of language evolved did this become possible. Once freed of the Tractarian vision of the function of language, the later Wittgenstein was better able to explicate a more liberal understanding of the nature of nonsense itself – one that attends to the wider aspects of the genuine possibilities for us in this regard.

This proposal is at odds with the extreme therapeutic readings, which must treat his remarks on ethics as nonsensical. Although such readings provide a useful counter to the doctrinal and theoretical readings, given that Wittgenstein expressly denied that there could be ethical 'doctrines' or 'propositions' they go too far by ruling out an understanding of his treatment of ethics in the way just described. We can make best sense of Wittgenstein's remarks on ethics only if we recognise that his *conception* of language evolved. Given that he places such great importance on the ethical aspect of the *Tractatus* – identifying it as being its very *point* – it can hardly be ignored. My proposal is that when considering the links and breaks between the early and later writings, we get a better grip on the issues he was grappling with in that early work when drawing distinctions in the broad domain of what was unsayable. It is with this in mind that Wittgenstein was driven at times to both allow and deny the existence of profound forms of nonsense. Despite being unable to incorporate this idea seamlessly into his thinking, recognising the ways he found it important is vital to understanding him and how his thinking progressed. Thus, as Koethe argues, if his early view of sense did not constrain his thinking with respect to these central topics:

> we should expect this attitude towards them to persist beyond the *Tractatus*. If on the other hand, their construal as nonsensical in the *Tractatus* is an artifact or consequence of the picture theory, then we should expect such concepts and discourse to survive the abandonment of that theory and to occur in his later writings in ordinary, unconceptualised forms.   (Koethe 1996, p. 39)

We can salvage the important point embedded in this remark by replacing Koethe's talk of 'the picture theory' for a non-theoretical variation that simply recognises that Wittgenstein was initially committed to a view about the general form of the proposition and the uniform function of language.

But, more than this, as his views about the nature of language opened up the office once performed by logical form was assumed by forms of life, the latter becoming his new metaphor for that which is the limit of all possibility and sense-making. Famously, and in direct contrast to the ideas that all propositions have a common form and that their unique essences are expressed only by their particular logical form, we are told that 'to imagine a language means to imagine a form of life' (*PI* §19). Considered thus, the move from logical form to forms of life was a natural, almost irresistible consequence of his growing interest in the distorting effects, not just of logical constants, but also of other forms of symbols, such as ordinary words and names. We can regard the approach in the later writings as a wider application of the proper method for treating philosophical problems, as exemplified by his method of breaking the spell cast by logical symbolism. It is against this background that he trades talk of logic for that of grammar. In his later period grammar performs the function of underwriting essence in just the way the combinatorial possibilities of objects were supposed to underpin the very substance or essence of the world. Echoing the concerns of the opening sections of the *Tractatus*, we are told:

Grammar tells us what kind of object anything is.   (*PI* §373)

Essence is expressed by grammar.   (*PI* §371)

But it should hardly surprise us that as Wittgenstein began to reconceive the nature of sense-making he was simultaneously driven to reconceive its *ground*: logical form. For if we remove the constraint that all language has a common form, defined by propositional bipolarity, with it goes the entire family of associated views, such as commitment to determinacy of sense, truth-functional complexity and atomism. This is because the idea that propositions have a general form is precisely what secures these ideas and gives them substance. They depend on the fact that *all* linguistic activity is to be understood as particular instances of modelling reality, as Wittgenstein initially held. This ensured that all propositions had a certain well-defined common form that lent shape to his vision of logic.

Put in transformational terms, in one sense something quite dramatic happens to the early account if we remove the idea that all propositions are essentially representative of facts. For without this anchor, it follows naturally that the possibilities of making sense should be seen in terms of a whole range of activities, mutually fixed by our nature and that of the world. What then of logic itself? He addresses this directly in the *Investigations* when he writes:

But what becomes of logic now? Its rigour seems to be giving way here. – But in that case doesn't logic altogether disappear? . . . The philosophy of logic speaks of sentences and words in exactly the sense we speak of them in ordinary life when we say e.g. 'Here is a Chinese sentence', or 'No, that only looks like writing; it is actually just an ornament' and so on. We are talking about the spatial and temporal phenomenon of language, not about some non-spatial, non-temporal phantasm.   (*PI* §108)

Thus, if we equate the early focus on logic with the latter focus on grammar, we ought to question as he did:

In what sense is logic something sublime?

For there seemed to pertain to logic a particular depth – a universal significance. Logic lay, it seemed, at the bottom of all the sciences. – For logical investigation explores the nature of all things. It seeks to see to the bottom of things and is not meant to concern itself whether what actually happens is this or that. – It takes its rise, not from an interest in facts of nature, nor from a need to grasp causal connexions: but from an urge to understand the basis, or essence, of everything empirical. Not, however, as if to this end we had to hunt out new facts; it is, rather, of the essence of our investigation that we do not seek to learn anything *new* by it. We want to *understand* something that is already in plain view. For *this* is what we seem in some sense not to understand.   (*PI* §89)

It would be wrong to exaggerate these differences without acknowledging the powerful continuities. For in another sense, since logical form was never a substantial construct to begin with, in many central respects it survives the transition unaltered. Despite noting the crucial differences outlined above, the notions 'form of life' and 'logical form' have many common features.

In gesturing at what lies at the bottom of our sense-making practices, Wittgenstein was clearly not trying to use them to make philosophical pronouncements about 'what there is' or 'what there must be'. Both remain outside the scope of the explicable, sayable or articulable and under no circumstances could the limits they embody be positively stated or charted. According to the *Tractatus*, although there would be many individual instances of sense-making, each expressing their own logical form, our inability to articulate these is what forces us to abandon any attempt to classify and catalogue distinct 'logical forms' in the way Russell had hoped. Such an idea, as we have seen, he thought worse than bankrupt. Hence, in speaking of logical form Wittgenstein does not give the notion any substance or boundaries, other than those provided by his understanding of the common nature of propositions themselves.

In all but the last respect, so it is too with the possibilities thrown up by our form of life. Just as logical form cannot be represented – ruling out the possibility of determining the limits of what we might encounter in the world in advance of inquiry – so too the idea of a form of life cannot be explicated. It can provide no *conceivable* boundary. It too is the very ground of all inquiry: the basis of all saying and doing. Thus we cannot anticipate the limits of what it is sensible to say by appeal to logical form or to forms of life, since neither are substantial notions – we can only explore such possibilities from *within*. His central insight, early and late, is that there can be no transcendental articulation of the limits of sense and possibility. In the same way that there is no way to define the limits of logical form independently of what falls out of particular acts of sense-making, there is no understanding forms of life from some theoretical hide *outside* the activities and practices that they ground. There is no getting behind, beneath or above a form of life for the philosophical purpose of providing an explanation or justification. It is for this reason that philosophers go seriously wrong in attempting to theorise and give explanations about what lies at the base of all our activities. Rather, they must be vigilant of transgressions of sense, occasion by occasion, without the aid of general rules that can be independently validated.[15]

> Grammar does not tell us how language *must be* constructed in order to fulfil its purpose, in order to have such-and-such an effect on human beings. It only describes and in no way explains.
>
> <div align="right">(<i>PI</i> §496; emphasis mine)</div>

Indeed, we can see this commonality even though he directly rejects his early view about what comes at the end of analysis in a variant of his famous remark that appears near the end of the *Investigations*, in which he tells us that forms of life are given. He writes:

> Instead of the unanalysable, specific, indefinable: the fact that we act in such-and-such ways, e.g. *punish* certain actions, *establish* the state

of affairs thus and so, *give orders*, render accounts, describe colours, take an interest in others' feelings. What has to be accepted, the given – it might be said – are facts of living [forms of life].

(*RPPI* §630; *PI* p. 226)

For these reasons, we must resist holding out hope for a further explication of the nature of our form of life by further characterising *what* is basic to our practices. For example, in looking at what is fundamental in this regard Stroll identifies 'several candidates . . . and all of them non-intellectual. Among these are acting, being trained in communal practices, instinct and so on' (Stroll 1994: 146, 158). He also speculates that the reason that Wittgenstein failed to carry out a more detailed analysis of these notions was that he only began to explore them seriously just before his death. But it was not lack of time that prevented him from going further in clarifying these notions. For Wittgenstein realised that what is fundamental to our practices is something that can only make itself manifest in and through the practices and activities in which we engage and the way in which we are inaugurated into them. Thus to the extent that our instincts, training and customs do characterise what is basic to our form of life it is not possible to cleanly distinguish them.

Confusion on this score also leads to fruitless attempts to identify the distinct contributions that the world, our communal practices and our more animal natures make to our form of life. It is true that Wittgenstein sometimes describes our form of life in relation to instinctive and natural responses as in *On Certainty* §§358–9; sections of that work which are prominently quoted by Stroll. In other places, Wittgenstein speaks of it in connection with the kind of sophisticated practices that depend on enculturation (cf. *PI*, p. 174). But it is a mistake to think that these views are somehow at odds or that they point to different manifestations of potentially conflicting forms of life. Wittgenstein's rare and seemingly unsystematic remarks on this topic serve to indicate that he thought our form of life grounds the possibilities for our existence on *both* these fronts, in different but complementary ways. They relate to one another in a nested way and are not in competition. Our natural, animal responses fund, but do not circumscribe, the full range of possibilities present in our sophisticated, cultural and communal activities.[16] More than this, talking of 'our' form of life is not only to gesture at both our natural reactions and our social education, but at *the world* as well, with which both are inexplicably and intrinsically bound up. How could we even imagine these separated? For the limits of the reality are only revealed through our active engagements with it.

Neither truth nor successful action rests *separately* on the world or our responses to it. They require the union of both – a union that takes place in what we do. This is, of course, not to say that our activities, such as adjudicating what it makes sense to say, do not depend on the way the world is. Wittgenstein is clear about this:

> And if things were quite different from what they actually are – if there were for instance no characteristic expression of pain, of fear, of joy; if rule became exception and exception rule; or if both became phenomena of roughly equal frequency – this would make our normal language-games lose their point – the procedure of putting a lump of cheese on a balance and fixing the price by the turn of the scale would lose its point if it frequently happened for such lumps to suddenly grow and shrink for no obvious reason.   (*PI* §142)

> If we imagine the facts otherwise than they are, certain language games lose some of their importance, while others become important. And in this way there is an alteration – a gradual one – in the use of the vocabulary of a language.   (*OC* §63; *PI* §230e)

The world constrains our practices, but it does not determine them; the possibility of change, transformation and development is ever present. We are often compelled to adopt new practices and new views as we discover unnoticed, or as yet unemphasised, aspects of reality. At other times we have more choice. Nevertheless, while there is a degree of latitude, it is neither that just anything goes nor that viable developments are *simply* a matter of choice. It is precisely because they are tied to our form of life that changes to our practices cannot be merely arbitrary. Wittgenstein makes this clear in his discussion of how we determine what is possible and what is not.

> 'So does it depend wholly on our ground what will be called (logically) possible and what not – i.e. what that grammar permits?' – But surely that is arbitrary! – Is it arbitrary? – It is not every sentence-like formation that we know how to do something with, not every technique *has an application in our life*; and when we are tempted in phi-

losophy to count some quite useless things as a proposition, that is often because we have not considered its application sufficiently.

(PI §520; emphasis mine)

Thus even though it is right to think of the transition of Wittgenstein's view of language from early to late as marking a shift from a focus 'modelling reality' to greater attention to 'human practices', there is a real danger of misunderstanding this in overly simplistic terms which obscure the deep continuity in his thinking. It is certainly not a shift from realism to idealism as many commentators hold, as I will argue more fully in Chapter 5. Wittgenstein's key insight, running throughout all his writings, is that there is no talking of 'reality' or our relation to it from a privileged or detached standpoint.

At this point it is particularly important to resist a certain relativistic reading, for the possibilities that are open to us cannot and should not be understood in terms of neatly specifiable and distinct 'language games'. Charting these would be possible only if we could review and critique such 'things' from without; but that is not an option. For if something is a genuine 'language game' it must always be possible, in principle, for us to enter into it or adopt it as our own, testing its merits from within. Anything that is so alien to us that we could not, even in principle, make sense of it could not be called a 'language game', a custom or a practice. This does not obliterate all local differences, but it does show that it is wrong to overemphasise these and that it is artificial, at best, to seek philosophical gain by observing that the different communities of various times and places do things differently. As Feyerabend neatly puts it, 'Potentially every culture is all cultures' (Feyerabend 1999, p. 33).

It is worth stressing this point if we are not to misunderstand Wittgenstein's approach. For McDowell is right to observe that 'Readers of Wittgenstein often suppose that when he mentions customs, forms of life, and the like, he is making programmatic gestures towards a certain style of positive philosophy' (McDowell 1998, pp. 277–8). Many think he is committed to a substantive 'social pragmatist philosophy of meaning', which relies on constructs such 'language games' that are defined by their 'rules'. It is this that allegedly gives definition to his supposition that 'meaning is use'. For example, as Travis, who ought be more circumspect given his views, puts it, 'Language games, we will take it, are abstract objects specified by their rules so that A is the same language game as B just in case any statement of A's rules is a statement of B's rules and *vice versa* . . . When we construct a language game, it and its rules are exactly whatever we say they are' (Travis 1989, p. 84). This idea of a set of rigid 'internal' rules allows us to think of meaning as precisely, yet normatively, defined by its correct use and that languages must be bound by their rules just as ordinary games are. If he had adopted this he would be advancing a position very like that espoused by many contemporary philosophers of language. The widespread appeal of this way of reading of Wittgenstein's later writings is partly down to Kripke; for although as an interpretation Kripke's exposition has been much criticised, its influence has none the less been felt even beyond the confines of Wittgenstein scholarship. Thus, it is common-place to hear the later Wittgenstein's contribution to philosophy summed up in the following way:

> Ever since Wittgenstein . . . it has been widely assumed the sense of an expression is to be somehow emerging from its use. Practically everybody who's anybody in modern Anglo-American philosophy has held some or other version of this sense-cum-use doctrine.
>
> (Fodor 1990, p. 161)

Likewise, his invocation of 'forms of life' is conflated with straightfor-ward acceptance of the doctrine of meaning holism or inferentialism, over which there is also a current broad consensus. In one form or another the received view is that concepts are individuated by their 'use' or that their possession conditions are determined by their inferential commitments and entitlements (although debates continue to rage over whether these should be understood; internally or externally – reduc-tively or non-reductively). Disagreement over these issues masks the extent to which there is a general underlying commitment to the idea that concepts are individuated by correct 'use', 'function' or 'inferential role'. For this reason is not unusual for Wittgenstein's name to be allied with thinkers such as Quine, Davidson, Brandom, Sellars and Rorty. Nor it is surprising that when condemning meaning holism Fodor and Lepore should directly target Wittgenstein's talk of 'a form of life'. They write:

> Meaning holism is, we're told, a very beautiful metaphor (we really were once told that, in those very words), a profound way of seeing things, a revealing picture of how the world might be, or even, heaven help us, a Form of Life . . . We don't know what to make of

this. Anyhow, we're pretty sure it's not the way we wish to do philosophy.   (Fodor and Lepore 1992, p. xiii)

Ironically, as a doctrine, 'meaning holism' is a pretty clear position. Although Fodor and Lepore rail against the use of loose or elusive metaphors, they find it quite easy to spell out the disastrous consequences that follow from holding meaning holism to be true. For example, they note that unless some internal limits are established then no meaningful content can be individuated without charting the way it relates to *every* other content. This suggests that although, in principle, each and every content can be 'precisely' or 'neatly' delineated as defined by its unique inferential liaisons, these would be impossible to chart in practice. Yet, how, then, could we know, with precision, what we mean on any given occasion? It is with this very same worry in mind, that Fogelin says, 'I wish to suggest that these non-contextualised appeals to wholes or totalities make no sense. I have no idea what could count as a whole culture or a whole language' (Fogelin 1994, p. 210).

For Wittgenstein, this would be no objection to his 'theory' for two reasons. First, given the practical purposes our concepts are meant to serve (including everyday scientific ones), the fact that we can specify them completely, whether finely or roughly, is no cause for concern. Wittgenstein has no intention of using concepts for a grander philosophical purpose, rather his aim is, in part, to understand their basis better. Thus, whether or not we can in practice precisely define concepts is not a wong for him. Second, and most importantly, he is not advancing a 'theory' that is at risk of refutation. Confusion on this score stems from and reinforces misunderstandings about his purpose in saying that 'meaning is use', and in introducing language games and relating these to our form of life. These notions are not, as many wrongly suppose, theoretical constructs.

In recognising that meaning is contextual, Wittgenstein is not subscribing to a doctrine that 'meanings' or 'propositions' are holistic such that we can understand them by simply charting their inferential connections. He explains, 'I am inclined to distinguish between the essential and the inessential in a game too. The game, one would like to say, has not only rules but also a *point*' (PI §564). To grasp the point of a 'language game' we must look not only at its intellectual dimension but also at the character and point of the surrounding practices and at their relation to our basic responses, as well. For example, we can only understand the nature of 'pain' by attending to all this. Thus:

The concept of pain is characterized by its particular function in our life.   (*Z* §532)

Pain has this position in our life; has these connexions; (That is to say: we only call 'pain' what has this position, these connexions).
                                                                    (*Z* §533)

Only surrounded by certain normal manifestations of life is there such a thing as an expression of pain. Only surrounded by an even more far-reaching particular manifestation of life, such a thing as the expression of sorrow or affection.   (*Z* §534)

We learn the word 'think' under particular circumstances.
                                                                    (*LWPPI* §41)

The surroundings give it its importance.   (*PI* §583)

The point is that he bids us to attend not just to the *use of words* but also to the practices that surround them. Hence he says: 'For a large class of cases – though not for all – in which we employ the word 'meaning' it can be employed thus: the meaning of a word is its use in language' (*PI* §43). This should be taken not as a theoretical proposal, but as methodological advice of the same sort he would have given during his early period about how to understand logical symbols. Certainly, he is not advancing a hypothesis or a dictum. Indeed, it is precisely because there are no fixed or surveyable rules for the correct use of concepts that define 'language games' that we are asked to imagine situations in which 'others' use concepts differently from the way we do for the express purpose of getting a better view of the grammar of our own language. It is because we lack a perspicuous representation of the working of our grammar that he places such importance on reflecting on language games and 'finding and inventing intermediate cases' (cf. *PI* §122). He reminds us that 'The language games are rather set up as objects of comparison which are meant to throw light on the facts of our language by way not only of similarities, but also of dissimilarities' (*PI* §130). This is all one can do in trying to capture the landscape of such a rough terrain. In 1948 Wittgenstein writes:

Nothing is more important for teaching us to understand the concepts we have than constructing fictitious ones.   (*C&V*, p. 74e)

Indeed, this is why he introduces us to the possibility of other language games that might surround the concept pain, to take the extreme case described in *Zettel*. He conjures up a tribe that employs two different concepts of 'pain', 'one is applied where there is visible damage and is linked with tending, pity and so on. The other is used for stomach-ache for example, and is tied up with mockery of anyone who complains' (Z §380). Accordingly, unless members of this tribe can locate some kind of outer bodily damage they will not regard the person as experiencing what we would call 'pain'. Their notion of what counts as pain cuts much more finely than would ours. Or, as Wittgenstein puts it, they, 'have concepts which cut across ours' (Z §379).

He says of them that their more 'public' understanding of pain is different, but related to ours. Hence to imagine it we would need to imagine many other connections different. Yet this in turn requires that we imagine many others facts as being different – not everything, of course, but quite a lot. For example, an indefinite number of other psychological facts and related practices would have to be otherwise if the analogy were to hold in just the way stated, although we cannot conceive of an exact list of which changes would be necessary. This can be seen straight away if we only consider that in making such a list we could either start, on the one hand, by imagining our reactions to pain to be quite different or, on the other, by imagining our reactions to other phenomena, such as warmth, as being quite different. A move in either of these directions would also have the ripple effect of making a great number of other connections and associations and activities live or die. Thus, an entire range of analogies would become appropriate or cease to be so (cf. Z §644). It is not possible to chart *all* such changes, which is why Wittgenstein only ever asks us to imagine localised 'language games' in restricted contexts. Although it seems we can do this – at a stretch – given the differences in our practices, it is only ever an exercise in imagination. To 'make genuine sense' of these activities would require the full picture, a complete sketch of this other 'form of life'. This is beyond us.

Nor are we not being asked to seriously imagine, *per impossibile*, an alien form of life. Rather, the imagined scenario is being used as a device to get us to reflect on the complexity of our own practice by way of comparison, and to recognise that it characterises an aspect of our form of life. In this way, imagining language games aids in the removal of the false pictures we may have developed. Thus, getting us to picture alternative language games serves as a dialectical tool. It is with this end in mind and not a theoretical one that he directs us to:

Let the use of words teach you their meaning.

(*PI* 220e, *LWPPI*, §856; cf. also 340)

This is why 'One cannot guess how a word functions. One has to look at its use and learn from that' (*PI* §340). We must be very careful in understanding what it is that he is trying to get us to describe when he tells us to focus on description not explanation. For it is a hangover of the urge to explain that tempts us to try to categorise what his descriptions aim at under some higher-order heading. For example, Gert proposes that he is interested in 'descriptions of descriptions', whereas Ebbs sees him as aiming at 'describing practices' (Ebbs 1997, p. 90). Even more generally Pears sees him as concerned with the 'description of the phenomenon of language' (Pears 1988, p. 218). The danger of such characterisations is that they can cause us to wrongly picture what is involved in the description of, 'language games or the use of individual terms' (Gert 1997, p. 221). Such proposals are very misleading in that they suggest that he was some kind of adherent to 'ordinary language' philosophy. Yet the fact is that Wittgenstein has no such easily designated target. He describes whatever is necessary to clarify the nature of that which we do not understand and only to the extent required to engender clarity. What unites his descriptions is that they serve *this* end, not that they all have some common object. I will have much more to say about this in Chapter 6.

It is important to be clear about this lest we misrepresent both what he was meant to be 'describing' and his purpose in doing so. For example, as Stroll observes, 'Most exegetes have interpreted him as saying that to give an explanation is to advance a theory and that advancing a theory is tantamount to searching for the essence of things. On this account, descriptions are alternatives to theories' (Stroll 1998, p. 103). But saying just this does not say enough. For even those who are clearly aware of Wittgenstein's views on these matters can find it difficult to understand what it is to engage in philosophy without advancing theories, doctrines or theses. Consequently, they hold that his descriptive approach is not really at odds with a theoretical one (understood in the right kind of way). Hence even Colin McGinn, who believes that Wittgenstein's approach is understood best as negative and therapeutic, claims that it is perfectly in line

to expound him as putting forward a number of themes and elaborating upon their implications and significance; and it will . . . do no harm to express these in the form of definite *theses* about meaning and related notions.   (McGinn 1984, p. 2)

It is true that Wittgenstein tells us only that if one tried to advance theses in philosophy, it would never be possible to debate them, because everyone would agree to them, not that it is impossible that one could advance philosophical theses full stop (*PI* §128). Following this line of thought, Koethe claims Wittgenstein's reason for rejecting the value of philosophical theses or theoretical explanations was that he had in mind an outdated and 'stereotypical' picture of philosophical theorising – one that few philosophers would today endorse.[17] To see this, Koethe proposes that we must consider the kind of 'theories' that Wittgenstein actually rejected. Chief amongst these are 'the semantic and metaphysical theories of the *Tractatus*' (Koethe 1996, p. 62). Cleansed of this limited conception of what a philosophical theory looks like, he holds, 'it is an exaggeration to regard the methodology of the *Investigations* as purely descriptive, free of anything that might be thought of as philosophical theorizing' (Koethe 1996, p. 6). Yet despite such gestures at softer renderings of what it is to advance a philosophical 'thesis' or 'theory', we are not given much detail about how such things compare with their harder, earlier cousins. Without further explication, such talk is bound to have misleading connotations. Specifically, it will not be acceptable if it encourages the idea that our philosophical quarry is something that we can regard as separable from the very activity of explicating it. What interested the later Wittgenstein were the very sorts of matters on which the adoption of an independent perspective is inappropriate, as it would be in trying to understand logic. It is precisely for this reason that he viewed the idea of philosophical theorising with such suspicion.

The point is that when Wittgenstein contrasts description with explanation, he is not offering his descriptions as an alternative means of getting at the very same target as philosophical theorists; since our relation to the target is in part what he wants us to rethink. Descriptions are therefore not straightforward alternatives to theories. But even if we are not misled on this score, we might still think the activities of offering philosophical descriptions and theories have other aspects in common. For example, Schulte likens his method of providing a perspicuous representation to the activity of an impressionistic painter. In his eyes, in attempting to correct our lack of a clear view of our grammar Wittgenstein allegedly 'uses complicated techniques which, by leaving certain details out of consideration, attempt to describe phenomena in the way they are normally seen by us and to draw our attention in this indirect manner to the peculiarities of *this normal way of seeing things'* (Schulte 1993, p. 26). In this regard, he cites Wittgenstein's own admission that he found it difficult to renounce all theory (see *RPPI* §723). Thus, despite being 'non-explanatory', Schulte's understanding of the descriptive approach 'does not amount to renouncing all analysis and systematic procedures' (Schulte 1993, p. 35). He supports this interpretation by focusing on material from *Remarks on Philosophy of Psychology: Volume 1* (starting at section 65) in which Wittgenstein makes a series of 'general' remarks that are seemingly meant to serve as a 'plan for the treatment of psychological concepts' (similar remarks are also interspersed throughout passages in *Zettel* beginning at section 472). He asks, rhetorically, 'what possible purpose might be served by these attempts to classify psychological phenomena or concepts' (Schulte 1993, p. 34)? His answer is that 'they owe their existence to his quest for the most general criteria defining our use of these concepts or entire classes of such concepts' (Schulte 1993, p. 34).

But despite this, there can be little doubt that it would be wrong to think Wittgenstein was seeking to identify such general criteria or to provide complete descriptions of specific phenomena. Rather, what drives his investigations should be understood against the background of his aim to get a clear view of 'something we know when no one asks us, but no longer know when we are supposed to give an account of it' (*PI* §89). For it is only this that is 'something we need to *remind* ourselves of' (*PI* §89). In this light, it is clear that he is not advocating a single method of clarification or striving after completeness or comprehensiveness.

> The description of word-usage. The word is uttered – in what context? So we have to find something characteristic of these separate occurrences, a kind of regularity. – But we don't learn to use words with the help of rules. How could I give someone a rule for the instances in which he is supposed to say he's in pain! – On the other hand, there is a ROUGH regularity in the use to which a person actually puts words.
>
> (*LWPPI*, §968)

So I shall say: It is not established form the outset that there is such a thing as 'a *general* description of the use of a word'. And even if there is such a thing, then it has not been determined how *specific* such a description has to be.

(*LWPPI*, §969; emphases original)

We are not at all prepared for the task of describing the use of e.g. the word 'to think' (And why should we be? *What is such a description useful for?*)

And the naïve idea that one forms of it does not correspond to reality at all. We expect a smooth contour and what we get to see is ragged. Here it might really be said that we have constructed a false picture.

(*Z* §111; emphasis mine)

It is not to be expected of this word that it should have a unified employment; we should rather expect the opposite.   (*Z* §112)

As an example think of the description of 'occasions'. Is it really clear that one has to understand the description of an 'occasion of grief'? For the occasions of grief are interwoven with 1000 other patterns. Is it clear that someone must be able to learn the technique of designating this kind of pattern? That he be able to pick an occasion of grief out of the other patterns the way we do?

(*LWPPI* §966)

Nor is the idea that he is seeking a general description more plausible if we focus instead on the phenomena that *underpin* our 'language-games'. Of these he writes:

One learns the word 'think', i.e. its use, under certain circumstances, which, however, one does not learn to describe.   (*Z* §114)

But I can teach a person the use of a word! For a description of the circumstances is not needed for that.   (*Z* §115)

I just teach him the word under particular circumstances.

(*Z* §116)

And now can I describe these circumstances? – and yet why not? I could give examples, that much is clear. *How can I learn to describe the circumstances*? Was I taught?   (*LWPPI*, §971; emphasis mine)

It should be of no surprise, then, that he also explicitly tells us that his interest in describing psychological phenomena 'is not of importance to me because I am keen on completeness. Rather because each one casts light on the correct treatment of all' (Z §465).

> And if I now imagine a list of such circumstances, who would be interested in it? – To be sure, individual aperçus are interesting. But would a listing which strove for inclusiveness be interesting? Would it be of practical use? – The game doesn't work that way at all.
> (*LWPPI* §973; cf. *PI* §133)

In this light, we can begin to understand better his purpose in offering up descriptions in terms of what he calls 'reminders'. To return to an early example, consider again the proposition ' "It is raining" is a proposition'. One way of making it intelligible, without thinking it expresses a metaphysical truth, is to see that it might be sensibly employed as an example designed to teach or reveal something about the nature of propositions themselves. So used, it is neither speculative nor hypothetical, nor does it *tell* the audience anything new about the state of the world, for without the requisite background knowledge already in place such an example would be pointless. Furthermore, anyone who did understand would simply 'agree with it'. At best such remarks serve as instructions, designed to educate or re-educate in the just way he later held 'There are physical objects' should be regarded as setting out a grammatical rule. It lacks the capacity to inform or misinform. But saying 'A is a physical object' is not nonsense when viewed as an instruction about the use of words. Its status only becomes odd or peculiar if it is modelled on a fact-stating proposition, for then we will be tempted to understand it as a statement of a metaphysical truth or a hypothesis about an extraordinary type of state of affairs, of the kind that is fit for philosophical theorising. Elucidations might then be used to initiate someone into a practice or to remind them of something about it they in some sense already know, but have seemingly forgotten or have never articulated.

We are reminded of just what is necessary to disabuse us of certain misunderstandings and to clarify matters. The procedure is meant to reveal aspects of our 'customary practice', it need not be comprehensive and, indeed, the very idea that there is a comprehensive 'description' or account of our *practices* – understood as giving us insight into the correct rules for applying words or concepts – is precisely one of the myths that Wittgenstein was trying to explode. There are no such general or final rules to articulate. This is why Wittgenstein's descriptions are always 'example-oriented' or 'case-oriented', as Stroll has emphasised.

> What we call 'descriptions' are instruments for particular uses . . . Thinking of a description as a word-picture of the facts has something misleading about it: one tends to think only of such pictures as hang on our walls: which seems to portray how a thing looks, what it is like. (These pictures are as it were idle.) (*PI* §291)

Thus what we are 'reminded' of, what is made clear, is not a comprehensive set of rules or descriptions since these were never part of our initial training, or in so far as they were they were supplemental. We are reminded of our training itself or its background, or at least some aspects of these. This is what it means to re-educate philosophers – to help them find their way home. This is what it is to 'bring words back from their metaphysical to their ordinary use' (*PI* §116). These reminders, therefore, neither provide nor make use of *new* information. There is no suggestion of a 'final, correct' description that could be used to simply replace some misleading philosophical picture.

Clarifying what it is he is trying to describe (or reacquaint us with) is vital if we are to understand properly why and in what sense he regards the ultimate target of his grammatical investigations to be conceptual. In saying this, he is not expressing an interest in the *merely* 'linguistic' over the properly 'metaphysical'. Rather, in rejecting the possibility of a privileged view of an independent metaphysical 'reality', he is making it clear that 'what there is' cannot be separated from our ways of understanding it. Philosophical investigations are neither *merely* factual nor super-factual, hence his claim that he is neither 'doing natural science, nor yet natural history' (*PI*, p. 230e). He remarks that:

> Philosophical investigations: conceptual investigations. The essential thing about metaphysics: it obliterates the distinction between factual and conceptual investigations. (*Z* §458)

It is in this context, not in support of some kind of linguistic idealism, that he contrasts the metaphysical and the conceptual. It is in this respect that a primary consequence of working through the imaginary exercises described above is that they help us to realise that 'We are not analysing a phenomena (e.g. thought) but a concept (e.g. that of thinking), therefore the use of the word' (*PI* §383). Such comparisons can help to break the temptation to try to observe the processes that go on when we are thinking; a temptation fostered by the thought that language simply serves to name objects. His comparisons with other possibilities nullify our need to examine that which the word 'thinking' names. It is with this in mind that he says:

> In order to get clear about he meaning of the word 'think' we watch ourselves while we think; what we observe will be what the word means. – But this concept is not used like that. (*PI* §316)

Here we can again see what is preserved from his early methodological approach. His concern is not only to remove the misleading picture, but also to gain an insight into the basis of our practices as they stand. In this respect, his use of language games is non-accidentally reminiscent of his use of truth-tables in the *Tractatus*, as described in Chapter 1. Equally, as with logic, in getting us to give up the idea that there is some process or thing that the term 'thinking' designates, Wittgenstein is also redirecting us toward what should be of interest to us when we wish to investigate the nature of our psychology. He writes:

> [W]e forget that what should interest us is the question: how do we compare these experiences; what criterion of identity do we fix for their occurrence? (*PI* §322)

> Look on the language game as the primary thing. (*PI* §656)

For these reasons, he contrasts the noting of language games with the advancing of explanations and conjectures (*PI* §§654–6). He regards our theoretical commitments as dangerous. They can mesmerise us and drive us to systematically misrepresent our practices. As he says, 'It often happens that we only become aware of the important facts, if we suppress the question "why?"' (*PI* §471). Knowing how we go wrong in seeking such explanations he warns, 'A main cause of philosophical disease – a one-sided diet: one nourishes one's thinking with only one kind of example' (*PI* §593). Deep-seated philosophical errors begin to take root in the fertile soil of attempted philosophical explanations, for focusing too much on just one aspect of a phenomenon can lead us to elevate it to the status of the essential feature. Thus when other, equally prominent features are noticed, they threaten to occupy this position, serving as counter-examples, or at the very least they require some other accommodation. In this way one can be led to intractable questions, contradictions or *ad hoc* claims that, in turn, spur on the production of further attempts at explanation. One is thus quickly drawn into an elaborate web of theorising, often without any clear means of evaluating the various proposals in play. But this process only obscures what we want to understand and takes us further and further away from genuine resolutions. This is why Wittgenstein remarks:

> When we do philosophy we are like savages, primitive people, who hear the expressions of civilized men, put a false interpretation on them, and then draw the queerest conclusions from it.
> (PI §194; cf. also §345)

> What we 'are tempted to say' in such a case is, of course, not philosophy; but it is its raw material. Thus, for example, what a mathematician is inclined to say about the objectivity and reality of mathematical facts, is not a philosophy of mathematics, but something for philosophical treatment.   (PI §254)

> Here the temptation is overwhelming to say something further, when everything has been described – Whence this pressure? What analogy, what wrong interpretation produces it?   (Z §313)

Attention to what we say and do is the only way to break free of this spell cast by a misleading picture and the commitments it inspires. The process requires not just removing the source of our puzzlement but being reminded – normally, by means of examples – of the conditions in which we deploy the concepts in question.

In important respects this is the same tack he took in his early approach to logic. Indeed, I hope to have demonstrated that his later view of language was a natural development and extension of his early approach into new territory. From this perspective, although the move from early to late involves a rejection of his early 'views' about the nature of language, it cannot be understood as a simple or straightforward rejection. In both periods his philosophical aim was always to get a clear view of what underpins our activities and his method for achieving this was always, in one way or another, to get us to attend appropriately to our practices.

Conclusion

In the next chapter I will consider two cases in which those who purport to be friendly to Wittgenstein's method have failed to take seriously this lesson. They fall back into seeking theories and explanations, or are in danger of doing so. I will illustrate this by considering two recent attempts to use his insights to help us better understand states of consciousness and rule-following, for it is instructive to contrast Wittgenstein's own approach to these topics with those of his so-called followers.

4
Without Explanation

Nonsense. Nonsense, – because you are making assumptions instead of simply describing. If your head is haunted by explanations here, you are neglecting to remind yourself of the most important facts.

Wittgenstein, *Zettel*, §220

Introduction

I hope I have now set out how Wittgenstein's approach to philosophy evolved, informed by his understanding of the nature of its concerns. In this chapter I will illustrate its virtues by contrasting it with approaches that seek to provide philosophical explanations. In particular, I hope to show the limits of the latter view of what philosophy can achieve by showing in what respect it is not possible to explain consciousness or resolve the rule-following paradox, as Wittgenstein's treatment of these phenomena is representative his general approach to fundamental topics.

Demystifying consciousness

Dennett has embarked on what he considers a 'demystifying philosophical investigation' with respect to the phenomena of consciousness (Dennett 1991a, p. 22).[1] In essence the strategy he has employed is one of getting us to 'trade in' our ordinary intuitions so as to soften us up for the first phases of a full-fledged 'scientific' explanation of consciousness in terms of sub-personal systems and their ontogenetic origins. His hope is that once we are freed from certain misleading metaphors about the mind, we will be receptive to such an explanation.

In concentrating on this first stage of his treatment of consciousness phenomena I offer a critique of Dennett's project in order to show how Wittgenstein also attempted to 'demystify' consciousness, but in a markedly different way. This is both important and ironic because in challenging our 'everyday' intuitions about consciousness, Dennett regards himself as following in Wittgenstein's footsteps. For example, he tells us that 'My debt to Wittgenstein is large and long-standing' and that 'what I am doing [is] a kind of redoing of Wittgenstein's attack on the "objects" of conscious experience' (Dennett 1991a, p. 462).[2]

My aim is to show not only that the 'reductive character' of Dennett's project is at odds with Wittgenstein's approach, but that its wider ambitions also break faith with it. Although they are good travelling companions up to an important crossroads, in the end their incompatible concerns take them in different directions. My hope is that we might begin to see good reasons for preferring Wittgenstein's 'road less travelled' by revealing the essential flaws that attend projects such as Dennett's attempt to *explain* consciousness. My ultimate aim is to throw light on the nature of Wittgenstein's approach to philosophical psychology, using Dennett as a foil. If successful, this will show precisely how that approach differs importantly from those advanced by many of today's philosophers and cognitive scientists.

Stuff and nonsense

When it comes to characterising the reality of psychological phenomena, many philosophers in the post-Cartesian analytic tradition see themselves as faced with a stark choice: to advocate either some form of dualism or some form of materialism. Dualists tend to divide into two main camps: those who support substance dualism and those who support property dualism. Substance dualists take minds to be logically distinct entities that are strongly independent of bodies. Standardly, they argue that minds must differ from physical substances because they 'stand beneath' entirely different types of attributes or properties – i.e. mental attributes or properties. On this picture other bodily organs are used as a model for 'minds', the main difference being that ordinary bodily organs such as hearts and livers are located spatially in the world while minds are not. Furthermore, if one thinks of the mind as some sort of non-physical entity or substance, then it is a natural next step to think of 'beliefs', 'feelings', 'moods' and their kin as objects, processes or states that inhabit the mental domain. Nevertheless, one could separate these two ideas and allow that although nonreducible 'mental' phenomena exist, 'minds', conceived as separate entities, do not. Those who take such a stand generally support a kind of 'property dualism'. Such a position is reasonably popular even today.

Strangely enough, treating the 'mind' as a home for 'mental episodes' is not logically tied to dualism. That is to say, this 'picture' of the mind as an extra non-bodily organ can get mixed up in a most unhelpful way with a crude materialism. This happens when one simply relocates the mind to the brain and treats mental phenomena as identical to types or token brain events. Such mind/brain events are then placed in a 'physical' chain of causes. They are designated both as the end result of incoming brain processes and as the starting point for outgoing brain processes. Appropriately, given the foundations of the modern debate, such a view has been dubbed 'Cartesian materialism'.

Asserting mental/physical identity is, of course, the natural response or reaction to dualism in its various forms – but it is little more than that. This simple 're-fitting' makes these materialists prone to misrepresent the nature of psychological phenomena in a new, perhaps more insidious, way. The mental objects, states, processes, events, and so on, which, in accord with dualism, would have inhabited the mind, have now simply become allegedly 'unmysterious' brain states, processes, activities and events. Nevertheless, all their interesting mental properties are somehow supposed to survive the transition.

What is interesting is that neither dualism nor materialism, as sketched above, tells us anything of much interest about the nature of mental phenomena. In fact, the debate over their physicality can obscure many important questions about their character. One of the initial problems in clarifying the nature of mental phenomena is that we find it hard to free ourselves of Cartesian-style thinking on these matters. For what thwarts both the materialist and the dualist when it comes to understanding the ontological commitments of common-sense psychology is that they 'accept a certain vocabulary and with it a set of assumptions' (Searle 1992, p. 2).[3] The main assumption is that it is justified to debate the ontology of 'mental' objects and processes without first deciding anything about their nature.[4]

Wittgenstein and Dennett are united in their rejection of such talk. For example, one of the primary stated aims of *Consciousness Explained* is to undermine the Cartesian legacy in the philosophy of mind. Dennett believes that most philosophers and those lay folk influenced by them conjure up images of an Inner (mental) Theatre complete with a Self who examines various Objects of Consciousness (pains, colours, figments of the imagination, etc.) whenever they think of the mind. They still think of our verbal reports concerning consciousness as based upon what the Self sees 'up on the screen'. Apparently, it 'introspects' mental items in a way similar to that in which we ordinarily inspect everyday things such as watches or pieces of china. Dennett hopes to undermine this Cartesian model of the mind. To this end he catalogues the kinds of traditional problems that such a view engenders through-out the chapters of his book. Such problems include the interaction problem, the problem of inverted spectra and problems concerning epiphenomenal 'qualia'.[5] However, he gives us an insight into his overarching reason for resisting the view by telling us that the 'funda-mentally anti-scientific stance of dualism is, to my mind, its most disqualifying feature' (Dennett 1991b, p. 107; see also pp. 106–8).

Wittgenstein is also particularly interested in the idea of the Inner (or 'states of consciousness' as he refers to them in the Preface of the *Inves-tigations*). Nevertheless, for him, the source of our misunderstanding about the nature of the Inner is not traced back to Descartes' doorstep – rather, it is generated by a primitive view of the operation of psycho-logical language.[6] For him the desire to reify the 'psychological' is bound up with the view that all language is essentially referential in nature. It is linked with the idea that the primary function of words is to provide names for objects. It is also tied to the notion that the essential aim of language is to effect a simple form of communication. For example, when I tell you what is 'going on inside me' I use a word like 'sharp pain' to pass on information. If you are acquainted with 'sharp pains' yourself, if you know what kind of things those words designate, then by analogy you gain an insight into my situation. For Wittgenstein, this picture of how language operates generates (and supports) the idea of an 'inner realm of mental events' which looks non-trivially like the 'mental realm' conjured up by Descartes' philosophy of mind.

The name–object view of language and the attendant metaphysics it inspires is the target of his celebrated 'private language argument'. That 'argument' is meant to show that the meaning of our sensation-terms cannot be based on any appeal to inner entities. Although it is much debated how to correctly interpret the *Investigations*' passages from §243 to §275 which allegedly make up the 'private language argument', I side with those who take Wittgenstein to be attacking the name–private object view of psychological language because it is incoherent. Even in imagining what would be involved in acts of private ostension it must be presupposed that an individual's 'signs' are meaningful *before* they engage in their private naming ceremony. But, as that very process is supposed to give these signs their meanings, one must face up to the insurmountable and unavoidable problem that even imagining sensations to be grouped under a type one must already have in hand some independent standard with which to identify and classify them. It is simply no good looking to 'objects' themselves to provide such a standard. Yet, in its absence, there can be no talk of being mistaken about whether or not a 'sign' hits its target. Thus, putative 'sensation labels' are robbed of any possible meaning.

What is important for our discussion is that in attacking the name–object view of language Wittgenstein rejects the default 'picture' of inner mental processes. Moreover, he realises that the name–object view of psychological language is not simply ill founded, it is responsible for preventing us from seeing our psychological situation aright. As he writes:

> The main difficulty arises from our imagining the experience (pain for instance) as a thing for which of course we have a name and whose concept is therefore quite easy to grasp.
> (*LWPP II*, p. 43e)

> The 'inner' is a delusion. That is: the whole complex of ideas alluded to by this word is like a painted curtain drawn in front of scene of the actual word use.　(*LWPP II*, p. 84e)

Wittgenstein wants us to get past this picture and attend to the situations in which we use psychological concepts. That is to say, he wants us to notice how, when and in what circumstances we actually make psychological ascriptions to others or give expression to our own psychological situation. It is precisely this concern that is embodied in the following series of typical remarks:

> The expression 'Who knows what is going on inside him!' The interpretation of outer events as the consequences of unknown ones, of merely surmised, inner ones. The interest that is focused on the inner, as if on the chemical structure, from which behaviour arises.
> For one needs only to ask, 'What do I care about inner events, whatever they are?!', to see that a different attitude is conceivable. – 'But surely everyone will always be interested in his inner life!' Nonsense. Would I know that pain, etc., etc. was something inner if I weren't told so?　(*RPP II* §643)

In the remark that follows shortly after this he makes some salient observations about how we respond to questions about the 'inner' lives of others:

> If we're asked 'What's going on inside him?' we say 'Surely very little goes on inside him.' But what do we know about it?! We construct a picture of it [the inner] according to his behaviour, his utterances, his ability to think.   (*RPP II* §650)

If we wish to avoid becoming bogged down in interminable metaphysical squabbles about dualism and materialism we must recognise that the term 'mind' does not refer to a kind of entity at all. We must realise that conscious states are not special kinds of 'object' – not even strange sorts of object whose *esse* really is *percipi*. Despite the difference in the origins of their worries concerning reified mental phenomena, Dennett and Wittgenstein can appear to be advancing somewhat similar positive accounts. More specifically, we might say the 'behaviourist' aspect of Dennett's 'personal' level understanding of consciousness has Wittgensteinian roots. For example, in one way or another, they both agree that concentration on outward behaviour and linguistic 'expressions' provides a better way for us to understand the nature of consciousness.

My ultimate aim in the next two sections is to reveal that this apparent similarity is in fact an illusion. It is certainly true that Wittgenstein and Dennett are allied in their attack on our tendency to reify 'conscious states' (where this term acts as an umbrella term for any number of mental phenomena such as feeling pain, seeing colours, experiencing dizziness, etc.). But even though they reject the idea of a reified mind, it is important to realise that they make their assaults on it from different directions and with different agendas. In the next sections I describe in some detail the road Dennett takes before comparing it to Wittgenstein's.

Dennett's new state of consciousness

In place of the Cartesian Theatre metaphor Dennett proposes what he calls the Multiple Drafts model of consciousness. He claims that 'heterophenomenology' will serve as the best means of neutrally analysing the conscious reports of ourselves and others. While engaged in heterophenomenology we effectively allow the subject to verbally 'describe for us the nature of his or her conscious experiences'. In reality, however, we let the subject generate a text about a 'notional' world and, on the whole, we give them authority concerning the nature of that world and what is found in it. Such notional worlds are analogous to fictional worlds.[7] In being so, 'The subject's heterophenomenological world will be a stable intersubjectively confirmable theoretical posit, having the same metaphysical status as, say, Sherlock Holmes's London or the world according to Garp' (Dennett 1991a, p. 81).

The 'texts' that are generated in these circumstances (and not something above and beyond to which they refer) effectively constitute consciousness. We need take the conscious experiences described in them no more seriously at the level of ontology than we would Professor Moriarty or the hound of the Baskervilles. To put it crudely, according to this view, conscious experience is treated as nothing over and above the very 'reports' we give, 'judgements' we make and 'beliefs' we hold about our putative experiences. Thus, consciousness is reduced to the 'intentional' in this fashion.[8]

Nor is Dennett satisfied with this reduction alone. He feels that we cannot fully 'explain' consciousness unless we somehow get beneath it. We won't have explained it until we give a naturalistic explanation of our ability to make 'speech acts', which purportedly act as expressions of our conscious experience. For he believes that 'Only a theory that explained conscious events in terms of unconscious events could explain consciousness at all' (Dennett 1991a, p. 454). His hope is, therefore, to explain how it is that our 'talk about consciousness' is produced by underlying sub-systems along with an ontogenetic explanation of how those sub-systems were formed. Thus, after having argued that the episodes of consciousness are nothing but the content of a coherently generated heterophenomenological text, Dennett's next move is to try to explain our ability to generate such texts from within a naturalistic framework. The essence of his theory is described thus: 'I am suggesting conscious human minds are more-or-less serial virtual machines implemented – inefficiently – on the parallel hardware evolution has provided for us' (Dennett 1991a, p. 218).[9] The virtual machine that gives rise to consciousness he calls a Joycean Machine. That is, one that is able to generate detailed texts concerning 'streams of consciousness', after the fashion of James Joyce's production of *Ulysses*.

This view has an important consequence: since Dennett does not believe that the Joycean software (i.e. that which turns us into conscious beings) is 'built in' he is prepared to argue that Joycean machines are the result of cultural design. Hence we get the result that consciousness is 'largely a product of cultural evolution that gets imparted to brains in early training' (Dennett 1991a, p. 219). At one point he even makes this intrepid remark: 'If consciousness is something over and above the Joycean machine, I have not yet provided a theory of consciousness at all' (Dennett 1991a, p. 281).[10]

This aspect of Dennett's account has been a major source of disillusionment for his readers, for as they see it such an admission amounts to a complete rejection of the idea that conscious states have any 'qualitative' content – a denial that there is anything that it is 'like' to experience certain forms of consciousness. They complain that non-human animals and infants surely have conscious awareness, even though they lack the ability to produce texts of a Joycean standard (see Bricke 1985; Lockwood 1993). The way Dennett jumps in response to this sort of criticism is instructive: he vacillates. In places, he seems to concede the possibility that consciousness might obtain even without a full-fledged Joycean text that would demand a linguistically mediated capacity for 'reportage'. He allows that 'Heterophenomenology without a text is not impossible, just difficult' (Dennett 1991a, p. 446). For example, he says of imagining what it is like to be a bat, the 'task would require us to subject ourselves to vast transformations . . . [but] we could use our research to say what these transformations would be' (Dennett 1991a, pp. 442, 444). In this case, our biological and ecological research would help by showing, 'us a great deal of what a bat could and could not be conscious of under various conditions' (Dennett 1991a, p. 444). That is, through empirical and controlled testing, ecologists may be able to tell me that bats can only be aware of moths (or whatever) at X distance under Y conditions. Naturally, such information will be of help to me in the course of devising a 'notional world' for the bat.

Elsewhere, he responds by arguing that our 'folksy' intuitions regarding animal and infant consciousness are simply not sacrosanct. For example, Fellows and O'Hear point out that 'an immediate reaction to the virtual software aspect of the multiple drafts model might be to say animals and human infants seem to be conscious perfectly well without the mediation of any culturally acquired "software"' (Fellows and O'Hear 1993, p. 80). Yet Dennett makes the ready reply: 'I agree; they seem to be. But are they? And what does it mean to say that they are or they aren't? . . . I claim that this question has no *clear* pre-theoretical meaning' (Dennett 1993, p. 147, emphasis original). This is the crux of the matter: in Quinean fashion, Dennett simply denies that we can make any 'pre-theoretical' sense of our shared intuitions about the general quality of conscious experience (non-verbal or otherwise).

The common thread to both responses is that we must not surrender, at any cost, the streamlined and principled criterion for consciousness that is provided by heterophenomenology.[11] A return to our rag-tag intuitions on this score could potentially lead to the admission of all kinds of nonsense and a re-vitalisation of the perplexing paradoxes of consciousness. But the price we pay for having this 'neat' criterion is that we must jettison some of our most deeply held intuitions concerning consciousness. One might expect that in doing away with the very idea of 'objects' of consciousness Wittgenstein must be advancing a revisionist line as well. But importantly he is not. On the contrary, he is concerned to 'leave everything as it is'. In the next section I want to examine what this amounts to, thereby revealing the superiority of his approach to the philosophy of psychology over Dennett's.

Wittgenstein's expressions

I have claimed that Wittgenstein offers an understanding of consciousness that differs significantly from that of his self-styled 'follower' Dennett. I said at the outset that I wanted to use Dennett's account to help throw light on Wittgenstein's position – showing in what ways that the latter's position is superior. In particular I hope to achieve this by revealing the naïveté inherent in Dennett's attitude towards the nature of psychological language. I maintain that the key difference between these two thinkers revolves around their attitudes towards the behaviour and speech acts that are regarded as deliverances concerning 'consciousness'. Wittgenstein is concerned to understand these as expressive in character, while Dennett hardly gives them any serious attention at all in his eagerness to engage in the larger project of 'explaining' consciousness. It is this that makes his treatment of consciousness thoroughly inadequate. It is because he lacks any positive account of how such language operates that, unlike Wittgenstein, he has trouble making room for the 'inner' after evacuating the Cartesian Theatre. Let me make my complaint more specific.

Despite having partially seen that it is a serviceable objection to Cartesianism to show that there are no mental items that are 'designated' by our talk of conscious experience, his very description of the heterophenomenological method nevertheless encourages the view that language, when it is performing its true office, is essentially referential in character. That is to say, he feels no discomfort in treating the deliverances concerning consciousness as referring to objects in the subject's notional world. The idea, as I understand it, looks something like this: we can make space for conscious entities so long as we don't take them too seriously at the level of *ontology*. This is why his account of consciousness is truly deflationary. Dennett's irrealism about consciousness is non-accidentally linked with the fact that he still treats talk of conscious experiences as 'kinds of report', whereas Wittgenstein does not. My objection to Dennett is that one will only feel the pressure to treat conscious deliverances less than seriously if one thinks that the purpose of language is simply to 'name' – hence having failed to name 'real' things we should think of this talk as naming 'notional' things.

What is worse, despite his appeal to 'notional worlds', he owes his reader an account of how we are able to interpret the content of the 'reports' that others make and the content of the 'beliefs' they hold. For he claims that the speech acts concerning consciousness are not just so much noise; they must be interpreted and he freely admits that the heterophenomenological 'process depends on assumptions about which language is being spoken, and some of the speaker's intentions' (Dennett 1991a, p. 75). But he gives us no 'explanation' as to how we are able to interpret these quasi-'reports' of others. For example, in collaborating to create your heterophenomenological world I hear you say, 'I see a purple cow'. But what is it that I take you to be saying? How I am to understand the meaning of that report? Is it referring to some item in your notional world? Dennett's answer is that it is 'because they know English, and this is what makes sense, obviously, in this context' (Dennett 1991a, p. 75). What is it about my knowledge of English that enables me to 'know what you mean'? It cannot be that I understand you because I know what kind of notional objects your words designate. For, to put the point succinctly, the private language argument will work just as effectively against objects in a 'notional world' as it does against the denizens of a 'private' inner world. Beetles in boxes are beetles in boxes, whether they are real or notional.

Having seen the folly of thinking that we are referring to private objects of experience when making utterances about our states of mind, Dennett fails to provide any plausible positive account as to how we might make sense of such utterances. This is so, even though, 'typically, he has subjects being conscious only of the content of their mental states' (Bricke 1985, p. 253). But if this is the case, why doesn't Dennett give more attention to the content of the 'seeming' reports about conscious seemings? He doesn't even begin to seriously address such questions other than by citing the fact that for most 'conscious beings' who speak the same language it will be unproblematic to determine what they mean. But having rejected the pre-theoretical out of hand, it is unclear how seriously we can take this appeal. Given his overall approach, to answer these questions properly requires a plausible *theory* of interpretation, not simply reliance on the idea that we all know that competent language users find it relatively unproblematic to understand such statements. Of course this is so, but if one is committed to giving a full explanation of the phenomenon, the question that looms large is: What underwrites this fact? Dennett is faced with a serious problem at this juncture because, whatever the merits of his reduction of consciousness to the intentional, his deep suspicions about 'meaning' lead him to support Quinean eliminativism about it. This leaves him without the resources to provide the whole story about, or in his terms the full *explanation* of, the philosophy of psychology.

Dennett's complete lack of concern for understanding the original basis and workings of psychological language is, in part, what crucially divorces his project from Wittgenstein's. Wittgenstein feels no pressure to address these sorts of issue because he rejects the idea of the 'reified mind' for very different reasons. Ironically, in failing to appreciate fully Wittgenstein's purposes Dennett is led to accuse his erstwhile hero of lacking the courage of his convictions in this very matter. Dennett applauds the famous remark, 'The thing in the box has no place in the language-game at all; not even as a something; for the box might even be empty' (*PI* §293). Nevertheless, he accuses Wittgenstein of 'hedging his bets' when he adds shortly after, 'It's not a something, but not a nothing either' (*PI* §304, Dennett 1990, p. 524, cf. also Rorty 1998, p. 124). Dennett, on the other hand, tells us that he is willing to take the bull by the horns and claims that in doing so he is more 'radical' than Wittgenstein.[12] But this sort of talk only reveals how little Dennett has really understood Wittgenstein's approach.

It is true that many find the 'not a something but not a nothing' remark to be deliberately and unnecessarily cryptic. But this stems from not understanding what Wittgenstein is acknowledging. Although he is partly restating his dismissal of the 'reified mind' – i.e. repeating that he is not prepared to treat consciousness as 'thing-like' – he is also making it clear that he takes our talk of 'consciousness' seriously just as it stands. But doing this does not mean we have to accept the idea that we are making reports about objects in a real 'inner' world nor reports about non-objects in some notional world, rather it is to give expression to our psychological situation. Unlike Dennett, at least Wittgenstein helps us to understand the role of language in this regard.

Once we give up on the myth of a 'reified mind' we cannot construe expressions of our psychological situation as being kinds of reports. We are not making judgements about 'inner objects' when we give expression to our 'inner' situation. We cannot treat these as being 'based' on some kind of inner evidence because the very idea of inner evidence is an oxymoron. We simply have no evidence to back up statements about our inner mental life. Just as the idea of 'inner' evidence is nonsense, it would be equally hopeless to think that we rely on 'outer' evidence when deciding such matters. I do not infer that I am in pain by first noticing a cut on my leg, nor do I decide this by noticing that I am having an 'inner' sensation of pain by some process of introspection. I simply feel pain, and say so. Psychological language is 'expressive' not 'referential'. This is why 'a lie about inner processes is of a different category form one about outer processes' (*LWPP II*, p. 33e).

Our linguistic utterances of pain are 'natural extensions' of, or replacements for earlier ways of expressing pain – i.e. shouting, bawling, etc. These are developments of more primitive modes of response that we share with animals. It is because psychological language is expressive that the basis of this sophisticated kind of language game is more to do with sincerity than accuracy (see Johnston 1993, p. 13). Accuracy presupposes some independent means of verification and that is precisely what we lack in this case. Hence, Wittgenstein encourages us to treat the speech acts concerning our 'inner life' as confessional in nature. He writes: 'What is the importance of someone making this or that confession? Does he have to be able to judge his condition correctly? – What matters here is not an inner condition he judges, but just his confession' (*RPP II* §562). He adds, 'confession is of course something exterior' (*RPP II* §703, 1967; §558).

But we may wonder: how are we to understand 'pretence' on a view that insists that 'nothing is hidden' and that psychological language is essentially expressive? For, of course, it is still possible that a person could be lying with their confession. What are they lying about? Here Wittgenstein reminds us that: 'Above all pretence has its own outward signs. How could we otherwise talk about pretence at all?' (*LWPP II*, p. 42e). Moreover, he makes it perfectly clear how we are to treat such cases when he talks about the role trust plays in dealing with another's psychology.[13] He writes: 'Do I pay any mind to his inner processes if I trust him? If I don't trust him I say, "I don't know what's going on inside him". But if I trust him, I don't say I know what's going on inside him' (*RPP II* §602; cf. also §604). That is to say, if I do trust him, I treat his utterances as being genuinely expressive – just as in a more primitive setting his facial or other bodily expressions would be transparent to me. If there is asymmetry between these cases, it is just the opposite of what one would expect if we were to think objects of consciousness exist. In the case where the subject is in pain, it is easy to see how we can get by with its expression; in the case of pretence, where there is no pain, we must treat the utterance as serving a different and potentially deceptive function. The point is that we need not return to the idea of a reified mind in order to make logical space for the possibility of pretence. In taking this line, Wittgenstein inverts the standard order of approach to these topics by getting us to rethink what it is we are trying to understand.

Doesn't this result in a reduction of the inner to outer behaviour? Wittgenstein constantly rejects this interpretation of what he is doing in many places in the later writings. I have collected but a few that make it clear that unless he is self-deceived, it is wrong to read him as sponsoring behaviourism in any form.

> The impression that we wanted to deny something arises from our setting our faces against the picture of the 'inner process'. What we deny is that the picture of the inner process gives us the correct idea of the use of [psychological] word[s]. (*PI* §105)

> 'Are you not really a behaviourist in disguise? Aren't you at bottom really saying that everything except human behaviour is a fiction?' – If I do speak of a fiction, then it is of a grammatical fiction. (*PI* §307)

> We have to deny the yet uncomprehended process in the yet uncomprehended medium. And now it looks as if we had denied mental processes. And naturally we don't want to deny them. (*PI* §308)

> But am I not really speaking only of the outer? . . . It is as if I wanted to explain (quasi-define) the inner through the outer. And yet it isn't so. (*LWPP II*, p. 63e)

Contrasting his ambitions with those of Dennett's enables us to see why he was not a behaviourist. In concentrating solely on the 'grammar' of our mental discourse while rejecting the name–object picture of language as altogether inappropriate in this domain, Wittgenstein was not thereby moved to equate 'consciousness' to talk of the outer behaviour of bodies. Rather, in showing why it is confused to offer any such explanations in this domain, he reminded us that to understand the expressive nature of psychological language requires attention to the way it is grounded in, and informed by, our form of life. In this way, as opposed to offering a new theory, he presents a more satisfactory view of the nature and importance of consciousness.

The vital thing to notice is that talk of 'our experiences' is not to be treated as analogous to the language we use when talking about physical objects. Psychological talk has its unique basis which must be attended to if we are to understand it. This is not immediately obvious to us. In other words, the strength of Wittgenstein's approach is that in rejecting the very idea of reified conscious states, he simultaneously attacks not only the name-object picture of language, but also the belief that explanations are appropriate in this domain. For this reason he is not even tempted to 'irrealism' about consciousness. He writes, 'The connection of inner and outer is part of these concepts. We don't draw this connection in order to magically remove the inner. There are inner concepts and outer concepts' (*LWPP II*, p. 62e). In this light, we can see that although Wittgenstein is often regarded as the grand guru of logical behaviourism, it is far more appropriate that Dennett don this title. For Wittgenstein, the inner is not demystified through elimination, it is demystified by attending to the nature of psychological language. In this way, our understanding of consciousness is, to use Mulhall's words, 'demythologized'.

What would Wittgenstein make of Dennett's 'demystifying investigation'? I think he would regard the latter's counterintuitive 'theory' as a bad response to a series of problems that rest on a house of cards. In offering us such a 'theory', Dennett is falling into the trap of trying to give 'new information' or a 'new discovery' to solve a philosophical problem when instead what is needed is a clearer understanding of the place of consciousness in our lives (cf. *PI* §§109, 90–2). Tellingly, by advancing his 'metaphysically minimalist' account of consciousness, which introduces us to such things as 'notional worlds', Dennett has simply generated a new sort of 'mythology' of his own. Rather than settling matters, his 'new set of metaphors' simply creates different will-o'-the-wisps to confuse the metaphysician. In contrast, Wittgenstein realises that philosophy finds peace when it understands the nature of the problems that concern it (and bedevil it). Thus, in taking the road he does, in the end we must regard Dennett as being mistaken in believing that he is, in fact, 'more Wittgensteinian than St. Ludwig himself' (Dennett 1993, p. 143). It is not that Dennett has been more honest and thorough in his application of Wittgenstein's method; rather, he has thoroughly misunderstood it. The first step is to free ourselves from philosophical myths, but the second is not to create new ones. Instead, if there is anything left for us to do it can be achieved only by attending to, not revising, our ordinary practices concerning psychology. We will not escape our philosophical problems by supplanting, surpassing or superseding these by advancing theories. This reveals the crucial difference in the character of their 'demystifying' investigations. To successfully demystify consciousness, Dennett thinks we need to develop a principled and revisionist theory of consciousness – but this will only lead to further muddles. What we require is a rearrangement of facts we already know. Understanding is achieved by our getting a clear view of them. This is Wittgenstein's general lesson about the purpose and method in philosophy, as I hope to illustrate with yet another example.

The rule-following paradox

Understanding how we are able to follow rules is yet another place in which we run up against similar limits. The overarching importance of this topic is underscored by the fact that it concerns not only a limited range of activities that come most naturally to mind when we talk of rule-following, but that it also impinges on our conceptions of meaning and truth quite generally. Thus we follow rules not only when we compute sums by adding 2 to a finite number series, but also when we judge, say, that a certain object belongs to the category 'apple'. Casting back to one of the themes touched on in the preceding chapter, Wittgenstein draws out this connection between meaning and rules in the following way:

> A meaning of a word is a kind of employment of it. For it is what we learn when the word is incorporated into our language.
>
> (*OC* §61)

> That is why there exists a correspondence between the concepts 'rule' and 'meaning'.
>
> (*OC* §62)

Nevertheless, there are serious questions about the viability of certain common views about what following a rule actually comes to in practice. If pressed to *explain* what this involves, on reflection, a standard reply is to point to some general rule to which we are attempting to be faithful; one that governs our particular attempts to apply it, and somehow stands over and above such attempts. Getting it right in the kind of cases cited above depends on our recognition of and successful alignment with independent standards that establish correctness conditions. It seems we are accountable to something beyond us that places a binding force on whether or not we have used our words or applied a rule appropriately or not. The correct steps are all somehow timelessly 'laid out in advance', there for us to take or not. It is in this way that rules seem to predetermine correct applications – past, future and present. At first blush, they appear to have a kind of 'contractual' status.[14] To accommodate this idea it seems necessary to postulate the existence of something independent that can act as a standard if we are to explain adequately what decides if a response is correct or incorrect. But this is only half the story, for we also need an explanation of how we gain access to this standard when it comes to saying which rule we are trying to follow. That is to say, we must somehow account for our ability *to grasp* independent standards if they are to 'instruct' and 'guide' us in our attempts to take the steps they demand. In short, then, there are two components to this answer of what following a rule involves. It appears that to follow a rule: (i) we must align ourselves to something against which success or failure can be independently measured, and (ii) it must be possible to specify what the rules require of us, at least on reflection. Only if this second condition is also met will it make sense to say that a rule guides us in our attempts to follow it.

This standard reply is frequently dignified with honorific epithets, such as: 'ordinary', 'natural', 'intuitive', 'commonsensical', 'innocent', 'naïve'.[15] The thought is that in making it, 'we "discover" the metaphysical picture lurking within our ordinary understanding of meaning' (Ebbs 1997, p. 38). However, this way of putting things might lead us to think that such a picture is built into our practice and obviously worthy of defence, which is contestable to say the least. More neutrally then, we can say that our first answers on this topic are likely to be encouraged by our use of such colloquial expressions as, 'grasping the meaning', 'seeing how to go on' and others of this kind. It is also worth noting that these too can be elevated to the status of *phenomena* requiring explanation, elaboration or elimination. Indeed, we must recognise the danger that in the course of trying to regiment such expressions, we will surrender to a temptation to 'put a fantastic mythological construction on [them]' (McDowell 1998, p. 258). The point is that we might come to think of a rule as something that can be brought before our minds, like a mental image – serving as a sort of talisman we can consult; one that enables us to 'fly ahead' and check our results. We will need something with 'queer' properties that can simultaneously fix meaning and act as a guide. It is with this in mind that Wittgenstein considers how one might imagine the processes involved in the grasping of rules, against which to compare our applications, as being akin to those of the operations of some kind of 'ethereal machine', one that, unlike us, *cannot* err or malfunction.[16] For what is required is a device that will do what no ordinary physical mechanism can. Only such thing could *embody* a rule (*PI* §§193–4).

Yet, just as some defenders of our ordinary understanding of consciousness disavow a commitment to specific 'pictures', defenders of the standard reply need not accompany their philosophical explanations with speculative trappings of the sort just discussed. The standard reply sketched above has other, more sophisticated incarnations, which have been defended on stronger grounds than the mere fact that it is encouraged by the use of certain colloquial expressions. For example, we find a core commitment to it forming the basis of Frege's account of rules, which was developed as a counter to formalist renderings of arithmetic. His primary complaint was that arbitrarily stipulated rules cannot provide the necessary warrant that permits us to claim we deal in truth-preserving inferences, for such trade requires appeal to laws that license certain connections between propositions that are quite independent of any of our practices or decisions. We need not rehearse the full details of Frege's account as its most basic elements were discussed in chapter 1. What is worth noting is that Frege was committed to his particular views about the objectivity of rules precisely because he held that it is only if arithmetical signs signify something beyond them that they can provide a genuine measure against which any specific application can be judged as correct or incorrect. To perform their offices such rules must be absolutely determinate and general. This being so, Frege argued that we cannot express the meaning of such signs by using limited definitions or demonstrations that incorporate only a finite set of examples. These lack the requisite precision and generality required to establish the true content of the governing laws. We are told that it is 'a mistake to see in such applications the real sense of the propositions; in any application a large part of the their generality is always lost, and a particular elements enters in' (*FA* §16). Consequently, it is only those definitions that *latch on* to something independent that are 'complete' in the required sense. Thus Medina – who convincingly argues that Frege was a primary source of influence on Wittgenstein's thinking about rule-following – identifies the core of Frege's thought in a way that frames the issues in a familiar way. He writes, 'the correct application of an arithmetical rule is not contingent on subjective judgement of its users; there must be a *fact of the matter* that determines each and all the applications of a rule' (Medina 2002, p. 93; emphasis original).

What becomes clear is that the standard reply goes hand in hand with a realist account of rule-following, whether or not we believe this to be something that is intrinsic to our ordinary thinking or the result of better-developed concerns and reflection. Establishing that the standard reply can issue from either of these sources is important because it ultimately matters to what we think is at stake in attempts to reply to the rule-following sceptic.

This creature embarrasses us by revealing that, despite our staunch convictions that we are following certain rules, we are unable to offer secure independent grounds for saying which ones these are. This worry is the focus of Kripke's infamous exposition of the famous paradox, which pushed concerns about rule-following into the philosophical limelight. His sceptic initially serves up the challenge it terms that make it look Goodmanesque, suggesting that we have no way of telling if our future uses will deviate from our past and current uses. Thus, picking up on the Fregean concern just noted, he starts by asking what could justify our claim that we have in the past been engaged in 'addition', given that we have never calculated with numbers greater than those of a certain magnitude. In his now famous example, it is stipulated that our alleged rule-follower has never yet added any numbers larger than 67 and 56. But this being so, how can we be certain that we haven't been carrying out operations in 'quaddition'? The rule for quaddition exactly mirrors that of addition, *except* in cases involving numbers greater than 67 and 56. When this is the case 5 is the correct result. However strange this may sound, it is at least logically possible that we have been following the rule for 'quaddition' all along. How are we to defend against this suggestion? What fact can we point to about ourselves that would establish that we are entitled to believe that we are 'adders' not 'quadders'? What gives us the right to say that the '+' sign denotes the arithmetical function 'plus' and not 'quus' – or, indeed, an infinity of other possible functions that we might imagine it to?

Faced with this, the search begins to identify a fact about the alleged rule-follower that will satisfy the sceptic. He is a patient listener. But given the nature of problem, he rejects the idea that our actual or possible applications can determine the rule that is supposedly being followed. Nor will he allow that any mental object, picture or image has the power unambiguously to relate to reality in the required way, for whatever we cite in this regard will always be completely compatible with a deviant interpretation of our actions. Likewise, it is no good appealing to our dispositions, for as the sceptic notes, they are always finite, whereas to solve the problem requires specifying a rule that has an infinite extension. Also, given that we are prone to err, it is impossible simply to read off the rule we are meant to be following by attending to our undifferentiated dispositions to act. On closer inspection, we discover the bankruptcy of each and every proposal and begin to despair of ever supplying the fact that justifies our conviction that we are indeed following *this* rule and not *that* one. Nothing we can marshal from either a first-person or third-person perspective seems to do the trick. The only honest conclusion seems to be that there simply are no facts about individuals that determine what rules they are following or what they mean by their words.

Wittgenstein's interlocutor proceeds in much the same way. He challenges us to say what kind of thing a rule must be such that it can guide us in understanding your applications. A range of proposals are entertained: from citing the familiar *feeling* that I know how to go on by pointing to past applications, to gesturing at general dispositions and inclinations to go on one way rather than another (see *PI* §§151–97). To close the gap between the rule and its applications it seems we need to identify something internally accessible, something we have internalised or something that is already built into the very fabric of our responses. Yet, nothing we dredge up from our phenomenology or that might plausibly underpin our outward responses manages to uniquely determine which rule we are meant to be following. None of these eliminates the logical possibility that, despite sincere protestations, one might be following a different rule altogether. Whatever I imagine I have 'in mind' or whatever responses or tendencies I point to – no matter how sophisticated – they will always be open to an alternative and equally justified interpretation of all the facts. In this way, Wittgenstein brings out the crux of the matter:

> 'But am I not compelled, then, to go on the way I do in a chain of inferences?' – Compelled? After all I can presumably go as I choose! – 'But if you want to remain in accord with the rules you must go this way.' – Not at all, I call *this* 'accord'. – 'Then you have changed

the meaning of the word "accord", or the meaning of the rule' – No; – who says what "change" and 'remaining the same' mean here?

However many rules you give me – I give a rule which justifies my employment of your rules.   (*RFM* I, §113; cf. *PI* §198)

The essence of the problem is seen most clearly on Wittgenstein's formulation; for any given description or interpretation of the rule there is always a competing, deviant one that fits all the facts equally well. Thus, barring special pleading, *there isn't anything* about us that we can point to that will settle the matter. Once we see the true source of the problem it becomes easy to see why none of the usual suspects can nail this down unambiguously. Hence, we can see that the sceptical result is guaranteed from the start. It is thus concluded that there is no interpretation to which we can appeal that will allow us confidently to identify which rule it is that we are supposedly following. The problem in accepting that we must somehow identify it by *other means* in order to justify our practices is that we are brought to realise that there is nothing to which we have access that can achieve this. The upshot seems to be that we legitimately ought to doubt anyone's sincere claims to be following rules.

Before considering how we might reply to this dark conclusion, it is worth digressing to air some differences concerning the way the matter is presented by Kripke's as opposed Wittgenstein's sceptic. It is unfortunate that Kripke's formulation has some misleading features since its popularity has somewhat occluded Wittgenstein's own. For example, because of it some have mistakenly thought the sceptical challenge to have a limited scope. Thus, in defending realism about rules, Pettit offers a non-reductive proposal that concedes much of the 'intuitive picture'. He suggests that we can make sense of rule-following by observing that 'an agent develops an independent disposition or inclination to extrapolate in a certain way to other cases: an inclination of which he may or many not be aware' (Pettit 1990, p. 10). This sort of inclination not only prompts the agent's responses, but also can be used to make manifest the rule they are attempting to follow, which can be revealed by means of examples. In this latter respect, 'the sort of inclination in question *serves like a description* of the rule, so far as it gives putative information about the rule: the putative information that the rule requires those responses, those ways of going on' (Pettit 1990, p. 11; emphasis mine).[17] To make this account credible it would be necessary to explain just how an inclination could have the status of a description and how exemplification could determine a unique description.

Moreover, as Pettit notes, the right kind of relationship between the inclination and rule would need to be specified.

There is reason to doubt that Pettit's proposal will deliver in these respects. But what is interesting is that he believes we can objectively determine which rules we are and have been following by appeal to our underlying inclination to go on in a particular way, even though he admits this would fail to determine a rule that extends over novel cases. But to suppose that this is some kind of advance is to underestimate the real force of the challenge (see also Shogenji 2000, pp. 504–5). The real problem is that there is an indefinite number of equally credible descriptions of the rules we are supposedly following, right here and right now, such that no *account* we give that standardised them will be non-arbitrary. How are we to determine which rule we are following by appeal to the limited set of examples we are inclined to employ? Doubtless confusion on this score is encouraged by the way Kripke presents his sceptical considerations, as it masks the deeper puzzle.

Moreover, his presentation has also wrongly led some to suppose the problem is *primarily* epistemological. This is because his sceptic does not begin by questioning the very idea of independent rules, but rather makes it seem as if the real puzzle is simply to decide how we can *know* which rule we are following. In turn, this can make it seem as if realism about rule-following has two *quite distinct* aspects: one 'ontological', the other 'epistemological'. It looks as if there is one question concerning how rules can exist as independent facts while having a normative status and a different question about how we can have knowledge of them.

Certainly, there is an intrinsic epistemological dimension built into the standard reply since in order to try to follow a rule at all one ought to have knowledge of the rule one is trying to follow and what this requires. As Wright observes, 'My assent to the rule, we feel, is always informative *for me*, as it were; I know what kind of pattern of use I am committing myself to' (Wright 2001, p. 28).[18] In deciding what such knowledge comes to we might consider the situation of someone who is still learning a particular rule. For we will be tempted to ask: What is it that enables them to 'grasp a general pattern of use' (Wright 2001, p. 34). In considering such cases:

> We move towards the idea that understanding an expression is a kind of 'cottoning on'; that is, a leap, an inspired guess at the pattern of application which the instructor is trying to get across . . . So the picture encourages, if it does not make absolutely inevitable, a drift

into the idea that each of us has some sort of privileged access to the character of their own understanding of an expression.

(Wright 2001, pp. 35–6)[19]

To make sense of this requires not only that we postulate the existence of rules, but that we also explain how we relate to them epistemically. The strategy of Kripke's sceptic is to attack this whole package of views by first pressing home the epistemic worry. Tactically speaking, if he successfully casts doubt on the legitimacy of our claim to be able to 'grasp' such rules, he will have undermined any clear rationale for postulating their separate existence in the first place. If we cannot distinguish the rule we are following from an infinite array of possibilities, what possible use would such rules be to us? If we do not have reliable access to them how can they guide or govern our applications? If we cannot answer the epistemic worry then the very idea of there being independent rules appears to be nothing more than idle fantasy.

But to think the challenge has only an epistemic focus is to conflate the sceptical *worry* with the *strategy* for engendering it. *A fortiori*, consider that even if we relax the requirement that the rule-follower must have knowledge of the rule they are following, the essential problem remains just the same. For example, we might hold that what justifies a person's belief that they are following a particular rule need not be something they can articulate for themselves. We might suppose that being guided by a rule only really involves a kind of implicit or tacit know-how, such that the fact that I am following this rule rather than that one is something that becomes manifest in my dispositions or inclinations. Given that I do not have uniquely privileged access to my dispositions, we might go so far as to endorse a completely externalist epistemology. Accordingly, we might accept that my belief that I am following a specific rule could be justified even if I am never in a good position to do this for myself. Perhaps it can be done *only* by appeal to evidence that is available third-personally. On the most liberal reading all that might be necessary to achieve this would be that, *at some point*, *someone* must be able to identify something about a given rule-follower that settles what rule they are meant to be following. This is one way of reading Kripke's insistence that, 'The "directions" . . . must *somehow be contained* in any candidate for the fact as to what I meant' (Kripke 1982, p. 11; emphasis mine). Of course, it has the consequence that even if there are objective facts about which rules I follow, these may not be facts I can identify for myself. This flies in the face of the idea that it is not possible to follow a rule unknowingly.

But even if we allow this, we come up against the very same problem. However one construes the epistemological issues, in the end it must be possible for *someone* to identify *something* about a given rule-follower that *explains* why it is the case that they are following *this* rule rather than *that* one. Thus, whatever one's epistemic predilections, what should not escape our notice is that at some stage it must be possible for someone to identify and give evidence about which rule is being followed. There would hardly be any substance to someone's claim to be following a particular rule if this could not be justified by anyone, from *any* perspective whatsoever. Yet, it is exactly this that the sceptic doubts. For these reasons, there is a strong consensus that the purely epistemic reading misunderstands the true nature of the sceptical challenge. It is in this sense that one often hears 'the problem is constitutive, not epistemological – its topic is the possibility of meaning, not our knowledge of it' (Boghossian 2002: 150; see also McGinn 1984, p. 149; Forbes 2002, pp. 16–17).

The apparent implications of failing to meet it are seen to be both devastating and pervasive. They are not limited to the domain of mathematics or logic (or to the kinds of realism associated with these). For it seems we are forced to conclude that there are no facts that determine what we mean by our words in any domain, but this is an intuitive requirement for the very possibility of meaning. Thus, unless we are prepared to reject that this really is a genuine requirement, we are forced either to solve the paradox or adopt some kind of eliminativism about meaning, accepting that 'All language is meaningless' (Kripke 1979, p. 71). The significance of dealing with this paradox is not lost on today's philosophers, who, noting it, might be forgiven for the hyperbolic tone of their assessments. Pettit is typical in this regard:[20]

> The magnitude of the challenge . . . can hardly be overstated. Deny that there are such things as rules, deny that there is anything that counts strictly as rule-following, and you put in jeopardy some of our most central notions about ourselves.   (Pettit 1990, p. 5)

For many, the whole point of underlining the importance of this problem stems from a desire to set it up as a worthy target for philosophical explanation. Indeed, this is natural enough if one adopts the view that it is the primary task of philosophy to solve such problems. A corollary of this is that all that really matters is to get clear about the features of the problem. Questions about its origins or the specific concerns of its excavator are, at best, of historical interest. The fact that many commentators hold such a view explains why they are not concerned about the way 'the problem' is presented. For example, this attitude lies behind Boghossian's avowal that his interest in 'the rule-following considerations' is not exegetical but, rather, 'almost entirely concerned with a retrospective assessment of the *philosophical* contributions' (Boghossian 2002, p. 141; emphasis original). The same assumption putatively justifies Pettit's way of setting up the issues, given that he makes it clear that in doing so he exercises 'some license [given that he does not] aspire to be an exegete either of Kripke or Wittgenstein' (Pettit 1990, p. 1). Still, ignoring these details can lead to a failure to recognise the full importance of the fact that it is only in a dialectical context that 'the problem' can come to light at all, a point which lends an important clue to how we might approach it.[21]

It cannot turn out that we do not follow rules, as the consequences would not just be problematic; they would be downright paradoxical. Considering the problem puts us in an uneasy situation. In fact, we cannot even state it without seemingly falling into performative incoherence: to understand the dilemma presupposes the very capacities it *seemingly* questions. For, as is frequently observed, even to pose Kripke's version of the paradox its readers begin by clearly distinguishing the meanings of 'quus' and 'plus'. This fact alone ought to make us suspicious of the legitimacy of the sceptical demand. This is why Kripke's sceptic can only approach the impossible conclusion indirectly and why his opening move is only to raise worries about our *past* applications. However, despite initially relying on our knowledge of what our words mean to set things up, the worry is, if the sceptic has done his job properly, we will eventually come to believe that we are not entitled to assume even this. Step by step, we seem to be driven from the frying pan into the fire. Since this cannot be a genuine result, it becomes clear that the paradox is *designed* to scupper our first intuitions about what rule-following requires, not to challenge the fact that we are following rules at all. It is *meant* to put us in the awkward position of casting doubt on what cannot be doubted – the fact that our words are meaningful – for the very purpose of getting us to think more clearly about what this involves. For this reason one misses the most important thing about the paradox if one fails to see that both Kripke's sceptic and Wittgenstein's antagonist operating within a dialectal context (see Ebbs 1997 pp. 11, 20–3).

In what follows I aim to establish that attempts to deal directly with this problem only generate a predictable pattern of inadequate defensive and revisionist responses. If it can be shown that there is a common reason why these must be condemned as inadequate *solutions* to the paradox, this will testify to the correctness of Wittgenstein's diagnosis that here again we are running up against the limits of philosophy, thereby vindicating his approach.

Straight and sceptical solutions

As we have just witnessed, both Kripke's and Wittgenstein's sceptics dismiss the claim that appealing to our dispositions could determine which rule we are meant to be following. Ignoring his contentious worries about the finiteness of dispositions, Kripke's sceptic effectively complains that this sort of move leaves no gap between the rule and its application, making error impossible. Thus, if we stick to a purely descriptive account we will wind up having to accept *everything* we are prone to do as part and parcel of the rule we are following – including what we would intuitively regard as mistakes. The dilemma is that in order to make room for the possibility of mistake, we will be driven to beg the question against the sceptic by simply helping ourselves to the very standard that appealing to dispositions was meant to uncover.

However, some commentators hold that the dispositionalist resources are not this meagre. To begin with, there is no reason to think of dispositions as something we could 'read off' the actual behaviour of a rule-follower. Using the simple case of saline water solubility, Forbes insists that the reason we need to use counterfactuals when specifying a disposition is precisely because they only manifest themselves in certain circumstances. Salt normally dissolves in water, but not in all liquids. It does not in petrol or benzene, as Forbes notes, which suggests that, 'if the appropriate contingent properties of water altered in some way, salt might no longer dissolve in it' (Forbes 2002, p. 21). However, this would not negate the truth of the original counterfactual claim about the propensities of salt. Drawing a lesson from this, Forbes rejects Kripke's argument on the grounds that it operates with a crude caricature. He concludes that dispositions cannot be understood in a straightforwardly descriptive way.

He claims that, appropriately understood, the dispositional proposal is more sophisticated than this and therefore fares better than Kripke makes out. To understand it correctly requires acknowledging that the dispositions associated with rule-following cannot be captured by our actual pattern of behaviour – as that allows no room for error – but only by a counterfactual pattern of behaviour that would become manifest under ideal conditions. Put otherwise, it does not ask us to focus on how we are disposed to perform *simpliciter*, but on how we would be disposed to respond in 'optimal' circumstances. In this way, the sophisticated dispositonalist does not make an indiscriminate appeal to the entire range of our responses, but only to a certain select class.

Contrasting the wider and narrower patterns of response would allow the requisite space to explain the normativity required for rule-following. In light of this distinction there is no reason to think that the mistakes to which we are prone stem from the very same disposition as the one that defines the rule we are meant to be following. Mistakes are shown to be less than ideal responses because we are disposed to correct them by revising them when they are pointed out. They reveal themselves as aberrations or deviations in this way. Of course, there is no guarantee we *will* always recognise and correct our mistakes – it is just that we *ought to*, all else being equal. For this reason it is normal for us to hedge the statements of the counterfactual patterns that characterise the rules we are following with *ceteris paribus* clauses. For example, we say:

> If someone has forgotten to carry, then *ceteris paribus* he should change his mind about the answer when reminded, or when the problem is given to him again with the sum of digits in the troublesome column computed separately and the left digit of the answer highlighted. (Forbes 2002, p. 24)

The hope is that once such absolutely ideal conditions are fully specified it will be possible to dispense with any qualifying caveats. But, is there any real hope that we could non-vacuously fill in all the *ceteris paribus* clauses? Boghossian has identified a serious technical flaw in the idea that this could ever be achieved when it comes to describing discursively based rules. Meanings are extremely promiscuous; they enter into countless inferential relations with each other such that it would not be possible to give a complete account of the rule for the correct use of any term without specifying which of an indefinite (if not infinite) number of potential liaisons were appropriate or not (see Boghossian 2002, p. 177). Given what would be involved in charting all such possibilities, the deep contextualist worry, which harps on a theme from Chapter 2, is that we would never be in a position to specify the ideal circumstances under which a specific rule-following disposition would manifest itself. Therefore, the sceptic would not be answered because it would not be possible, in practice, to specify exactly which rule we were following in a way that would accommodate any possible challenge.

Even less plausible is the thought that we could capture the rule by means of a description that employed only non-semantic and non-intentional vocabulary. This requires characterising, '*in non-intentional and non-semantic terms*, a property M such that: possession of M is necessary and sufficient for being a disposition to apply an expression in accord with its correctness conditions' (Boghossian 2002, p. 169; emphasis mine). At this point, it is worth underlining just how very limited the resources are for doing this. If we did not distinguish such patterns on the grounds that one exhibits greater regularity than another, what other purely naturalistic means might we employ to distinguish the 'right' pattern (see Hutto 1999, chs. 2 and 3)? Unless we can say how it is possible to determine which class of behaviours is the select class without begging any questions, then, its sophistications notwithstanding, the dispositionalist proposal smacks of a 'Just So' story.

It is here that, once again, we are brought face to face with the really deep aspect of the sceptical challenge: to identify the sought-after pattern on independent, principled grounds that would nevertheless justify our everyday accounts of the rules we are following. No matter how systematic or chaotic our patterns of behaviour, there is no alternative way of designating such responses as 'failures' or 'successes' that is both independent of our ordinary intuitions and yet can accommodate them non-arbitrarily.[22] For even if absolutely none of my responses, internal or external, accorded with the correct application of a given rule, it would not follow from this that I was not trying to apply it correctly. As Wittgenstein stresses, 'there is no sharp distinction between a random mistake and a systematic one' (*PI* §143). As before, the moral is: given that rule-following is a necessarily imperfect business, whatever interpretation we offer there will always be another that is equally consistent with all the facts. Once again, it Wittgenstein who gets right to the heart of the matter by asking:

> How can the word 'Slab' indicate what I have to do, when after all I can bring any action into accord with any interpretation?
> How can I follow a rule, when after all whatever I do can be interpreted as following it? . . . (*RFM* VI §38)

To take this seriously means we cannot rely on any pre-theoretical knowledge we may have of the meaning of terms, for the difficulty is to identify the rule against which such irregularities can be classified as such, without begging the question. The point is that once we put our ordinary understanding into the hazard we are no longer entitled to rely on it to characterise this or that action as 'checking' or 'correcting' behaviour in the easy way described above. If we cannot appeal to our common sense of the obvious to defend such proposals there is no other alternative, yet principled means of doing so. This is why struggling with this problem so often leads to smuggling – our workaday intuitions creep back in without being noticed, playing a supporting role in saying which responses are to count as acts of correction or deviations from the rule. Unless we can develop and evaluate such proposals without any implicit reliance on what we already know about our practices, they will remain just what they appear to be: *ad hoc* and question-begging.

Anticipating continued failure on this front, revisionist concessions to the sceptic might begin to look attractive. Recognising the legitimacy of the original sceptical demand and accepting that it cannot be met in any straightforward way, Kripke notoriously responds to it by giving a deflated answer in the form of a *sceptical* solution. He abandons all hope of finding some constitutive fact about individuals that justifies their avowals about which rules they follow or what their words mean. Nevertheless, the conclusion is not that there are no facts about what is meant and what is permissible, it is just that, rather than being determined by some independent standard to which individuals might have private access, these turn out to be facts about what a community of speakers will tolerate. We are offered a different account of what decides whether a pattern of response is correct or incorrect. For to be dignified as such, to borrow Blackburn's apt term, depends on whether or not they come into conflict with what is agreed upon by the community. This kind of possibility provides the friction needed to enable the possibility of error and thereby the possibility of meaning. We are told:

> All that is needed to legitimize assertions that someone means something is that there be roughly specifiable circumstances under which they are legitimately assertable, and that the game of asserting them under such conditions has a role in our lives. No supposition that 'facts correspond' to those assertions is needed.
>
> (Kripke 1982, p. 78)

Wittgenstein finds a useful role in our lives for a 'language game' that licenses, under certain conditions, assertions that someone means 'such-and-such' and that his present application of a word 'accords' with what he 'meant' in the past. It turns out that this role, and these conditions, involve reference to a community.

(Kripke 1982, p. 79)

All this is in keeping with Kripke's reading of Wittgenstein, according to which the main purpose of the rule-following passages is to secure the publicity of rules by providing a conclusive argument against the very idea of a private language.

Some have complained that this line of reply makes no real advance on the central problem. For example, it is easy to imagine that an entire community might hold that it is using a term correctly, when in fact is it not. On these grounds, Blackburn objects, 'If my community all suddenly started saying that 57 + 68 = 5, this fact does not make me wrong when I continue to assert that it is 125. I am correct today in saying that the sun is shining and daffodils are yellow, regardless of what the rest of the world says' (Blackburn 2002, p. 39). Unless we are independently assured that custodians of the community are themselves 'correct' in their applications they cannot held to be reliable indicators of the right standard. On this basis, we are led to ask: What fact about the community determines whether it is in line with the correct pattern? To allow this question is damning, though, for if we accept the need to meet this condition, then the same old worries about rule-following and meaning are resurrected, only now replayed at the level of the community as opposed to the individual. We are meant to see from this that what is sauce for the goose or the gander, is sauce for the whole flock.

But advocates of a sceptical solution will complain that this objection is misguided, as it seriously underestimates the radical nature of their position. In making the concession to the sceptic they are prepared to bite the bullet and hold there are no independent facts that underwrite truth and meaning. There are only facts about which responses a community will permit and which it will not. To say this is, of course, explicitly to abandon any interest in defending our naïve picture. In this sense their move is thoroughly reactionary and revisionist: it is meant to replace our intuitive picture. It is offered in the same spirit as Dennett's new theory of consciousness. We are pushed into reconceiving what makes meaning possible. In this respect, Kripke's dialectical argument also functions like Dennett's softening-up exercise, paving the way for a new model theory of meaning while at the same time getting us to reconsider what needs explaining, so as to reduce the explanatory burden. To opt for a sceptical solution is to reject the possibility of an independent standard underlying truth and content: the aim is to make sense of 'truth-talk' by other means. This is what distinguishes it from a straight solution. Understood rightly, its proponents maintain that, counter-intuitive or not, the only sense we can make of such talk is in terms of its sociological import. As Bloor explains:

> When routines break down, then collective decisions and choices must be made to re-establish them under the new conditions. Authority may be needed to maintain the cohesion of usage, and to cope with any divergent tendencies . . . But from where does authority derive? There is no higher court of appeal than the community itself . . . There is nothing else to consult. We can't say 'consult the world'. (Bloor 1996, p. 371)[23]

The role of authority as it relates to the notion of training and customary practice deserves greater scrutiny. For we might ask: About what is the teacher authoritative? About what exactly are we 'consulting' the community? On pain of abandoning the sceptical solution, we must not attempt to make sense of authority by appeal to anything other than the fact that certain of us are charged with deciding what is to be tolerated as 'acceptable responding'. It cannot be that instructors somehow have correct 'rules in mind' that enable them to determine if the student has 'got it right'. For such imagery, promoted by expressions like 'He tried to get the idea across', would be a retreat to the postulation of pre-existing and independently established meanings that are privately owned and passed about or otherwise commonly grasped.

But if we reject this, we are left with a question about what it is that the community's surrogate considers us to have mastered when it is agreed that we are 'adding correctly'? Once again, whether or not we think this a good question, to accept the sceptical solution is to deny it can be answered. Unable to appeal to the traditional notion of content, we are left with nothing but responses that conflict or not. 'Right' turns out to be whatever the society happens to find acceptable. This clearly fails to do justice to our ordinary notion of truth.[24] In this light, the sceptical '*solution*' seems to be throwing out the baby with the bathwater. Whatever attractions it may have, they derive entirely from the manifest failure of the straight solutions: it gets all its life from a lack of alternatives. For this reason it makes sense to review other options.

For example, we might be encouraged to adopt a non-reductive explanation, averring the existence of primitive meaning facts. McGinn
canvasses just such a response. He objects to the assumption that the
sceptical argument must end with the acknowledgment that 'there are
no semantic facts, when the correct conclusion ought to be that semantic facts cannot be reduced to non-semantic facts' (McGinn 1984,
p. 151). Given that at least some concepts must be taken as primitive,
without being regarded as mysterious, he holds that we can answer the
sceptic by simply appealing to facts about what we ordinarily mean
by our words. Thus, in claiming to overcome the paradox in a straight-
dealing way, McGinn boasts that 'The irreducibilty thesis is one kind of
straight solution to Kripke's skeptical problem' (McGinn 1984, p. 164).[25]
Blackburn's reply adds a projectivist twist but remains in certain key
respects similar to McGinn's in rejecting the possibility of reduction,
while still hoping to provide an explanation.

> Following through the problem of answering the paradox leads to
> sympathy with a basically 'anti-metaphysical' conception of rule-
> following. We simply cannot deliver, *in other terms*, accounts of what
> constitutes shared following of a rule, or what the fact of a rule, or
> what the fact of a rule being in force 'consists in'. In my view this
> invites a *projectivist explanation* of these kinds of judgement, although
> also in my view *we cannot conclude that it is improper to talk of the facts
> of the case.*   (Blackburn 2002, p. 44; emphases mine)

Although it is good to see the stirrings of resistance against the sceptical challenge, merely offering non-reductive explanations does not go far
enough, as these would never satisfy the sceptic. It is quite unclear how
claiming that there are irreducible meaning facts adds up to an explanation if it provides no independent means of vindication. To accept this
leaves us none the wiser as to what actually justifies our discursive practices since talk of primitive meaning facts brings no greater explanatory
resources to bear than we might give by simply insisting we just know
what we mean.[26] How, then, is the non-reductive reply anything more
than a mere reiteration of what we already take ourselves to know? Isn't
this, to use Quine's phrase, merely to acquiesce in our home
language? Despite promising to put sceptical worries to bed, non-
reductionism is objectionable because it only masquerades as having
answered the paradox. The more secure move is to take the further step
of denying the legitimacy of the sceptical question altogether.

Wittgenstein's stance

How do these responses to the paradox compare with Wittgenstein's own? As might be expected, he is not at all interested in providing a solution of any kind, sceptical or otherwise. To understand why we must realise that his 'target is not the very idea that a present state of understanding embodies commitments with respect to the future, but rather *a certain seductive misconception of that idea*' (McDowell 1998, p. 223; emphasis mine).[27] Accordingly, we have once again been 'dazzled' by a picture of what it is to understand something or to follow a rule. This is yet another paradigm case in which we become befuddled due to a certain committed way of looking at things. Difficulties mount up precisely when we try to make these 'intuitive' ideas more philosophically respectable. In this way we are led to produce ever more elaborate, but ultimately forlorn, proposals. The point is that even if our speculations about such things flow naturally enough, they are not inevitable. As Wittgenstein insists, there are no *musts* in philosophy.

As we have seen, in this particular case the villain of the piece is a particular 'intellectualist' picture of what rules are and of what it is to 'grasp' them. Defenders of this account must face the paradox precisely because it is not possible to provide unassailable *interpretations* of the rules we putatively follow. From a distance, there is always room to reinterpret which rule is being followed; nothing we say, think or do can unambiguously specify which is correct with iron-clad determinacy, eliminating other logical possibilities. Echoing the remark from the *Remarks on the Foundations of Mathematics* quoted earlier, Wittgenstein famously proclaims:

> This was our paradox: no course of action could be determined by a rule, because every course of action can be made out to accord with a rule . . . What this shows is that there is a way of grasping a rule which is *not* an *interpretation* but which is exhibited in what we call 'obeying the rule' and 'going against it' in actual cases.
>
> (*PI* §201)

This being so it should become clear that, at base, rule-followers cannot and do not rely on interpretations when following rules.[28] Picking up on the anti-intellectualist tenor of his remark, a clear link can be discerned between this late treatment of rule-following and his early views on meaning, as set out in Chapters 2 and 3 of this work. The point being made here is familiar to the *Tractatus*; we cannot capture what is correct in the use of words by means of a general rule or description. In this regard, it is useful to compare his early reticence about providing examples of elementary propositions with the following later remarks:

> How do I explain the meaning of 'regular', 'uniform', 'same' to anyone? – I shall explain these words to someone who, say, only speaks French by means of the corresponding French words. But if a person has not yet got the *concepts*, I shall teach him to use the words by means of *examples* and by *practice*. – And when I do this I do not communicate less to him than I know myself.   (*PI* §208)

> But is that *all*? Isn't there a deeper explanation; or mustn't at least the *understanding* of the explanation be deeper? – Well have I myself a deeper understanding? Have I *got* more to give in the explanation?
> (*PI* §209)[29]

To take Wittgenstein seriously on this front requires abandoning the idea that what is embodied in a practice can be uniquely specified in terms of a proposition or description that captures the sense of a general 'rule', which might be used to serve certain philosophical purposes. Of course, this is not to deny that we employ rules, orders and the like on a regular basis in our everyday practices, but it is to reject the idea that these can be elevated to the status of entities that can independently predetermine meaning. What we are left with is the realisation that there is no 'circumspect' or 'surveyable' description for the correct rule for the use of most words:

> If I tell someone 'Stand roughly there' – may not this explanation work perfectly? And cannot every other fail too? But isn't it an inexact explanation? – Yes; why shouldn't we call it 'inexact'? Only let us understand what 'inexact' means. For it does not mean 'unusable'.
> (*PI* §88, 98–9)

Again, in line with a key theme of the preceding chapter, what sets limits for our use of terms and concepts is not to be understood as stated by some general rule that governs the applications under its care, rather such limits are 'fixed' by the *role* these play in our lives. He makes his views on this explicit in the following interchange:

'Then according to you everybody could continue the series as he likes; and so infer *any*how!' In that case we shan't call it 'continuing the series' and also presumably not 'inference'. And thinking and inferring (like counting) is of course bounded for us, not by an arbitrary definition, but by natural limits corresponding to the body of what can be called the role of thinking and inferring in our life.

(*RFM* I §116)

We begin to see that what the 'intellectualist' picture demands is impossible. It cannot be a condition of our ability to use and understand language successfully that we are able to grasp absolutely determinate 'meanings'. This idea is shown to be ill founded on other grounds as well. For, on pain of regress, learning how to use concepts could not require this of us in the initial stages. Learning to follow a rule cannot presuppose the very sort of intellectual capacities it is meant to engender. Instead, by attending to what is involved in such cases, we discover that it depends on the teacher and student having certain common tendencies to respond to similar things, with the latter willing to accept the authority of the former – at least while being taught. Such tendencies are based upon, but not confined to, our common natural reactions and instinctive responses. These constitute our first nature and provide the, 'preliminary steps towards acting according to a rule' (see *RFM* VI, §43). In this respect:

> Following a rule is analogous to obeying an order. We are trained to do so; we *react* to an order in a particular way.
>
> (*PI* §206, emphasis mine)

> What has the expression of a rule – say a sign-post – got to do with my actions? What sort of connexion is there here? – Well, perhaps this one: I have been trained to react to this sign in a particular way, and now I do so react to it.
>
> (*PI* §198)

> And then I shall act without reasons.
>
> (*PI* §211)

In the most basic cases, all one can do when teaching is to give examples and hope that the student catches on. For example, in teaching simple arithmetic, the only method is to show again and again what it is to add various numbers, perhaps using different types of unit. It is natural to say that, when successful, the student is able to 'see how to go on' but it is precisely at this point that we must beware of falling into myth-making. For if 'seeing how to go on' is taken too literally, it will encourage the very picture that wants resisting: that of an interpretation somehow settling what needs to be done in all our applications. Demonstrations only go so far. They cannot tie down a unique interpretation in the form of a general description that details the essential nature of the rule. Still, in learning how to add, the student will either come to 'see' what is required or not. It is just that this 'seeing' should not be understood as involving the grasp of a proposition or the fix on an interpretation, but rather as something that manifests itself in the pattern of the student's responses, if they are satisfactory (cf. *PI* §§208, 235).

It is through such training that a shared sense of the obvious is developed. The medium in which a novice becomes an autonomous speaker is necessarily a social one; rule-following does not occur in isolation or without an established custom (see Stueber 1994, p. 21; M. Williams 1998, p. 210). This is why, paying homage to Aristotle, we ought to regard such training as the means through which we develop a communal 'second nature'. The following remark is typical of Wittgenstein's way of underscoring the essentially social side of learning to following a rule:

> If one of a pair of chimpanzees once scratched the figure | - - | in the earth and thereupon the other series | - - | | - - | etc., the first would not have given a rule nor would the other be following it, whatever else went on at the same time in the mind of the two of them.
>
> If however there were observed, e.g, the phenomenon of a kind of instruction, of shewing how and of imitation, of lucky and misfiring attempts, of reward and punishment and the like; if at length the one who had been so trained put figures which he had never seen before one after another in sequence as in the first example, then we should probably say that the one chimpanzee was writing rules down, and the other following them.   (*RFM* VI §42)

Here he is noting certain essential features required for learning and following rules: rules which ultimately make possible our saying anything at all. In this respect, 'Following according to rule is FUNDAMENTAL to our language game' (*RFM* VI §28). However, there is danger of thinking that such claims attempt to provide a replacement theory for the 'intellectualist' picture that Wittgenstein demolished. To think this would be to misunderstand the status of his remarks and his dialectical purpose. For what we learn by confronting the paradox is that there is no way to deal with it adequately if one's commitment to explanation is unshakeable; we can neither surrender to the sceptic nor answer him directly. The point in exposing our vulnerability on this front is meant to get us to see that we have no option but to take for granted the fact that our words are meaningful. It is not that we are meant to realise that certain answers to the sceptic are inadequate, but rather that there is something deeply confused about his whole line of questioning. In this light, the mistake is made in taking the very first step of accepting the challenge. But this step is also the most deceptive because it appears to be totally innocuous. The irony is that, in giving our first answers, it hardly seems we are making theoretical moves at all, as opposed to merely expressing what 'everyone thinks' about rule-following and meaning.

Wittgenstein's purpose, therefore, is not to help us to *escape* the sceptic's trap, but to get us to resist it altogether by showing us that such worries and the philosophical attempts to answer them are *both* idle and confused. For taking such doubts seriously and attempting to quell them require an alienation from the very activities that make doubting and questioning possible at all. In trying to answer the sceptic we go wrong immediately by making, 'an objectifying move . . . [which] leads us to adopt an external perspective on our own assertions and judgements' (Ebbs 1997, p. 37). Or, put more carefully, we are provoked *to try* to make such a move since it is not a genuine possibility that we can do so. There simply is no principled way of saying 'from the outside' – from a theoretical distance – what our words mean or which rules we are following in a way that would content the committed sceptic. Bearing all this in mind, Wittgenstein's reflections not only get us to see that there is no prospect of giving a 'philosophical solution' to the paradox, they also make us realise that the paradox itself is one of our own making. It is the product of our misguided attempt to do more than is possible, through a failure to recognise the true limits of inquiry. This is not a retreat into scepticism or nihilism; his aim is much more subversive than that. Minar captures the point by noting that through such considerations, 'the paradox is thrown into doubt' (Minar 1991, p. 214; see also Goldfarb 2002, pp. 104–7).

To free ourselves fully from such confusions it is not enough to rid ourselves of particular misconceptions, we must also surrender certain philosophical ambitions. With respect to such a fundamental concern as rule-following, there is simply no prospect of advancing or defending philosophical theories or explanations at all. It is not just that Wittgenstein lacks an interest in giving explanations of this phenomena, as is sometimes suggested, rather he realises that here one runs up against the limits of what can be explained or justified.

> 'How can one follow a rule?' That is what I should like to ask.
> But how does it come about that I want to ask that, when after all I find no kind of difficulty in following a rule?
> Here we obviously misunderstand the facts that lie before our eyes.
>
> (*RFM* VI §38)

But freed of misleading pictures and confused explanatory ambitions, Wittgenstein's reminders of what 'lies before our eyes' are neither advanced in the form of a theory nor do they add up to one. For as he also says:

> What we are supplying are really remarks on the natural history of man, not curiosities; however, but rather observations on facts which no one has doubted and which have only gone unremarked because they are always before our eyes.
>
> (*RFM* I §142; cf. also *PI* §129)

It is hardly surprising then that one will find his contributions woefully in need of amplification if one fails to understand this point. For example, Bloor believes that Wittgenstein was advancing them as part of a theory, and complains:

> We need more than a generalized awareness of the importance of social processes: we need a specific understanding of what is meant by the word 'institution'. The same applies to Wittgenstein's reference to conventions and customs . . . so far the statement of the sociological aspect of Wittgenstein's theory has been relatively undemanding. It is now time to probe more deeply. We must find an illuminating way to characterise the central, sociological concepts on which the theory depends.
> Here we must brace ourselves for a shock. Wittgenstein at no point explained or defined the words 'custom', 'convention' or 'institution'.
>
> (Bloor 1997, p. 27)

Bloor goes on to say that despite the fact that Wittgenstein's, 'conclusions are plausible and predictable, they are also disturbingly minimal, hardly adding depth to our understanding of the theory' (Bloor 1997, p. 27). Of course, we will only be 'shocked' by the inadequacy of Wittgenstein's 'theory' if we wrongly imagine that his offerings were meant to constitute one. It should be clear by now that this was never his interest. To note that rule-following activities are grounded in training, customs and habit does not constitute a communitarian or sociological theory of meaning. At this point it is usual for Wittgenstein to be charged with advocating 'quietism'. Yet, without refinement, this attribution will not do, for as we have just seen, he is prepared to make revealing observations about issues of fundamental philosophical concern. Although we would be unable to appreciate these if we were still under the spell of certain confusions, it is simply untrue that he is completely silent about such matters. Nor, without the restrictions of the Tractarian conception of the limits of sense in play, is there any reason he ought to be mute about such topics. In light of this, it is pertinent to ask: About what is Wittgenstein 'quiet' and in what sense?

In addressing this, Brandom's work provides a useful contrast precisely because although he openly credits Wittgenstein with inspiring the idea that meanings must be explained in terms of their use, he also rejects 'other features of his thought – in particular his theoretical quietism' (Brandom 1994, p. xii).[30] Before we can decide who is in the right on this issue it is important to shed light on what such quietism actually comes to by comparing what we are given by Wittgenstein, in the form of non-theoretical observations, with what is promised by Brandom, in the form of a theory. The key question is: In what way, if at all, do Brandom's offerings constitute a *theoretical* or *explanatory* advance over Wittgenstein's?

Brandom's project in *Making It Explicit* seeks to provide non-reductive explanations but of a different sort from those discussed at the end of the previous section. Despite this, the reason he is not a 'quietist' is that he does not regard the normative aspect of our linguistic practice to be 'primitive or inexplicable' (Brandom 1997, p. 154). One of his primary ambitions is to show that the norms inherent in our mature discursive practices are socially instituted. Thus he accepts that they depend for their very existence on the way one *regards* another's actions.[31] That is to say, norms get their life from the practical attitudes adopted, which are revealed in the ways in which we respond to one another. In illustrating this, he focuses heavily on the imposition of sanctions.[32] These

come into play when 'implicit' rules are transgressed, even if participants in such practices are never in a position to articulate them.[33] In
the simplest pre-linguistic cases the attitudes of taking, or treating, a
given performance as correct or incorrect is manifest in reprimanding
behaviour. In the crudest cases, sanctioning might involve the direct
punishment of an offender, for example, beating them with sticks for
not showing a certain leaf before entering a certain hut. But what distinguishes Brandom's approach is that he is not interested in unpacking the notion of sanctions in more behaviouristic terms by appeal to
such notions as 'positive and negative' reinforcement, which may leave
room for yet further reduction. For him, someone's being faithful to or
violating a specific norm is best understood in terms of the effects it has
on other normative statuses, conferring or removing other obligations
or entitlements. Hence he claims it 'is compatible with the sanction paradigm that it should be "norms all the way down"' (Brandom 1994, p.
44). Thus Brandom is a non-reductionist only in the sense that he stops
short of 'bald naturalism'. What distinguishes his approach from cruder
naturalist attempts to 'theorise' about meaning is that, 'No attempt is
made to eliminate, in favour of non-normative or naturalistic vocabulary, the normative vocabulary employed in specifying the practices that
are the use of a language' (Brandom 1994, p. xxii, 1997, p. 154). Instead
we are told, 'The *via media* pursued here eschews intentional or semantic specifications of behaviour, but permits normative and therefore
social specifications of what is in fact linguistic behaviour' (Brandom
1994: p. xv).

Certainly, Brandom provides a useful counter to purely representationalist approaches by showing how pragmatic and semantic aspects
of meaning are first united in use.[34] Still, it is difficult to see how this
aspect of his account is anything more than the recognition of the fact
that the attitudes involved in mature linguistic practice have as their
precursors attitudes of the kind exhibited in equally irreducibly normative and social non-linguistic practices. The trouble is that this
cannot be the basis of Brandom's anti-quietism, as Wittgenstein also
notes it. His remarks make clear that he is aware that our capacity to
follow rules and engage in reasoned discourse are part of a sophisticated
form of life which is inescapably social and norm-bound. Moreover,
in a different way, so is the rudimentary animalistic form of life in
which it is rooted. Indeed, Brandom says that, 'One of Wittgenstein's
most important claims is that the practices in which the norms that
articulate meanings and their uptake in understanding are implicit
must be *social* practices' (Brandom 1994, p. 53). The difference is that

Wittgenstein did not think this revelation constituted a philosophical explanation. Certainly, it does nothing to explain or justify our discursive practices in a way that would silence a genuine sceptic. Nor, in line with Bloor's charge of minimalism, is observing this deep enough to warrant talk of an explanation of some other sort. Consequently, we might wonder afresh, what exactly gives Brandom's self-proclaimed theorising an explanatory edge that Wittgenstein's observations lack?

Brandom makes clear that his aim is to make our discursive practices less mysterious by showing: (i) how 'linguistic norms are instituted by social practical activity, and (ii) by 'explaining what is actually expressed by normative vocabulary' (Brandom 1997, p. 154). So far, we have only considered one part of his account. Hence understanding what is involved in basic norm-conferring social activities such a 'sanctioning' is meant to reveal how norms first come into being while, at the same time, explicating the basis of such normative notions as: 'is committed', 'is permitted', 'ought' and their kin. But this is not where Brandom's story ends. For his express purpose is to build up resources to enable him to deal with what he calls 'the fanciest sort of intentionality', that found in our distinctively linguistic practices (Brandom 1994, p. 7). The basic idea will be familiar to fans of conceptual role semantics; a given propositional content is defined by its particular set of inferential and practical consequences. However, Brandom's twist is that, in line with his view of simpler normative practices, he regards the contents of thoughts and speech acts, of those who give reasons and make claims, as conferred by the attitudes of those who participate in the complex practice of keeping track of the commitments and entitlements of claimants. So by revealing what is *particular* to the structure of this sort of explicitly conceptual activity, Brandom can further his project of making 'linguistic intentionality less mysterious' by providing an account of what 'sentient creatures would have to be able do to count as sapient as well' (Brandom 1994, p. 7). Thus it would to be premature to decide that nothing much is explained by acknowledging that our linguistic practices have an intrinsically social and normative basis. To see the fruits of Brandom's account, we need to look beyond its roots to its branches.

In doing so we immediately encounter its most distinctive feature; the claim that we can best understand the structure of discursive practice by thinking of the conferment of conceptual contents in deontic score-keeping terms. The sketch he gives of the features of assertional and inferential practice is complicated and highly systematic. But this should not blind us into thinking that this aspect of his account supplies it with the requisite explanatory edge. For he openly says that it is not designed to explicate 'our actual practice but an idealization of it. Simplified and schematic though the model may be, it should nonetheless be recognizable as a version of what we do. The model is intended to serve as the core of a layered account of linguistic practice' (Brandom 1994, p. 161). The point is that even if, for the sake of argument, we accept that thinking of discursive practice in deontic score-keeping terms succeeds in explicating its *actual* structure, it would, at best, still be only *descriptive* of what lies at the heart of such practice. Consequently, whatever insight it may shed or mystery it may dispel, it could not serve to address the fundamental *philosophical* concerns that Wittgenstein identified.

However, he also makes clear a further explanatory ambition when he writes:

> The book is an attempt to explain the *meanings* of linguistic expressions in terms of their use. The explanatory strategy is to begin with an account of social practices, to identify the particular structure they must exhibit in order to qualify as specifically *linguistic* practice and then to consider what *different sorts of semantic contents* those practices can confer on states, performances and expressions caught up in them in suitable ways.
>
> (Brandom 1997, p. 153; final emphasis mine)

Indeed, Brandom leaves us in no doubt that it is on just this matter – in his attempt to say what is distinctive about the conferring of representational as opposed to purely expressive contents – that he sees himself as breaking faith with Wittgenstein. He writes:

> The later Wittgenstein reminds us again and again that we must not assume that all sentences have the expressive job of saying how things are, or that all terms have the job of picking out objects. But he has remarkably little to say about just what these expressive roles consist in and how we are to distinguish them. One of the core projects of *Making It Explicit* is to do just that, by starting with an account of the pragmatics of inference and assertion in terms of social deontic scorekeeping practices, and then moving to an account of the representational semantic dimension of sentences and subsentential expressions in terms of substitution-inferential commitments and their anaphoric inheritance. Surely this is a laudable explanatory ambition – one whose pursuit ought not be ruled out in advance

by theoretical quietism, however principled. The *only* real question is to what extent the attempt is successful.

(Brandom 1997, p. 190)[35]

According to Brandom's own admission, the real test of whether his account has any genuine explanatory power boils down to whether or not it is 'in the end successful in ... baking an objective cake out of social ingredients' (Brandom 1997, p. 200). But what is the prospect of *explaining* normativity of the sort involved in conferring representational contents? He has no illusions about what success in this project requires. He is aware that to explain the objectivity that is presupposed by our conceptual practice requires making sense of our ability to talk of facts that are 'independent of what we, even all of us forever, take those facts to be' (Brandom 1994, p. 53). This requires making room for a kind of normativity that is of an altogether different order from that involved in our simpler practices. Thus he contrasts conceptual norms with the expressive sort described above precisely on the grounds that while the latter can be seen to depend wholly on the attitudes of participants, the former cannot. That is to say, with respect to other kinds of norms, it makes no sense to imagine that the community's all-in practical assessment could be mistaken, whereas this is a live possibility in the case of conceptual norms. Immediately after underscoring this distinction, Brandom acknowledges that accounting for such objectivity is his 'primary challenge' (Brandom 1994, p. 54).

Ultimately, he hopes to meet it by explicitly endorsing Davidson's account of how conceptual objectivity emerges in and through the context of interpretation, in the interplay between interpreters, each of whom must distinguish in practice how things *are* from how they are merely *taken to be*. Understanding this is crucial for making a claim that confers commitments that claimants are not always in the best position to judge. Brandom emphasises the importance of *de re* illocutions in enabling the possibility of contemporaneous disagreement and, indeed, future reassessment (see Hutto 1999, ch. 5, ss. 2.2–2.3). These act as intersubjective linchpins, enabling us to compare how another *takes things to be* against the way in which *they are*, as seen by us. This does not descend into a mere clash of 'perspectives' because for something to be an objective judgement it must always be attended by the possibility that its assessment may be awry. This is ensured by the fact that 'any existing practice can be rationally criticized ... There is no Archimedean point, independent of all practices, from which to criticize any of them. The world only comes into view through the deployment of some concepts or others' (Brandom 1997, p. 201).[36] Hence, he eschews the very idea of a final, all-in community perspective on how things stand independently of us. Rather, on his account:

> Sorting out who should be counted as correct, whose claims and applications of concepts should be treated as authoritative, is a messy retail business of assessing the comparative authority of competing evidential and inferential claims . . . no perspective is authoritative as such. There is only the actual practice of sorting out who has the better reason in particular cases.   (Brandom 1994, p. 601)

For this reason, Brandom promotes an *I–Thou* conception of inter-subjectivity, which he regards as fundamental to the possibility of a community of concept-users, as opposed to the other way around. How does all this compare with Wittgenstein's way of accommodating objectivity? Although Wittgenstein recognises the social dimension of language, he nowhere appeals to communal conventions to make sense of it. He explicitly rejects the thought that meaning and truth rest on prior 'agreements', thereby repudiating any consensus or convention-alist theories of such. Indeed, he goes further by making it clear that these get matters back to front.

> 'So you are saying that human agreement decides what is true and what is false?' – It is what human beings *say* that is true and false; and they agree in the *language* they use. That is not agreement in opinions but in form of life.   (*PI* §241; emphasis original)

The upshot is that we must realise that all the necessary distinctions are made *within* our practices. It is with this in mind that we should read the following exchange in which he makes clear how he would accommodate objectivity:

> 'But mathematical truth is independent of whether human beings know it or not!' – Certainly, the propositions 'Human beings believe that twice two is four' and 'Twice two is four' do not mean the same. The latter is a mathematical proposition; the other, if it makes sense at all, may perhaps mean: human beings have arrived at the mathe-matical proposition. The two propositions have entirely different *uses*.
> (*PI* p. 226e)

Like Brandom and Davidson, he rejects attempts to explain the objectivity of meaning by appeal to community assessment or by simple appeal to a ratification-independent world. Of course, refusing to make the choice does not prevent him from recognising that, 'If you draw different conclusions you do indeed get into conflict, e.g. with society; and also with other practical consequences' (*RFM* I §116). Rather, the point is that there is no prospect of a deeper account of the basis of our linguistic practices in the sense of understanding better what makes our use of words correct or incorrect. Thus Brandom is wrong to think that the *only* real question is whether his explanation is successful. Given that, in the end, it shares so much with the non-explanatory approaches of Davidson and Wittgenstein, we can also ask: In what respect it is really an explanation at all?

Building on the central insight of the *Tractatus*, we can see that just as there can be no general science of logic, the laws of which designed to explain or externally justify our inferences, so too there can be no explanation of the kind of objectivity embodied in our rule-following practices. There is no getting below or behind what we do that would permit the sort of explanations that would answer to the *philosopher's* needs. At this point, Wittgenstein tells us that 'I have exhausted the justifications' and 'my spade is turned' (*PI* §217).[37] There is no getting below this point for beyond it questions of 'truth' and 'falsity', 'interpretation' and 'misinterpretation' do not arise. It is only because he rejects the very possibility of giving explanations and justifications of this sort that it would be correct to call Wittgenstein a quietist. The problem is that if we remain committed to a certain picture of what is possible in philosophy, we will fail to acknowledge any genuine limits, resulting in confused attempts to provide philosophical explanations that show themselves to be unworkable, misleading and ultimately unsatisfactory.[38] The alternative is to respect Wittgenstein's injunction not to dig below the ground, recognising that:

> Giving grounds, however, justifying the evidence, comes to an end.
> (*OC* §204)

Conclusion

Knowing where to stop is not easy. Even some of Wittgenstein's most astute and sympathetic supporters, who shun attempts at philosophical explanation, continue to fall prey to the desire to say more. For example, McDowell clearly sees the folly of endorsing realism and anti-realism, but like Brandom he too fears that matters cannot rest here since he holds that rejecting the idea of a wholly independent relation between rules and words does violence to the robust sense of 'objectivity' that our ordinary dealings enshrine. Thus, in response to Wright, he claims:

> If the notion of investigation-independent patterns of application is to be discarded, then so is the idea that things are, at least sometimes, thus and so anyway, independently of our ratifying the judgement that that is how they are. It seems fair to describe this extremely radical consequence as a kind of idealism.
>
> (McDowell 1998, p. 222)

He holds that in rejecting the notion of ratification-independence, Wright threatens not only a mistaken metaphysical realism, but also an essential ingredient of our intuitive notion of the objectivity of meaning. As we have just seen, the practice of determining what is true must allow for the possibility of *everyone* being mistaken about how things stand. McDowell hopes to make room for this aspect of our intuitive picture – the idea of an independent standard of the right kind – without falling back into *philosophical* realism. Furthermore, he also thinks this is something that can only be understood by giving appropriate attention to our practices.[39] Thus, he writes:

> The key to finding the indispensable middle course is *the idea of a custom or a practice*. How can a performance both be nothing but a 'blind' reaction to a situation, not an attempt to act on an interpretation (avoiding Scylla); and be a case of going by a rule (avoiding Charybdis)?   (McDowell 1998, p. 242)

He is quite clear that this appeal to practices is not meant to address any explanatory needs.[40] Thus, taking slight issue with Wittgenstein, he says:

> There is indeed room to complain that Wittgenstein reveals a need for something he does not give, or does not give enough of. But what we might ask for more of is *not a constructive account of how human interactions make meaning and understanding possible*, but rather a diagnostic deconstruction of the peculiar way of thinking that makes such a thing seem necessary.
>
> (McDowell 1998, p. 278; emphasis mine)

Even so, McDowell goes too far in another way. For although the production of a theory of meaning expressly holds no attraction for him, he is prone to employ suggestive metaphors that encourage further philosophical elaboration, speculation and development in much the way Dennett's talk of 'notional objects' does. Instead of being content simply to expose the misleading picture and the confused agenda that leads to it, he goes on to talk of such things as:

> the obvious and surely correct reading: that *hearing a word in one sense rather than another is hearing it in one position rather than another in the network of possible patterns of making sense* that we learn to find ourselves in when we acquire mastery of a language.[41]
>
> (McDowell 1998, p. 260)

The danger of saying such things is that they tempt one to go further. Thus, if one were to take this kind of acoustic metaphor too seriously, it easily gets elevated to the place held previously by 'seeing how to go on'. By this route one is easily led to endorse new philosophical pictures sponsored by the same old type of confusion. Against this, Wittgenstein's moral stands out clearly. For he anticipates our tendency to go wrong at just this point:

> Our mistake is to look for an explanation where we ought to look at what happens as a 'proto-phenomenon'. That is, where we ought to have said: this language-game is played.
>
> (*PI* §654; cf. also *LWPPI* §873)

As we shall see in the next chapter, this advice is particularly pertinent in understanding his way with realism and idealism.

5
Before Realism and Idealism

> Really 'The proposition is either true or false' only means that
> it must be possible to decide for or against it. But this does not
> say what the ground for such a decision is like.
>
> Wittgenstein, *On Certainty*, §200

Introduction

For all that has been said in the preceding chapter, there is still a need
to confront openly an important residual issue; that is, the question of
whether rejecting the idea of the possibility of an independent stance
on our practices, necessarily entails some form of transcendental or linguistic idealism. For example, according to Anscombe's test, a position
constitutes a form of linguistic idealism if it gives a positive answer to
the question, 'Does this existence, or this truth, depend on human linguistic practice?' (Bloor 1996, p. 356). Some, such as Bloor, propose to
make giving a positive answer to this question more palatable by noting
that, 'with an appropriate understanding of "idealism", there are such
elements and very important ones, [which are] are consistent with also
seeing Wittgenstein as a naturalistic thinker' (Bloor 1996, p. 355). But I
hold we must not assimilate Wittgenstein too readily into the idealist
tradition, even if we are prepared to recognise the subtleties in that
family of views that welcome friendly comparisons.

I hold rather that in both his early and late periods, Wittgenstein
recognised that there is what we might call an 'internal', yet inexpress-
ible and inexplicable, connection between thought, language and the
world; the limits of possibility with respect to these ultimately run
together. In particular, the basic vision of the relation between thought,
reality and logic in Wittgenstein's early work is not abandoned in

his later period. Hopefully, I have already independently motivated this reading, but in this chapter I hope to establish this case even more firmly and finally to dispose of the crutch of the 'inside/outside', 'internal/external' metaphors.

To achieve this, I focus on Bernard Williams proposed 'model' for reading Wittgenstein's later philosophy as set out in his paper 'Wittgenstein and Idealism', in which he claims to have exposed its transcendental idealist character.[1] By this he roughly means that Wittgenstein's later position is idealist to the extent that it disallows the possibility of any independent reality that is not contaminated by our view of things.[2] Furthermore, he thought it was transcendental in the sense that 'our view of things' is not something that we can explain or locate in the world.[3]

What makes Williams' interpretation of Wittgenstein unusual in the literature is that rather than claiming that Wittgenstein moved from realism in his early period to idealism in his later one, he holds that Wittgenstein is an idealist in his later period precisely because his views on this topic have not altered in the transition. I agree that many of the continuities that Williams finds between the *Tractatus* and the later writings exist, but I reject the claim that it follows from this that he sponsored any form of transcendental idealism in his later period precisely because I hold that he did not do so in his early period. I make this case in several stages and on two different platforms. First, I give a brief description of the underlying basis of Williams' interpretation. Second, I defend its general thrust against a critique issued by Malcolm. Finally, without disputing the views ascribed to Wittgenstein by Williams, I argue that acceptance of them does not make one into a transcendental idealist. I show this in two ways. On the one hand, I reveal the non-trivial resemblance between Williams' Wittgenstein and Donald Davidson, who is a self-styled realist. On the other hand, I set out exegetical reasons for thinking that if the continuity that Williams sees between the *Tractatus* and the later writings actually exists, then it provides reason in itself not to regard Wittgenstein as an idealist.

Williams' Wittgenstein

What leads Williams to think that the later Wittgenstein is a transcendental idealist of sorts? His train of thought makes these mainline stops:

(a) There is evidence that Wittgenstein was a transcendental idealist in the *Tractatus*.[4]

(b) In Wittgenstein's later writings there is a transition from the solipsistic 'I' to an all-embracing 'we' which still 'contains an important element of idealism'. (Williams 1974, p. 79)[5]

Let us consider the evidence in support of (a). Williams sets out three tenets of the position he thinks is espoused in the *Tractatus* which essentially make it a form of 'transcendental idealism'. Here is a paraphrase of those tenets:

(1) The limits of my language are the limits of my world.

(2) The limits of language must be staked out from the 'inside'.

(3) The 'I' that forms the limit is not something in the world.

As Williams sees it, (1) and (2) establish the idealistic nature of the Tractarian position, while (3) secures its transcendental character. Hence, having *prima facie* established (a) by appeal to these well-known remarks, he goes on to concentrate on the continuity between the *Tractatus* and the later writings on this front.[6] In fact, he claims that the only important change is a shift in Wittgenstein's use of pronouns – a move from the first-person singular 'I' to the first-person plural 'we', primarily motivated by an argument against 'private language'.[7] This is a move from thinking that a lonely solipsistic subject forms the limits of the world to adopting a thoroughgoing anti-individualism in which 'our shared form of life' comes to constitute that limit. Effectively, this is a move from solipsism to an 'aggregate solipsism' (cf. Williams 1974, pp. 82–3).

This, so Williams claims, accounts for the vague and indefinite use of 'we' in Wittgenstein's later writings (see Williams 1974, pp. 79, 90, 92). His proposal is that Wittgenstein's use of 'we' shifts from referring to particular human groups, which are the objects of attention or comparison, to referring to an overarching stance from which we make our comparisons. This kind of referential ambiguity reminds one of the ambiguity that arises when one tries to 'make sense' of solipsism (i.e. to give it expression in ordinary language). Using some devices of the *Tractatus*, we can say that the problem is that the ordinary referent of 'I' is not identical with what it refers to when it plays the role of a metaphysical limit. When one attempts to express solipsism, the clash between these two notions becomes acute. One attempts to describe the solipsist 'I' – the 'metaphysical' subject – while mistakenly keeping the 'psychological' subject in mind. This is why Wittgenstein thought it possible that solipsism could be shown to be correct, but it could not be expressed. Crucially, on Williams' interpretation 'we' sometimes has a transcendental use in Wittgenstein's later writings, paralleling the uses of 'I' in the *Tractatus*.

Bearing this in mind, there are two main questions that form the focus of the sections to come. First, is Williams' interpretation of Wittgenstein's later work plausible? Second, if we accept Williams' interpretation, does this entail that the later Wittgenstein was a transcendental idealist of a linguistic sort? I shall attempt to answer these questions with a 'yes' and a 'no' respectively.

The failure of Malcolm's critique

Malcolm attempts to undermine the basis for Williams' interpretation, dismissing the charge that Wittgenstein was a transcendental idealist by directly challenging the claim that Wittgenstein's use of 'we' is 'vague or indefinite', denying that its reference vacillates (Malcolm 1982, p. 251). He writes:

> In Wittgenstein's writings the reference of 'we' is precise. The reference is always to some actual human group or society, in contrast with another real or imagined one. I do not find 'a we which is not one group rather than another in the world' but is instead 'the plural descendant of that idealist I of the *Tractatus*'.
>
> (Malcolm 1982, p. 254)

Malcolm's point is that because the 'we' – or more precisely 'we's – of the later work always designate some particular human group in the world, there can be no sense in thinking of them as being of the same order as the metaphysical subject denoted by the 'I' of the *Tractatus*. His strategy is to attack Williams' interpretation at its root, resisting the idea that there is a simple continuity in Wittgenstein's thought on the matter of transcendental subjectivity between the early and later periods. Without the assumption of continuity on this front, it would seem that the charge of linguistic idealism as applied to the later works fails to be plausible.

Furthermore, Malcolm also claims that when using the pronoun 'we', Wittgenstein always had some specific group in his sights *because* the very purpose of his 'us and them' comparisons was to help us to see that 'our' use of concepts is not the only way they might be used

(Malcolm 1982, p. 261). So in contrast to Williams' idealistic reading that sees Wittgenstein as always moving around 'within our form of life', Malcolm insists that the whole point of cross-tribal comparisons is precisely to give us a means of stepping outside of it. The comparisons are made for the reflective purpose of enabling us to get a clearer, more objective view of our concepts. He puts the point as follows:

> In describing forms of life, world-pictures, language-games, real or imaginary, that differ from our own, we are enabled to reflect on our own concepts and *to see them objectively*; we distance ourselves from our concepts and *view them from outside*; as it were.
>
> (Malcolm 1982, p. 262; emphases mine)

He attempts to marshal support for his reading by pointing to the wealth of examples drawn from *On Certainty*, *Philosophical Investigations* and *Zettel*. For example, Malcolm recounts the extreme case of cross-tribal comparison discussed in Chapter 3, in which the concept of pain is imagined to be restricted, only applying to cases in which 'there is visible damage'. Malcolm makes much of this example because it allegedly provides evidence that we can imagine another 'form of life' that is not 'trivially' conditioned by our own way of seeing things.[8] This sort of case might seem to provide a paradigm case of our stepping 'outside' our own form of life. For, if Malcolm is correct, the narrow notion of pain used by this imaginary tribe is remarkably dissimilar to our own – so much so that he claims their attitude toward pain, 'would *seem* incomprehensible to us' (Malcolm 1982, p. 255; emphasis mine).

The crux of the matter is: What should we make of this talk of *seeming* incomprehensibility? Malcolm's way of coming to terms with it is to draw two sorts of distinction: one between 'description' and 'understanding' and another, paralleling it, between 'language games' and 'world pictures'. He allows that other language games can be compared and that we can 'objectively' describe them while holding that we will fail to understand other world-pictures because these will be incomprehensible to us.

To help see what is at stake here it will be useful to draw some distinctions of our own. To put things in to sharp focus, it helps to see that Malcolm must either be supporting a strong or weak reading of incomprehensibility vis-à-vis the possibility of imagining other forms of life. On a weak reading the claim that another is 'incomprehensible' has the same kind of force as in everyday phrases like 'I can't make sense of you at all' or 'I don't understand you'.[9] We use such language – not when we are completely baffled by another – but when some aspect of what they are doing confuses us. It is only against the background of a general understanding that we could find another's actions odd or puzzling. For, to employ a variant of an oft-quoted Davidsonian moral, too much incomprehensibility will leave us with nothing to be confused about.[10]

Yet, in order to sabotage Williams' reading and make sense of getting 'an outside view', Malcolm must be pushing for something stronger. But the very idea of 'incomprehensible world pictures' that would support such a stronger reading is incoherent. To make this point vividly, we might consider the Wittgenstein-inspired project of Rodney Needham. He hoped to expose the fact that many translators and anthropologists, despite taking care to understand 'alien' cultures, are nevertheless often in this process, too quick to ascribe uncritically their own psychological states to those they interpret. Needham hoped to make us aware of our tendency to use ourselves as models for others, focusing on the nearly universal bias of describing the psychological attitudes of certain exotic peoples in terms of their 'beliefs'.[11] By enjoining us to examine the true history of the concept 'belief', he intended to illustrate graphically why we would be ill-advised to attribute this type of psychological attitude to people who have not shared in the same intellectual history as English-speakers. For instance, he claimed that the Chinese word *hsin* does not easily translate into 'the modern sense of "belief" which the concept came to have under Greek and Latin influences' (Needham 1972, p. 23). The reason for our inability to translate the word, he suggests, is due to the fact that the Chinese concept 'belongs to an autonomous psychology that in some regards appears to frame a *radically* distinct view of human capacities and their relationship to the nature of things' (Needham 1972, p. 37; emphasis mine).

If we take Needham at his word the Chinese operate with a set of 'strongly incomprehensible' psychological concepts. Indeed, it would appear wrong even to describe this difference in this way, given the standard connection between 'beliefs' and 'concepts'. In this light, it is a wonder that Wittgenstein could even have managed to imagine the practices of the tribe with a 'narrow concept of pain'. The point is, we should feel inclined to agree with Root that this kind of incautious, 'rhetorically extravagant' talk of 'radically distinct views' is best seen as hyperbolic (Root 1986, p. 299). For if others are genuinely so radically different that we cannot even describe their 'perspective on things' in any coherent way, then we have designated nothing worth calling a perspective (cf. *PI* §207). As Root nicely puts the moral of Davidson's 'The Very Idea of a Conceptual Scheme': 'One cannot show that a mind is indescribable by proceeding to describe it' (Root 1986, p. 300). If this is right then the very idea of strong incomprehensibility is, indeed, incoherent.[12]

We can now see that Malcolm's critique of Williams is caught on the horns of a dilemma. He can only opt for the strong reading of incomprehensibility at the cost of incoherence. Yet, if he hopes to discredit Williams' interpretation by suggesting that Wittgenstein endorsed the possibility of 'incomprehensible world pictures' in the weak sense (which is what I think he intends), then he won't have done enough to expose the implausibility of that interpretation. For such a view is consistent with Williams' position that the comparisons between ourselves and others in the later works are not really comparisons between different human groups; rather, they are explorations of our one and only set of concepts – even if the boundaries of those concepts are loose-fitting. Namely, on a weak reading of 'incomprehensibility', it is still possible to see the later works as an insider's exploration of 'our' homely concepts, exposing their limits and exploring new possibilities (to avoid confusion we might speak of the limits of concepts, *per se*, and give up the quibbles concerning ownership). On this reading, it turns out that consideration of alien forms of life is just to take up a reflective stance with respect to our own ways of proceeding, but adopting such a stance does not require us (or even allow us) to 'step outside our own form of life': At least, not in any dramatic sense.

Moreover, there is strong evidence that Wittgenstein's position only implies adherence to the weaker view. For example, the 'narrow' concept of pain used by the tribe in *Zettel* can be seen as a deviation or restrictive version of our usual concept of pain (even if it is heading in an 'unusual direction').[13] In the remark that follows the passages referred to by Malcolm, Wittgenstein acknowledges that the imagined deviations cannot be too great. He writes:

> But in that case isn't this man just overlooking something that is there? – He takes no notice of it and why should he? – But in that case his concept just is fundamentally different from ours. – *Fundamentally* different? Different.   (Z, §381; emphasis original)

Ultimately the possibility of different concepts will be predicated on differences in upbringing or in the having of quite different instinctive responses.[14] Thus, we are told:

> I want to say: an education quite different from ours might also be the foundation for quite different concepts.   (Z §387)

For here life would run on differently. – What interests us would not interest them. Here different concepts would no longer be unimaginable. In fact, this is the only way in which essentially different concepts are imaginable.   •   (Z §388)

The problem is not that there is no basis for finding this more moderate reading of Wittgenstein in Malcolm, but rather that if one did adopt this more moderate understanding of incomprehensibility, then one cannot dismiss Williams' reading so easily. Endorsing the weak reading of 'incomprehensible' fails to discredit the plausibility of Williams' proposal for it makes the gap between us and the others too limited to warrant talk of 'an outside view'. If anything, the above considerations serve to highlight a particularly attractive feature of Williams' interpretation. For it, at least, holds out the promise of allowing us to make sense of the reflective activity that is the basis of Wittgenstein's comparisons themselves. Let me stress that if we accept the weak reading, then the stance we can adopt in such cases is at best reflective, never thoroughly 'objective'. Yet if such reflection is possible, it requires a vantage point that encompasses both the foreign and the domestic perspectives. How else, we might ask, is it possible to consider and compare them both? This provokes the further question: Who is in a position to compare 'our' take on things with that of the others? When talking of making 'ourselves' objects of comparison we must always leave the 'synthesising subject' who does the comparing out of the picture. Any attempt to turn that subject into an immediate object of attention lands us in an infinite regress of subjects. This suggest that the very act of comparing different language games with our own requires our having to take up a transcendental perspective – even if it is only temporal in character.

As Lear points out, 'Wittgenstein was of course trying to deny the possibility of a transcendent perspective from which one can view our form of life' (Lear 1986, p. 279). According to Lear, Wittgenstein's evident lack of attention to this topic is one of the main failings of the later works.[15] In fact, he ruefully suggests recognising this very lacuna may have been the reason why Wittgenstein regarded his later work as 'unfinished'.[16] This sets the stage for Lear himself to 'finish' that philosophical project – to develop a more coherent 'transcendental anthropology', one that answers the question: 'How are we to understand reflective philosophical activity when it goes on within a form of life?' (Lear 1986, p. 282).

Alternatively, what seems to be a lack of concern on Wittgenstein's part can also be seen as a natural consequence of his knowing where to stop seeing explanations. In saying this, we might want to help ourselves to what is best about Williams' interpretation and draw a direct parallel with the *Tractatus*. In doing so, we can see the later works as supporting the idea that sometimes when doing philosophy 'we' does not refer to any actual groups of people in the world, but rather denotes the perspective we adopt when taking the reflective stance. Such a 'we' cannot be employed in the 'ordinary sense', hence it resembles the Tractarian 'I' which is used to designate the metaphysical subject – the one that could only be shown but not stated.[17] This frees us from the regress for we can simply accept that, at bottom, the 'subject' that compares cannot, at the same time, be an object of scrutiny or comparison.[18] If we accept this then, *contra* Malcolm, the pronoun 'we' is ambiguous in just the way that Williams' suggests. That is to say, in any given case, it is intelligible to ask: Are we the observers or the observed? The ambiguity arises because coherency demands that, in some sense, we are both.[19] In at least this respect, Williams' interpretation seems to offer a coherent and not implausible way of reading the later writings. I repeat: obviously, reading Wittgenstein by Williams' lights is *one way* of dealing with this apparent tension.

The really important question to ask is, can we accept what is right about it without following its lead with respect to issues of realism and idealism? If we adopt Williams' model, do we have to read Wittgenstein's later works as committed to a linguistic form of transcendental idealism? I think not. To show this I will initially consider the work of Donald Davidson, whose position on these matters, I suggest, fits Williams' interpretation of the later Wittgenstein quite snugly. Only then will I attend to Wittgenstein's own remarks on these matters.

A Davidsonian comparison

If we accept that Williams' interpretation is a plausible way of reading the later Wittgenstein, at least on the aspect just identified, we are still left with the question: Is what we might call the 'transcendental' side of Wittgenstein's philosophy necessarily idealistic in character? The big question, however, is whether or not this attribution is in fact warranted. One way of resisting the idea that it must be is to consider the work of Donald Davidson. For there is a non-trivial resemblance between Davidson's position and Wittgenstein's on all the issues which, according to Williams, add up to make the latter an idealist. For example, we find Davidson endorsing the idea that our language is the best guide to metaphysics,[20] that ultimately our way of seeing things is the only way of seeing things,[21] and that the basis of language cannot itself be explained, since it is a transcendental condition of 'experience' (broadly construed).[22] From this it certainly looks as if Davidson ought to support the kind of 'aggregate idealism' that Williams attributes to Wittgenstein. Therefore, it is interesting to note that although he openly sponsors the trio of tenets that Williams regards as embodying Wittgenstein's idealism, Davidson is a self-styled realist. How can that be?

Davidson has tried to make clear the modesty of his 'realism' in a number of places (see Davidson, 1986a, 1986b, 1990b). His commitment to realism is directly connected to his views on radical interpretation in that he has argued that we learn to interpret others in a social environment on the basis of what is provided to us by the world. It helps if we consider the position of the radical interpreter who has nothing but his observations and principles of charity to go on when interpreting others. As Davidson stresses, in such a situation, 'what can be observed, of course, is speech behaviour in relation to the environment, and from this certain attitudes toward sentences can be fairly directly inferred, just as preferences can be inferred from choices . . . From such acts it is possible to infer that the speaker is *caused by* certain kinds of events to hold a sentence true' (Davidson 1990b, p. 318; emphasis mine).[23]

In light of this remark, it is worth digressing to make clear what role causality plays in the process of interpreting speech acts. This is important because some philosophers may be misled into thinking that an invocation of causality at this juncture is at odds with the overall non-reductive nature of the account. For instance, Evnine thinks that Davidson's invocation of 'causal talk' is at odds with his 'interpretative hermeneutic project [which] goes with an idealist theory of content' (Evnine 1991, p. 175).[24] The worry is that if the triangulation required for interpretation is thought of as a kind of causal nexus, then this surely opens up a necessary gap between what causes my thought and what my thought is about – a split between what is given and how I interpret it.

But the worry that a Davidsonian approach to interpretation will go the way of 'crude causal theories', thereby resuscitating the scheme/content distinction, is unwarranted. It is certainly true that in talking of 'causation' and 'correspondence', Davidson is endorsing the idea that there is an independent world, which in some sense we 'confront'. In this sense, Evnine is right to think that there is a gap between what causes a speaker's utterances and what the speaker means by those utterances. Nevertheless, Davidson holds that, viewed as a divide between a lone subject and the world, such a gap is unintelligible. In order to make sense of it we must realise that the very idea of an objective world that is independent emerges in the course of interpretation. The subject/object split (or scheme/content distinction) only has life in an intersubjective, social context.[25] It is only in such a space that we can employ the normative criteria needed for treating utterances as truth-bearing or not.

Truth, and the notion of an objective world, develop in the process of learning from, and interpreting the utterances of, others. We might say the concepts of truth and objectivity emerge when communicators establish public criteria for the assessment of reports made by others.[26] Moreover, these notions are basic and inexplicable.[27] Or, to put the point in the context of concerns just raised about Davidson's use of 'causation', we must realise that we can only make sense of a 'gap' between the subject and some object as a 'gap' found within the world, within experience.[28] It is during interpretation, by 'triangulating', that we are able to determine what causes another to use their words as they do (and whether they use them correctly or not).[29] We can see, then, that the causes of which Davidson speaks are already incorporated, non-reductively, into the social context of interpretation. But this is not to say they are 'constructed' by society.[30] Therefore, although Davidson speaks of causality, objectivity and correspondence, it is vital to notice that the role these concepts play in his work is nothing like that which they play in traditional correspondence theories of truth and reference which he, himself, calls absurd (Davidson 1986b, p. 307).[31]

Moreover, as the notions of objective truth and error arise only in the context of interpretation and against the background of intersubjective normativity, subjectivity and objectivity emerge together. Davidson's way of expressing this is to say, 'the foundations of knowledge must be subjective and objective at once' (Davidson 1986b, p. 327). We might make use of Heidegger's term here and say they are equiprimordial (Heidegger 1962, s. 43, 200). I take this also to be what Heidegger means when he says, 'the world is disclosed essentially along with the Being of Dasein' (Heidegger 1962, s. 43, 203). The choice of words is important here. Notice Heidegger says the world is 'disclosed' to us and not simply 'constructed' or 'created'. Likewise his student, Gadamer, explicitly adopts a similar line: 'The agreement about things that takes place in language means neither a priority of things nor a priority of the human mind' (Gadamer 1976, p. 78). This is what frees Davidson from idealism. For he too thinks it would be a mistake to think that reality is dependent upon us even though ours are the only standards for interpreting it (cf. Putnam 1987, p. 12).[32]

I hope it is now clear why it would be wrong to tar Davidson with an idealist brush even though he supports the views that Williams attributes to Wittgenstein. This should reveal, at the very least, that it is possible to hold such views without committing oneself to 'idealism' *per se*. In the final section I will consider some of Wittgenstein's remarks – found in both the later writings and the *Tractatus* – which should lead us to doubt that he ever sponsored transcendental idealism.

Wittgenstein exegesis

Wittgenstein and Davidson substantially agree in that they both regard contact with the world and its objects as crucial to the mastery of 'language', even though the former's view of language mastery is less 'intellectualist' than is Davidson's.[33] Whereas Davidson regards coming to recognise the conditions under which another's utterance will be true as being all-important to interpretation, it is clear that Wittgenstein wished to consign the idea of an assertional model of language to his past.[34] Consider this remark:

> Children do not learn that books exist, that armchairs exist, etc. etc.,
> – they learn to fetch books, sit in armchairs, etc., etc.
>   Later questions about the existence of things do of course arise. 'Is there such a thing as a unicorn?' and so on. But such a question is possible only because as a rule no corresponding question presents itself.
>   *(OC*, §476)

Although it may be that Davidson and Wittgenstein have different understandings about precisely how it is that we are related to the world (or perhaps Davidson's encompasses elements of both Wittgenstein's earlier and later selves in this regard), it is quite clear that concerning transcendental realism and idealism, they stand together. Like Davidson, Wittgenstein is continually trying to steer clear of the positions occupied by philosophers of both these camps. He makes this clear in a remark from *The Blue Book* in which he openly says that 'the common-sense man . . . is as far from realism as from idealism' (*BBB*, p. 48).[35] Also, in *Zettel* he remarks:

> One man is a convinced realist, another a convinced idealist and teaches his children accordingly. In such an important matter as the

existence or non-existence of the external world they don't want to teach their children anything wrong.

What will the children be taught? To include in what they say: 'There are physical objects' or the opposite?   (Z, §413).

But the idealist will teach his children the word 'chair' after all, for of course he wants to teach them to do this and that, e.g. to fetch a chair. Then where will be the difference between the idealist–educated children and the realist ones? Won't the difference only be one of battle cry?   (Z, §414; see also *RPP II* §§338–9)

Wittgenstein's point in these passages is that the divide between these two philosophical positions is, practically speaking, uninteresting.[36] Both stances are effectively indistinguishable when we consider them in the realm of the ordinary. He is drawing our attention to the fact that addenda such as 'and there are mind-independent objects' and 'and there are no mind-independent objects' are paradigm examples of how philosophical language idles.[37] It is as if, when enumerating what exists in the world, we start by making an ordinary list of things we find in it; but the philosopher goes on to suppose that it makes sense to put 'reality' on the list as well, as if it were yet another item. But this requires us to make sense of a 'general' notion of 'reality' itself. But, what does this idea really come to?

A reality corresponds to the word 'two' . . . Should we say this? It might mean almost anything.   (*LFM*, p. 248)

What is 'reality'? We think of 'reality' as something we can *point* to. It is *this, that*.   (*LFM*, p. 240)

Arthur Fine also recognises this use of language as a symptom of the diseases of metaphysical realism and idealism. As he says, all 'the realist adds [to a core acceptance of ordinary existence claims] is a desk-thumping, foot-stamping shout of "Really!"' (Fine 1984, p. 97). Likewise, the idealist (or anti-realist) only contributes to 'the core position a particular analysis of the concept of truth' (Fine 1984, p. 97). But, Fine points out, it is possible to take our ordinary claims at face value – without such addenda. He labels this the 'natural ontological attitude' and there is reason to think Wittgenstein exuded it. The point is that to be unimpressed by the posturing of the metaphysical realist is not the same as endorsing, in any ordinary sense, the view that there are 'no mind-independent objects in the world'. It is to hold that talk about mind-independent objects is simply to talk about the familiar items of our quotidian world – such as tables, armchairs, etc. That is why such a position is a piece with the verdicts of common sense even if it is at odds with so-called *common-sense philosophy* of a realist character.

So where does this leave us? How can we make sense of Wittgenstein's blatant dismissal of idealism? How does this square with Williams' interpretation? I think that rather than denying the link between the early and late writings, it forces us to re-examine the allegedly idealistic character of the *Tractatus*. Indeed, I maintain that Williams' key exegetical mistake is *the way* in which he focuses on the idea that the 'limits of language are the limits of the world and that they cannot be staked out from both sides' (cf. Williams 1974, p. 78). Naturally, this way of expressing the view is encouraged by Wittgenstein's talk of 'limits' in the *Tractatus* (cf. *TLP* 4.114, 5.6–5.62, 6.45). It is certainly true that this image of being 'inside' is directly linked with Wittgenstein's vision of reality as a 'limited whole'. But while it is often observed that we cannot even make sense of what lies behind such limits, it is less frequently noted that it also follows that there is also no substance to the idea of being inside them either.[38] The entire metaphor breaks down. Yet I think it is this figurative usage that is responsible for generating the confusion that makes Wittgenstein's position appear to be transcendentally 'idealistic'. Importantly, I think it is no accident that Williams also describes Wittgenstein's later understanding of our place in the scheme of things with reference to this very metaphor. Thus, he freely talks of our 'moving around reflectively *inside* our view of things' (Williams 1974, p. 85; emphasis mine). Even though I have allowed myself to talk in this way at various points in this book, ultimately if we press this metaphor we find it really makes no sense.

It may help to see the confusion it engenders from a slightly different vantage point. In an article concerning Davidson's transcendental arguments, Maker rather nicely sets out the story of philosophical development with respect to the issue of transcendental subjectivity in a way that demonstrates the misuse of the inside/outside metaphor (cf. Maker 1991, pp. 348–52). He begins the tale with the original postulated dichotomy between the realms of the subjective and the objective – that to which we have access and that to which we hope it corresponds. As he points out, the age-old epistemic problem generated by this picture is that nothing we can have subjective access to could ever count as evidence for what is objective. Anything we come in to genuine contact with is by definition subjective, hence cannot provide uncontaminated evidence of an 'objective' standard. This is how the postulation of a truly objective realm serves as a breeding ground for scepticism. At this point, 'transcendental' thinkers come in to save the day – for they attempt to 'get us to rethink the idea that subjectivity can be properly understood as something we are trapped within, forever cut off from an objectivity lying beyond' (Maker 1991, p. 349). Such philosophers reject the very idea of a subject/object split (conceived as being outside of, or prior to, experience) as a myth. The subjective and objective need no 'bridge' to link them since they are not in fact separated in the way the original picture suggests.

It is worth attending to the way Maker describes the second stage in the development of these ideas. He tells us: 'Transcendental thinkers ask us to *interiorize* objectivity' (Maker 1991, p. 349; emphasis mine).[39] Of course, that is the natural way to express the situation if one still has in mind the picture of a subject/object split. From that starting point, it looks as if the proper way to describe transcendental arguments is as trying to force the 'objective' world into the realm of the 'subjective'. But, of course, when we draw this picture clearly it becomes evident that such a description is inappropriate. Having dragged the world fully into the subjective realm we are left with nothing that can any longer be called 'subjective' or 'objective' in the philosophically dramatic sense presupposed by the original picture.[40]

As Maker shows, if we follow out the programme of 'radical subjectivism', it becomes clear that the subjective/objective split cannot be sustained and we also lose the sense that we are somehow 'trapped' within our view of things (Maker 1991, p. 356). As he writes, it is 'a radical or thoroughgoing subjectivism – a subjectivism without limits – that leads to a satisfactory objectivism' (Maker 1991, p. 356). The echoes are unmistakable. I believe that this is the very manoeuvre which Wittgenstein had in mind when speaking of 'following solipsism out strictly'. What I have tried to do is graphically illustrate his claim that 'solipsism, when its implications are followed out strictly, coincides with pure realism' (*TLP* 5.64).[41] Once the subjective (whether in singular or plural) and the objective merge on equal footing, there can be no more sense to be had from the old inside/outside metaphor of our relation to reality.

It helps to see this if we also note that, while it is common to take notice of Wittgenstein's diminishing of the subject by focusing on the solipsistic passages of the *Tractatus* that he also cut the world down to size in precisely the same fashion is equally important but often over-looked. Rée is one of the few authors to draw explicit attention to this issue.[42] For, as he points out, not only is the self not encounterable in experience, the world too is absent when we go looking for it.[43] To use the language of the *Tractatus*, all we ever find are 'facts' that can be pictured in propositions – 'The world is the totality of facts' (*TLP* 1.1). The world shrinks away just as, 'The self of solipsism shrinks to a point without extension and there remains the reality co-ordinated with it' (*TLP* 5.64).

To sum up, in drawing a connection between Wittgenstein's earlier and later self, Williams has failed to grasp how 'radical' Wittgenstein's early project really was with respect to its rejection of philosophical the-orising, including the sort that makes it seem as if we must endorse either realism or idealism. The big change in the later writings is not a dismissal of the Tractarian stance on this, but rather a proper following through on what is required by that stance. In the later material Wittgenstein begins to practise what he had been preaching. The tran-scendental twaddle, which shows itself to be idle, is entirely cut out, not 'mentioned': rejected. As he famously writes:

> When philosophers use a word – 'knowledge', 'being', 'object', 'I', 'proposition', 'name' – and try to grasp the *essence* of the thing, one must always ask oneself: is the word ever actually used in this way in the language-game which is its original home?
> What *we* do is bring words back from their metaphysical to their everyday use'. (*PI* §116)

A major symptom of our going awry philosophically is the free and easy use of such 'super-concepts'. It is simply not possible for us to with-draw from our ordinary use of words – to get outside everyday practices and review them from on high. If we could do this we might be able to debate whether our epistemic and metaphysical situation is idealistic or realistic but there is no place for us to stand in order to have such a debate. If we come to see this, and are thus cured of our philosophical tendency to bump our heads against the limits of language, the unan-swerable question about whether realism or idealism is the right view will cease to plague us.[44] It is this kind of realisation that brings about, 'The real discovery . . . the one that gives philosophy peace, so that it is no longer tormented by questions which bring *itself* in question' (*PI* §133).[45]

Conclusion

The upshot is that once we see the real nature of the continuity in Wittgenstein's approach, it becomes clear that he never sported transcendental idealism, if such 'idealism' must allow for the *possibility* of some radically 'other' or 'outside' take on things. If one denies this, there really is nothing at stake between the realist and the idealist. Importantly, this is not to say we are not always speaking of, and interacting with, 'mind-independent things' that exist in a world that is neither 'composed' by us, nor obedient to our concerns. This is why the claim that the world is 'constructed' by us – that it is our 'product' – is nonsense and why not just anything goes. Once again:

> Our language only works, of course, when a certain agreement prevails, but the concept of agreement does not enter into the language game. . . .   (Z §430)

> Does human agreement decide what is red? Is it decided by appeal to the majority? Were we taught to determine colour in that way?
> (Z §431)

The crucial point is that we can never take the impossible step outside our own form of life – because there is no such place to step. Unless we imagine ourselves in the position of a philosophical God, there is no sense in our sponsoring either metaphysical realism or idealism. In the next and final chapter, I conclude by comparing this way of approaching philosophy with certain contemporary offerings in order to establish some of its positive features and important implications.

6
Description Alone

> Philosophy simply puts everything before us, and neither explains nor deduces anything. – Since everything lies open to view there is nothing to explain. For what is hidden, for example, is of *no interest to us*.
>
> Wittgenstein 1953, §126

Introduction

Many philosophers take exception to Wittgenstein's bold injunction that 'we may not advance any kind of theory. There must not be anything hypothetical in our considerations. We must do away with all explanation, and description alone must take its place' (*PI*, §109). In alarming contrast to the endeavours of most contemporary philosophers we are warned that, 'In philosophy we do not draw conclusions. "But it must be like this!" is not a philosophical proposition' (*PI* §599; cf. *CV*, p. 6e). Philosophers tend to be strongly divided in their views about the worth of this kind of approach. Sometimes it is applauded for its anti-metaphysical virtues, as in Pleasants' remark below:

> Wittgenstein came to relinquish the idea that philosophy could, or should, claim to reveal 'the way things are' . . . I advocate taking entirely seriously the descriptive approach he commends.
>
> (Pleasants 2000, p. 292)

But just as often it is condemned as being nothing short of a betrayal of critical philosophy – a lowering of our sights. In this light, it is seen as the abandonment of a much more creditable and noble end: that of distinguishing appearance from reality, of getting at the true nature of things.

> I cannot see any reason for accepting . . . [Wittgenstein's] belief that philosophy, as such, must never criticize, but only describe.
>
> (Dummett 1993, p. xi)[1]

In the rush to judgement, such praise and condemnation are often issued with little or no attention given to the nature and function of Wittgenstein's descriptions. For example, it is rarely discussed what such descriptions are descriptions of, and why he holds that they alone can achieve his philosophical end or indeed what that end is. These are the important questions that need addressing if we are to understand and properly assess his infamous remark.

Descriptions as reminders

It is often assumed that Wittgenstein is eschewing explanation in favour of an utterly passive description of *the* correct use of our concepts, along the lines advocated by ordinary language philosophers or social anthropologists. Ironically, if this were so, then he would have thought that philosophy had the same end and methods as many traditional philosophers suppose it to have. He would have been pursuing a straightforwardly conservative programme. The thought that he was is no doubt promoted by some of his remarks, such as the following:

> It is not our aim to refine or complete the system of rules for the use of our words in unheard-of ways.   (*PI* §133)

Moreover, it is also encouraged by his slogan: 'Philosophy only states what everyone admits' (*PI* §599; cf. *CV*, p. 6e). Yet, we must not be misled by this claim. For, as the previous chapters make clear, its more precise formulation would be that philosophy only states what everyone would admit, if they were not held captive by a theory or picture. For, as Wittgenstein also reminds us, 'when . . . we have got a picture of our ordinary way of speaking . . . we are tempted to say that our way of speaking does not describe the facts as they really are' (*PI* §402).

To think Wittgenstein's approach is 'uncritical' on these grounds is seriously to misunderstand it. It is just that, rather than directing his criticisms at specific philosophical proposals with an eye to replacing them, he targeted the very tendencies towards explanation that lead us to offer such proposals. His intention was to ward off certain confusions to which we fall prey when we reflect on our ordinary doings. Bearing this in mind is crucial when it comes to thinking about the status of his correctives. There are plenty of cases in which Wittgenstein adopts a 'prescriptive' tone in the course of re-educating us; reminding us of the home of our concepts. For example, he often leads by saying, 'You want to say X', and goes on to probe further, asking, 'But in ordinary cases is the concept ever used like that?' Indeed, he clearly states:

> It is only in the normal cases that the use of a word is clearly prescribed. (*PI* §142)

This sort of remark creates the illusion that he is interested in describing what is stable and, more importantly, *correct*, in our actual use of concepts; something that could serve as a standard.[2] But this idea rests on a mistaken 'picture' of the nature of concepts, according to which we are tempted to imagine the rules governing them as reified, ideal patterns of response. This image is often inspired by popular intellectualist renderings of the doctrines of meaning holism and inferentialism. Recalling the discussions of Chapters 3 and 4, it is evident that Wittgenstein's method could not require a description of '*the*' rules that define the correct use of concepts.[3] Given this, it should be abundantly clear that it cannot be our ordinary rules for the use of concepts that Wittgenstein is trying to make perspicuous when he speaks of getting a clear view of our grammar.

It should also be clear that, along with the rejection of the idea that the normative dimension inherent in our use of concepts can be captured in the form of a statable rule – understood as a kind of interpretation or description – goes any hope that philosophy can discover some kind of fixed essence which determines the correct use of our concepts. This is why, in supplying his reminders, he never puts us in mind of correct rules for using concepts but rather of *normal cases* and circumstances of their use, case by case, by means of examples. That is to say, he describes *situations* in which the words are normally used. This is what gives his approach a critical edge, but it neither involves nor requires specifying the correct rules for the use of each concept. This can make it look as if his aim is to prosecute some kind of empirical investigation (cf. Kindi 1998, p. 298). Yet, although the examples he cites point to contingent features of our actual practices, his method is not empirical – we are being reminded of the grounds for the use of particular concepts and the occasions of their *proper* employment.

For example, he often directs us to consider the circumstances under which we first learned our concepts. One important difference between this sort of case and those involving our mature practices, such as high science, is that initially we learn the norms for the use of our concepts relatively uncritically and without challenge. When we first learn our concepts, no serious doubts about their correct application enter, for if everything were tentative for us, we would never get to a stage where there was anything to doubt. Thus:

> We teach a child 'that is your hand', not 'that is perhaps (or probably) your hand.' That is how a child learns the innumerable language-games that are connected with his hand. An investigation or question, 'whether this is really a hand' never occurs to him. Nor, on the other hand, does he learn that he *knows* that this is his hand.
>
> (*OC* §374)

In this sense, it is quite appropriate to say that Wittgenstein's descriptions are designed to re-educate us. It is with this purpose and target in mind that we should understand his concern with 'description'. These observations ought to be enough to quash the charge that Wittgenstein is a straightforwardly conservative, uncritical thinker. However, in order to demonstrate that his rejection of explanatory approaches to philosophical problems is not simply the product of a negative malaise it is worth considering the prospects of alternative forms of philosophy that attempt just this. By highlighting the problematic features of these, Wittgenstein's recognition that philosophy has certain limits appears in a much more positive and less defensive light.[4] Moreover, such a review reinforces the very aspects of his approach I have just underlined.

Conceptual analysis and essence hunting

The general assumption about what it is to engage in philosophy is very clearly put in the opening lines of Paul Moser's book, *Philosophy after Objectivity*. There he writes:

> Philosophers of all stripes have theories to offer, for better or worse ... Theories in philosophy, whether good or bad, aim to explain something, to answer certain explanation-seeking questions ...

What is being? What is thinking? What is knowledge? What are we?
... Rare is the philosopher with no theory whatever to offer. Such
would be a philosopher without a philosophy ...

(Moser 1993, p. 3)

In fleshing out this idea it is tempting to think that philosophical
explanations must be analogous to those in more ordinary and scientific domains. That is to say, a philosophical theory starts life in the form
of a speculative proposal about what defines some important topic,
taking the form of a conceptual analysis, traditional or otherwise (cf.
Beaney 2000). It is frequently observed that although these proposals
must necessarily be couched in linguistic terms, the very point of
distinguishing 'conceptual' from merely 'linguistic' analysis is meant to
remind us that the philosophical target is always how things *really* stand
with respect to the subject under scrutiny, not just how we happen to
talk about them. Like the early Russell before them, contemporary conceptual analysts are not interested in words, but what lies behind them.
Jackson employs a colourful analogy to make this point. He says, 'When
bounty hunters go searching, they are searching for a person and not a
handbill. But they will not get very far if they fail to attend to the representational properties of the handbill of the wanted person'(Jackson
1998, p. 30; see also p. 33; Miller 2000, p. 234).

However, unlike empirical hypotheses, the testing of a philosophical
theory cannot proceed by ordinary experimental methods. Instead,
philosophical hypotheses must face the tribunal of counter-examples
and testing through thought experiments[5] to establish their credentials.

> When an analysis is proposed, it becomes open to the method of
> counterexample. The analysis of X, to the extent that it is clear, has
> implications for what does and does not fall under the concept. The
> analysis is then tested to see if the things which it implies are X's
> really are and if things which it implies are not X's really are not. If
> one can find a genuine X that the analysis claims isn't or a non-X
> that the analysis claims is, then one has found a counterexample and
> the analysis is refuted. (Miller 2000, p. 245)

In the light of such testing, the original hypothesis is either refined
or abandoned. In this respect, it is thought that the responses we are
inclined to make to possible cases provide the appropriate constraint
for philosophical, as opposed to other kinds of empirical, theorising.

That is to say, analytic philosophers focus on 'agreed intuitions, those shared intersubjectively' in their attempts 'to justify the objectivity of particular intuitions' (Gomila 1991, pp. 85–6). For example, we are told:

> Our dispositions to use or refrain from applying the words which express concepts are the *objective evidence* we have for what those concepts are. Intuitions may be merely subjective manifestations of publicly shared linguistic dispositions.
>
> (Miller 2000, p. 235; emphasis mine)[6]

We can see from this that the methodological plausibility of conceptual analysis depends on our acceptance of the idea that our agreed intuitions can provide the right sort of constraints for the *assessment* of speculative philosophical proposals about the nature of important concepts. That intuitions are used to play this sort of role is borne out not only by rare explicit statements of method on the part of analytical philosophers, but even more revealingly by their actual practice.[7] For example, in tracing the legacy of what he calls 'counter-example philosophy' as passed down from classical to contemporary thinkers, Bishop provides a representative but hardly comprehensive list of its recent practitioners. He writes, 'Consider just a fraction of these: David Lewis on convention (1969) and on causation (1973), Alvin Goldman on knowledge (1967), H. P. Price on meaning (1957), Carl Hempel on explanation (1948), Wesley Salmon on causation (1984) and Hilary Putnam on mental states (1967)' (Bishop 1992, p. 267).

But there are several problems with the idea that conceptual analysis might proceed as suggested above. First of all, concepts are classically thought to be tightly defined in terms of necessary and sufficient conditions and there is reason to think that this view of concepts is still 'held by the overwhelming majority of conceptual analysts' (Brown 1999, p. 36). This makes sense because seeking a decisive result – such as 'the' correct analysis of a given concept – requires there to be some fixed, determinate, hard target. But, as is well known, this account of concepts has been seriously challenged.

The model might best suit concepts deployed in established forms of mathematics in which the use of strict 'definitions' in terms of necessary and sufficient conditions is commonplace, making the concepts in question appear to be near enough immutable. But to think that concepts in general have this sort of clean-cut order is clearly a mistake (see Brandom 2000, pp. 88–9). In the light of these considerations, we should take seriously and respect the different circumstances in which we use our concepts and the purposes for which they are used. Although some concepts may lend themselves to rigorous, tight definition, the majority do not. Outside mathematics, not only do we get by quite well without such strict, determinate contents, it would be hard to see how we could get by if we were saddled with them.[8]

What reason is there to think that philosophically important concepts, such as 'knowledge', 'thought' and 'reality', are tightly defined in this way? The evidence from our failure to provide an agreed analysis of them and the rampant disagreements about their 'essential' features suggests quite the opposite.[9] With clear Wittgensteinian overtones Brown reminds us of a different understanding of concepts: 'members of a conceptual community often have concepts that are related to each other only by a family resemblance – which may occur among intensions and extensions. These family resemblances, not a set of identical concepts, bind the community together' (Brown 1999, p. 43). Moreover, as he notes, this leaves open the possibility that disagreements in our intuitions about the correct definition of such central concepts are likely to emerge because, in considering possible scenarios, one begins to imagine a vast range of different circumstances in which our concepts may be legitimately used. A single concept may have many different uses, which is something to which the classical account of the nature of concepts is insensitive. Putting the moral slightly differently, Brown holds that in many cases conceptual analysts 'are not attempting to analyze the same concept' (Brown 1999, p. 56). Of course, if one accepts this basic line of reply, then debating whether a concept is the 'same' or not is ultimately a practical matter. I will say more about this below.

This alerts us to a very serious concern about the project of conceptual analysis: the claim that it is conducted on objective grounds. For we may wonder how our intuitions are meant to provide an independent check on philosophical speculation. Is this idea really plausible? For example, consider a parallel worry about using proofs and arguments to settle issues of substantial philosophical concern objectively.[10] Proofs are meant, *par excellence*, to provide 'arguments independent of the prejudices or the goodwill of the audience' (Feyerabend 1999, p. 51).[11] But how can they achieve this given that the acceptance of a conclusion depends on our current conceptual commitments as revealed by our evaluation of the facts. Feyerabend illustrates the general problem by considering Parmenides' argument for a monistic account of Being and its later rejection by Democritus and Aristotle. In both instances, the success of the proof and its putative refutation were built into the reception of the premises that supposedly enable us to draw our final conclusion. In this case, the success of these arguments was dependent on the understanding the proponents had of the 'reality' of change. In both cases, whether these conceptions were *taken* as established fact or not was decisive. In devising his proof, Parmenides was aware of the common view that things change, even though he denied it (his first premise), whereas Aristotle bases his counter-argument on accepting it.[12] We can see from this that the success of proofs involves making practical decisions; it is never the result of purely objective processes. Consequently, what constitutes a proper counter-example depends on our normative assessment of what we are willing to accept as such. This being so, logical reconstructions of our reasoning at best provide a means of articulating or making explicit our commitments; they do not have the power to settle disputes with any objective authority. *Contra* their advertised properties, logical arguments cannot decide things for us on their own; like any other mode of persuasion, whether we ultimately accept or reject an argument's conclusion depends on our evaluation of it. But such evaluations cannot be based on any kind of *independent* check, which is precisely what makes doing serious philosophy so difficult. Miller sums up the overarching hope and underlying problem neatly in the following passage:

> One of the attractions of the old method of analysis was that it gave philosophers the impression that they could decisively refute some philosophical hypotheses and that, to this extent at least, philosophy could become progressive instead of endlessly debating the same issues without resolution . . . Looking for counterexamples is something every philosopher knows how to do and it provides the comforting illusion that one's opponent has really been refuted. But the illusion evaporates when one takes a sufficiently broad perspective on the controversies as they really unfold. Whether something is really an *X*, as opposed to being an *X* according to the proposed analysis, is determinable solely by appeal to intuition. And the flimsiness and variability of those intuitions come to light as soon as there is any serious controversy over any weighty philosophical issues.   (Miller 2000, p. 245)

With this in mind, Feyerabend proposes that we reverse our standard conception of the genesis of argument, for 'it was not the argument that produced the conclusion . . . but the conclusion . . . [that] produced the argument' (Feyerabend 1999, p. 75).

This should make us suspicious of the idea that there could be an identifiable independent standard against which to assess the correctness of any given analysis. But without such a standard, there is no independent acid test for determining whether or not an analysis is correct. In what sense is it right to think of such analyses as a kind of theorising? In what sense could they potentially yield explanations? At best, it seems the products of traditional forms of conceptual analysis are descriptive, as opposed to genuinely explanatory. This is, of course, ironic in the light of the standard objection that Wittgenstein's approach lacks ambition.

We can see the seriousness of this problem by asking which intuitions are meant to provide the standard against which we can evaluate our analysis of concepts. Without some established criteria for this we run the risk that if it should turn out that there is no general agreement, this would 'suggest that concepts are idiosyncratic and that conceptual analysis is a form of autobiography' (Brown 1999, p. 34). Jackson is prepared to court controversy on this front, treating the matter as an entirely empirical issue.[13] He sums up the point of conceptual analysis in the following way: 'What we are seeking to address is whether [something] *according to our ordinary conception*, or something suitably close to our ordinary conception, exists' (Jackson 1998, p. 31). Usefully, he goes on to ask: 'But how should we identify our ordinary conception? The only possible answer, I think, is by appeal to what seems most obvious and central [about the concept in question], as revealed by our intuitions about possible cases' (Jackson 1998, p. 31). Thus he says, 'My intuitions about possible cases reveal my theory . . . Likewise, your intuitions reveal your theory. To the extent our intuitions coincide with those of the folk, they reveal *the* folk theory' (Jackson 1998, p. 32). Our agreed ordinary conception takes on the status of a folk theory of the subject matter in question. In seeking to characterise our common conception it is not necessary to accept any and all responses as equally valid. For example, a person's first thoughts on a topic may be poorly developed and misleading. Still, it is possible that the intuitions of some will be at odds with those of others, even after careful reflection and debate. Jackson is happy to admit this. Yet he maintains, that it is the *typical* or common responses to possible cases, refined and tutored, that we ought to take seriously as defining 'our' ordinary conception.[14] Of course, his hope and expectation is that our intuitions will not turn out generally to be at odds. Indeed, what makes identifying the 'ordinary' conception so easy is that 'often we know that our case is typical and so can generalize from it to others' (Jackson 1998, p. 37). Even though it is unlikely that everyone's intuitions on a given topic will agree, Jackson can be sanguine about his prediction in the light of the fact that general agreement will be ensured by systematic training and teaching. No doubt this is what allows us easily to identify aberrant responses, much as our teachers identify illegal moves in the application of concepts. At least, this is so in uncontroversial cases.

Nevertheless, as the concepts in question are not straightforward, it is easy to put pressure on the idea that 'all members of a conceptual community must share a set of concepts', or in Jackson's terms, that, for most concepts, there is *a* defining folk theory or *an* agreed ordinary conception. Why should we believe that such a singular conception exists, even at the quotidian level? In line with the idea that concepts are best understood in terms of family resemblance, and therefore across contexts of use, it may be questioned whether it makes sense to talk, without qualification, of 'a' conceptual community at all (see Brown 1999, p. 45). For example, in some contexts concepts that we might intuitively identify as being the 'same' can turn out to have distinct *uses*. If this is right, 'conceptual communities' will turn out to be nothing but a collection of individuals with common interests, projects and practices. This raises the question: what do we think we are analysing? Is it *the* concept of X or *our* concept of X? And, if the latter, whom does the pronoun 'our' denote? It follows that there will not be clean definitions of most concepts – even our most central ones – as long as, we use 'our' with wide enough scope to refer to 'all of humanity' (Brown 1999, p. 55). Indeed, this is the likely explanation for widespread disagreement about and divergent analyses of important philosophical concepts (cf. Miller 2000, pp. 235–6).

Serious concerns can also be raised not only about the truth of the claim that there are shared ordinary conceptions, but also its peculiar status in the analytic literature. For example, Brown asks why it should be upheld in the light of the major and perpetual disagreements amongst philosophers concerning the correct analysis of important concepts. Interestingly, he notes, 'the usual response is to maintain [the existence of a shared conception] and conclude that the fault lies with individual conceptual analysts so that, at best, all but one of those who disagree must have gotten the analysis *wrong*' (Brown 1999, p. 39; emphasis mine).[15]

At this point, we must ask afresh: In difficult cases such as these, whose intuitions about possible cases are to be privileged in assessing whether an analysis is correct or not? Considering this question may lead us to question the conservative idea that it is philosophy's job to uncover and articulate our 'ordinary conceptions' on important topics. Even imagining we could identify such a thing, why should it provide the appropriate measure for our thinking about such topics?[16] This is especially pertinent since, if Wittgenstein is right, we have a pervasive tendency to find misleading pictures of our use of concepts intuitively appealing. But surely the task of philosophy is to determine what *the* right understanding of our important concepts is, not what we happen to think it is. To borrow Jackson's idiom, we can ask: If philosophy is simply theorising, why should we expect our 'folk theory' about a given topic to be our 'best theory'? As Brown observes, 'there are many concepts of interest to philosophers and associated with words widely used in ordinary talk, but for which we should have little concern with their everyday versions' (Brown 1999, p. 51). Indeed, at least some 'everyday concepts should be replaced for philosophical purposes' (Brown 1999, p. 51).

This throws up yet another problem, the fact that even our everyday concepts tend to evolve over time. This connects with another of Feyerabend's reasons for being cautious of proofs. He complains that they promote a kind of 'simplification' for to function properly they require 'stable and unambiguous concepts' (Feyerabend 1999, p. 57). Making concepts stable and unambiguous is costly – it requires that they have the stillness of death. Feyerabend puts the point beautifully by remarking that 'Clarity is . . . a property of corpses' (Feyerabend 1999, p. 78). As he notes our concepts are 'well defined only when the culture fossilises' (Feyerabend 1999, p. 79). Hence, there is a problem with the very idea of conceptual analysis even if we overlook the fact that it is not in tune with the existence of many different *current* uses of what might be counted at the 'same' concept. Apart from underestimating the importance of this synchronic diversity, it is also out of synch with the fact that, unless we have reached the end of inquiry, our concepts are subject to diachronic development.

Thus, even if for the sake of argument we were to accept Jackson's claim that 'our' ordinary conception can defined by the 'typical' set of intuitions of most people, statistically determined, and that it provides the 'right' target for our analyses, this would at best define a universal standard for a correct analysis of a concept *at a given time*. This is serious, since one of the main attractions of conceptual analysis is that it promises to reveal something of *lasting* importance about the topics it scrutinises – at the very least, even if it fails to *explain* our concepts, it is thought that it might still be a means of discovering their essential nature. But the promise that it might is predicated on the assumption that the concepts to be analysed are not in a continuous state of flux.[17]

Concepts, even important ones, are not immutable. Rather, they are tied to our practices, which are open to potential change and development. Recognising that they are generally on the move puts paid to the idea that there are eternal standards against which to judge the adequacy or success of any proposals about the correct philosophical elucidation of our concepts. If concepts are continually subject to change, how can investigating them enable us to understand the 'essential' features of their extensions? If this is right, it turns out that to think conceptual analysis can proceed in anything like the *traditional* way described above is an illusion. Moreover, even if it could, it raises the question: If there is no fixed, final characterisation for most concepts – if they differ according to particular human groups – what is the point of explicating them? For what purposes would we seek to engage in this kind of descriptive inquiry? If our concepts are open to development and are not underwritten by what is 'eternal, unchanging', it follows that our philosophical conclusions on any substantial matter will not be final. There is no point in trying to decide, once and for all, what is or is not 'possible' in advance or from on high. We can see from this that the source of the problem with traditional approaches to conceptual analysis is not just endorsement of the idea that the main purpose of philosophy is to investigate what is 'essential' about phenomena, but also holding that this would yield some final, fixed result.

However, once we are freed from the illusion of stability, another activity for philosophers suggests itself. That is the development and refinement of our concepts and even development of alternative concepts, as opposed to the mere description of existing ones. The thought is that our concern should be with the 'development and clarification of concepts that are in accord with overall scientific and philosophical aims' (Brown 1999, p. 49). This move has found favour with a number of recent authors. Thus, praising Sellars, Brown widens the scope of the former's motto to read: 'Philosophers have hitherto sought to understand "meanings": the task is to change them' (Brown 1999, p. 55).[18] Nor is Brown alone in adopting it. For example, we are told:

> Analytic philosophy is finished. Philosophy, I hope, is not. The discipline as I see it has a glorious and successful past and much to contribute to *human progress* in the future. The future does not lie in naturalism. Philosophy should respect science, but it should not attempt to be science.
>
> (Miller 2000, p. 249; emphasis mine)

From analysis to revision

Brandom carefully distinguishes the 'explication of concepts' – from the analysis of meanings, seeing only the former as the proper task of philosophy. As he regards it, the most important difference, is that, 'where the analysis of meaning is a fundamentally *conservative* enterprise (consider the paradox of analysis), I see the point of explicating concepts to be opening them up to rational *criticism*' (Brandom 2000, p. 77).

Even though the making of our commitments and entitlements explicit necessarily involves an important degree of idealisation, Brandom rejects intellectualist renderings of this activity in favour of a pragmatic one, despite his open endorsement of a version of conceptual role semantics. In line with the discussion of Chapter 4, he regards the explication of our concepts as getting clear about our *practical* commitments and entitlements. As these are generally unnoticed and unarticulated they have a subterranean influence on us, which needs to be brought into the light: these must be examined, challenged and replaced or removed, if necessary.[19] Philosophers need not regard themselves as simply uncovering what is 'already there' or as questing after 'essences'. Rather, they are playing a primarily revisionary role in developing our ideas and practices. Explicating our underlying commitments and entitlements would then be like erecting signposts for practical and rational scrutiny. These would prepare the way for the review and potential revision of our concepts, by showing one clearly what is in fact entailed by certain ideas. Here philosophers behave not as final arbiters. They simply prepare the ground for this kind of practical activity. In this, work in philosophy provides the basis for, and the means of, critical reflection. It is only by understanding current commitments and entitlements properly that one can rationally *argue* for change. At the very least, the process provides a platform and spur for the development of new habits.

Consideration of Brandom's approach takes us full circle as it attempts to restore something like the Hegelian focus on dynamic conceptual development – *sans* the Absolute Idea, *sans* an attachment to subject-predicate logic.[20] The role of philosophy will be to make explicit the possibilities in our concepts/world, hence to stake out their consequences. As with Hegel's dialectic, logic – although now conceived differently – is seen as playing a central role: one that gives philosophy a privileged place in the development of concepts. It paves the way for the rational assessment of our conceptual entitlements and commitments, enabling them to be clearly expressed and rendered explicit, eventually enabling us to rid ourselves of inadequate or defective concepts that infect our thinking. Thus, Brandom also tells us:

> Logic is the organ of semantic self-consciousness. It brings into the light of day the practical attitudes that determine the conceptual contents members of a linguistic community are able to express – putting them in the form of explicit claims, which can be debated, for which reasons can be given and alternatives proposed and assessed. The formation of concepts – by means of which practitioners can come to be aware of anything at all – comes itself to be something of which those who can deploy logical vocabulary can be aware.
>
> (Brandom 1994, pp. xix–xx)

To treat this project as Hegelian puts it as odds with those that regard Hegel's ambition for absolute knowing as an attempt on behalf of the subject to give a true *description* of itself. For example, it is with this latter reading in mind that Bowie makes sense of Heidegger's rejection of Hegelian idealism. He writes: 'The point of *both* the idealist *and* the materialist views for Heidegger is that they assume a final, articulable ground, either in the self-certainty of the subject, or in a physicalist reduction of that subject to its material ground' (Bowie 1999, p. 362). But Hegel need not be read as committed to the existence of an Absolute Idea. According to Houlgate's modest reading, self-determination is a quest for absolute knowing which is a form of self-knowledge that emerges through our *activity*. This understanding is made compelling if we recognise that concepts, for Hegel, are not to be identified with determinate, reified patterns. Nor is it necessary that we have a complete grasp of what concepts entail in order to explore them rationally, for that is something we are seeking to discover. Self-determination on this reading is something like the gentle unfolding of our possibilities of being, an expression of our freedom. In this respect, it can look very like Wittgenstein's explanation of forms of life.[21]

Nevertheless, on either reading, it would seem a defining feature of both Hegelianism and neo-Hegelianism that philosophical progress is an ambition. By these lights, philosophy's task remains rationalistic and progressive. Hence Brandom's claim that:

> *Making* the tradition rational is not independent of the labour of concretely *taking* it to be so. To be adequate, each such Whiggish rewrit-

ing of our disciplinary history *must* create and display *continuity and progress* by its systematic inclusions and exclusions.

(Brandom 2000, p. 76; third and fourth emphases mine)

The idea that philosophy is primarily about the rational revision and development of our concepts has been growing in popularity. Thus, it has become common to think its aim is the 'construction of *better* concepts' (Brown 1999, p. 57; emphasis mine). Or to be told that 'Philosophers should propose new concepts and evaluate them solely in terms of their utility ... Utility trumps intuition' (Miller 2000, p. 240). Yet, what assurance is there that such developments are 'better' or 'more useful'? On what basis is this judged? Shorn of an ambitious understanding of something that might play the role of absolute knowledge, can we make intelligible talk of progress and betterment? In the absence of some independent standard, what do such assessments actually come to? How is it to be decided that our concepts are rationally improving?

For example, Bishop rightly notes that, if there are 'no rules' about 'which revision is more successful than another', the very idea of conceptual progress is brought into disrepute. Despite this he interestingly rejects the thought that philosophy should provide empirical theories, maintaining it should provide non-empirical ones instead. In so doing, 'theory-choice should be governed by the same sorts of normative principles as are empirical theories' (Bishop 1992, p. 273). But if, as argued above, appeal to thought experiments, argument and intuitions does not adequately constrain such theorising, then there is no anchor for such 'theorising' that parallels the role experiment plays in the empirical sciences. Hence, if we want to continue to speak, in good faith, of philosophical progress, we must identify some other, more credible constraints on the development of our concepts.

The rise of scientific naturalism

Given these concerns, it is hardly surprising that naturalism has emerged as *the* dominant form of philosophy, favoured by the inheritors of the analytic tradition. In awarding 'the results of empirical science the centrality formerly enjoyed by intuitions', it promises to supply real constraints on conceptual development, which permit us to talk of progress (Miller 2000, p. 231; cf. also p. 233). Unlike those who see philosophy as providing a privileged vantage and means to get at 'real essences', naturalists agree that there is no perspective 'other' than that provided by language from which to view matters. Any distinctions must be drawn and justified *within* our existing and developing practices. Philosophers, who crave an independent measure by which to judge, once and for all, the worth of their explanations, crave the impossible.

Nevertheless, like revisionist philosophers, naturalists believe that concepts and practices are always on the move, having the potential for improvement. But unlike other revisionists, they hope to provide a firm assurance that such developments are in fact progressive. They hold, above all else, that the methods of the science are the best and most rigorous that we have. It is thus a short step from dismissing the idea of higher philosophical perspective to the acceptance that there is no perspective higher than that provided by science. This is what opens the way for a very ambitious naturalism, according to which science is seen as having a privileged place in ensuring all genuine conceptual development. It is our highest court of appeal on such matters. Amidst all *our* activities, it is first among equals. Russell captured this mood long ago:

> This brings me, however, to a question of method which I believe to be very important. What are we to take as data in philosophy? What shall we regard as having the greatest likelihood of being true, and what as proper to be rejected if it conflicts with other evidence? It seems to me that science has a much greater likelihood of being true in the main that any philosophy hitherto advanced (I do not, of course, except my own) . . . We shall be wise to build our philosophy upon science.   (*LA*, p. 339)

Such too is the creed of today's scientific naturalists. Quine made this approach attractive when he revealed the analytic/synthetic distinction to be bankrupt. We can see the methodological implications of his famous move in the following claim:

> If there is no proper distinction between analytic and synthetic, then no basis at all remains for the contrast which Carnap urges between ontological statements and empirical statements of existence. Ontological questions then end up on a par with questions of natural science.   (Quine, 1966, p. 211)

With the collapse of this distinction, everything becomes an empirical matter to be decided by appeal to our best theories. Everything is open to revision, including 'logic' itself. Still, should one discover a contradiction in one's thinking, the right first move would be to alter one or other background commitments and not to challenge the law of non-contradiction. Although for Quine this more radical move is always in some sense possible, abandoning such a central plank would result in the collapse of nearly all our practices – certainly our linguistic ones.

Quinean holism ensures that there is always a way out if one's presuppositions or assumptions lead to nonsense: to surrender these background tenets or certain others. This can often be achieved by changing associated concepts. On this view, it is always possible to make such adjustments. It is common for its supporters to charge Wittgenstein with ignoring the prospect that scientific and philosophical progress might go hand in hand. It is often thought that an obstinate and unwarranted anti-theoretical attitude caused him to overlook this possibility for the refinement and improvement of our categories.[22]

'Wittgenstein speaks of the resolution (or dissolution) of a philosophical puzzle as one in which the puzzle "completely" disappears; and leads to the "vanishing of the problem". This is just what conceptual change produces' (Klagge 1989, p. 324). In saying this, Klagge distinguishes what he calls 'scientific' and 'conceptual' resolutions to philosophical problems. An example of a scientific resolution would be a naturalistic 'straight solution' to the rule-following paradox, in that if viable it would meet the particular demand by supplying the appropriate facts. Klagge is prepared to agree with Wittgenstein that in many cases a scientific solution to a philosophical problem will not be forthcoming. But this still leaves open the possibility that we might dissolve philosophical problems by revising our conceptual criteria or by replacing troublesome concepts in the process of developing our scientific theories. As he puts it, 'Science not only discovers new facts, but in doing so . . . it can affect old concepts. Science can be relevant to the resolution of philosophical perplexities by provoking a conceptual resolution of them' (Klagge 1989, p. 325).[23]

This being so, why shouldn't philosophy simply proceed after the fashion of science? Put simply, if we are open to the possibility of radical change in our scientific conceptions, then why should we also think that philosophy can deal with its troubles in this way? That is: when faced with paradox, why shouldn't philosophical problems be 'resolved' by revisionary methods? Why shouldn't philosophy be concerned with this sort of positive, systematic and progressive development of our concepts?

After all, philosophers have helped to clarify issues by drawing unseen distinctions.[24] To point to just a few cases, consider the way in which Spinoza's conflation of reason and cause and Locke's conflation of ideas and concepts have been challenged. Offering such critiques is typical of philosophical practice, but in doing so is one not contributing to the development of concepts and theories? Moreover, why shouldn't philosophy help to bridge gaps between different disciplines by introducing fertile metaphors, as is often the case in science (see Hutto 2000, ch. 7). For, apart from playing a vital role in oiling the learning of new concepts, sometimes these are *created* and old ones developed and extended by means of analogy.[25] On what grounds should we deny that philosophers have sometimes contributed mightily to the development of concepts in just these ways? The removing of conceptual confusions would be like the clearing of rubble before exploring new ground. Thus revising our concepts can be seen in the service of this higher end. Why shouldn't philosophers regard themselves in Lockean terms as those for whom it is 'ambition enough to be employed as an under-labourer in clearing the ground a little, and removing some of the rubbish that lies in the way of human knowledge' (Locke, *Epistle to the Reader*). I don't think Wittgenstein would deny this, so long as the scope of this claim were limited. But naturalists make a much stronger claim, which Papineau sets out clearly below:

> Traditionalists will allow, of course, that some philosophical problems, problems in applied philosophy, as it were [can be solved by the uncovering of further empirical evidence]. But they will insist that when we turn to 'first philosophy', to the investigation of such fundamental categories of thought and knowledge, then philosophy must proceed independently of science.
>
> Naturalists will respond that there is no reason to place even first philosophy outside science. They will point out that even the investigation of basic topics like thought and knowledge needs to start somewhere, with some assumptions about the nature of the human mind and its relation to the rest of reality. Without any assumptions to work from, investigation would be paralysed. And the obvious strategy, naturalists will argue, is to begin with our empirically best-attested theories of mind and its relation to reality, and use these as a framework within which to raise and resolve philosophical difficulties . . .   (Papineau 1993, p. 3)

At first blush, this may make it appear as if we have a simple *choice*: either describe without explanation or refine our concepts through reduction and revision, incorporating them within a broader explanatory scheme. Why doesn't Wittgenstein regard the latter as a legitimate task for philosophy? Certainly he does not deny the possibility of useful and radical shifts in our conceptions. For example, he writes:

> What a Copernicus or a Darwin really achieved was not the discovery of a true theory but of a fertile new point of view.
>
> (*C&V*, p. 18e)

Indeed, he is known for claiming that our concepts have a rich play in them, as he states in numerous places:

> The extension of the concept is not closed by a frontier . . . For how is the concept of a game bounded? . . . Can you give the boundary?
>
> (*PI* §68)

> When language games change, then there is a change in concepts, and with the concepts the meanings of words change.   (*OC* §65)

Moreover, at times, his remarks about the ultimate limits of what is possible in this regard sound quite Quinean. Consider Quine's remarks about the limits of theory choice:

> We hope to *choose* in such a way as to optimize future progress. If one of the sentences is purely mathematical we will not *choose* to revoke it; such a move would reverberate excessively through the rest of science. We are restrained by a maxim of minimum mutilation . . . I make no deeper sense of necessity anywhere. Metaphysical necessity has no place in my naturalistic view of things, and analyticity hasn't much.   (Quine 1991, pp. 269–70, emphases mine)

Wittgenstein appears to join him in rejecting a 'metaphysical' understanding of necessity. He says such things as:

> Do not say 'one cannot', but say instead: 'it doesn't exist in this game'.
>
> (*Z* §134)

> For there is also something like *another* arithmetic. I believe this admission must underlie any understanding of logic.   (*OC* §375)

This can make it appear as if Wittgenstein ought to agree that there are no secure bounds that constrain how our concepts might change. Yet since, unlike Quine, he does not appeal to anything like scientific method to ensure that such developments progress steadily, we might wonder how Wittgenstein protects against the prospect that 'anything goes'. As Klagge says, 'From what Wittgenstein says, it sounds as though changes of criteria are more or less immediately possible, so that *we may choose* which phenomena are to count as criteria' (Klagge 1989, p. 322; emphasis mine). We can see from the emphasis on 'choice', in both Quine's and Klagge's remarks, that the question that really troubles naturalists is: What, if anything, ensures that concepts simply do not shift randomly and without direction, as a matter of whimsy? But despite such accusations, Wittgenstein is very much alive to this concern, only he gives a different answer:

> 'So does it depend wholly on our grammar what will be called (logically) possible and what not – i.e. what that grammar permits?' – But surely this is arbitrary! – It is not every sentence-like formation that we know how to do something with, *not every technique has an application in our life.*   (*PI* §520, emphasis mine)

> But how can I decide what is an essential, and what an inessential, accidental, feature of the notion? Is there some reality lying behind the notion, which shapes its grammar?   (*PI* §562)

He illustrates the importance of attending to the *purpose* of our activities by discussing how we might decide what defines the role of a playing piece in a simple game. For here is a clear case in which we cannot understand this by simply attending to the rules that determine which moves are legal and illegal. As he says, 'So I am inclined to distinguish between the essential and the inessential in a game too. The game, one would like to say, has not only rules but also a *point*' (*PI* §564; emphasis original). It is by attending to this that we understand what is essential to it, not because we have divined something metaphysical but because we understand the purpose of the rules we use. As he remarks, 'But after all, the game is supposed to be defined by the rules! So, if a rule of the game prescribes that the kings are to be used for drawing lots before a game of chess, then that is an essential part of the game. What objection might one make to this? That one does not see the point of this prescription' (*PI* §567). Similarly, by focusing on the purpose for which we use our concepts, as opposed to the rules that might define them, we can be confident that they will not develop arbitrarily, even if they are not constrained by purely 'rational' or 'scientific' methods.

In emphasising the role certain applications have in our lives, Wittgenstein is focusing on what is fundamental in what we do. Here again, we are reminded that our form of life informs our activities, lending purpose to them. But given that 'form of life' is not a substantive notion, as argued in chapter 3, it cannot dictate. This does not mean that there are no limits – only that a certain, rigid picture of what defines them – his own early *picture* of 'logical necessity' which was tied to his understanding of the nature of the proposition – is not legitimate. It is not that there is no logic; it is just that we cannot describe its bounds independently of what we do. Not being substantive, *it* is not subject to change. He writes: 'And everything descriptive of a language-game is part of logic' (*OC* §56). In this way, Wittgenstein is able to acknowledge *possibilities* that are in some way both necessary and contingent, without advancing a metaphysics.

Wittgenstein acknowledges a teleological aspect to 'what we do' that, not being part of our concepts, remains constant and that shows itself through our activities. We will only be able to make sense of conceptual change if we focus on the underlying point of our various activities and not merely 'rules' alone. For example, consider again the important use of analogies and the role they play in the explanation and extension of our concepts. Feyerabend uses Achilles' rejection of the Homeric conception of honour in order to illustrate just this. The situation is that Achilles has withdrawn from the war against the Trojans because he is dissatisfied with the part played by Agamemnon in the battle. Messengers have been sent offering appropriate recompense to restore honour and repair the situation. Yet, Achilles' rejects it and in his anger formulates the idea that honour and its trappings are necessarily separate, a thought apparently, as yet, unthinkable to his contemporaries.[26] The question is: Has Achilles simply begun to spout nonsense? No. For, guided by analogies relating to their current understanding, his audience can be drawn into his way of seeing things and might join him in a new understanding of honour and virtue.[27] Indeed, over time, this was how new ideas on these topics began to take root even though they were not initially as well defined as their predecessors.[28] Has an old concept been replaced or just developed? I agree with Wittgenstein in thinking that it is a practical question, not a philosophical one, whether or not a concept has changed (cf. *LWPP I*, pp. 873 ff, 930).[29]

Ambiguities and possibilities for change are always present in our language and practices, since they draw on the abundance the world avails us. This way of regarding matters enables us to make sense of Achilles' new observations about honour, such that in exploring them we do not find that he has fallen into talking nonsense. To hold that he must have is an artefact of focusing too much on 'stable' periods of discourse as opposed to 'periods of change'. Feyerabend is absolutely right that 'Speaking a language or explaining a situation, after all, means both *following* rules and *changing* them' (Feyerabend 1999, p. 125; emphases original). Many things can motivate such change, none of which is simply the result of purely intellectual developments. As we have seen, anger can play its part, but there are other motivating factors, such as forgetfulness and boredom.

To accommodate the possibility of conceptual development as opposed to replacement, we must surrender the inferentialist idea that concepts are defined along a single axis.[30] Put otherwise, we must surrender the idea that, at least in theory, they can be captured in very tight enclosures with pre-set boundaries established by the full set of their appropriate conceptual liaisons, such that any use that takes them outside of these boundaries results in a loss of sense or a change of meaning. Again, we are put in mind of the importance of attending to the point of our practices. Wittgenstein reminds us:

> Grammar does not tell us how language must be constructed in order *to fulfil its purpose*, in order to have such-and-such an effect on human beings.   (*PI* §496; emphasis mine)

In this light we may doubt the claim that the sciences, individually or collectively, operate with a special method or methods that would afford them pride of place with respect to *all* forms of conceptual change. Although proofs in logic and mathematics are useful, why should we accept that, because certain methods are successful for a limited range of purposes, they can apply equally well in all domains? Without a satisfactory answer to this question it is an arbitrary choice to elevate the sciences above all other domains. There can be no grand philosophical justification for deferring to the 'sciences' on all such matters, as naturalists admit. Yet some think to justify this type of approach by claiming that there will be a future, coherent absorption of all legitimate disciplines into a single, unified science, through the painstaking process of conceptual revision and theoretical reduction. At best this is a hope, and a dim one: It is not an argument for naturalism. For although in some domains, such streamlining reductions have occurred, there are many cases in which the divergent methods in sciences cast doubt on the idea of a future unified science (see Hutto 2000, chs. 6 and 7).

Nor can such deference be justified by pointing to the fact that the sciences reliably produce what are deemed to be 'successful' results in their specific domains. For, in the absence of philosophical justification, this could be said of *any* practice that reliably produces results that we find agreeable. It is only by appealing to our needs and what we find acceptable that we can safely ignore the sensitive issue of how, at any given stage, we can legitimately talk of scientific 'progress' as opposed to 'mere change'. What is the criterion of adequacy or success in the scientific development of concepts? How do we know if an analogy is fertile and appropriate as opposed to misguided? Without appeal to our background needs, talk of aligning our concepts so as to achieve a *'best'* fit with our other theories or appeal to 'inference to the *best* explanation' is vacuous.

Clearly, Wittgenstein did not always think it a mistake to seek explanations or to use analogies. Indeed, he is forever drawing our attention to analogies with 'samples', measuring rods and signposts in his later work (cf. Goldfarb 1997, p. 81). But he makes us ask: Why should we think *this* is a legitimate extension – or an appropriate use of analogy? How can we tell when it is appropriate to extend a concept by analogy – when is this successful or not? In exactly which respects does the analogy work and in which not? Not every analogy is fertile and development is not always possible or needed in every case. Sometimes analogies mislead, inspiring nothing but nonsense and confusion.[31] Once we forgo the dream of a unified science and come to realise that our more homely needs are what should drive conceptual development wherever it occurs, it becomes clear that in many cases, *contra* the expectations of revisionists, there is no genuine need to develop or revise our existing concepts. As Wittgenstein remarks:

Why don't we form a simpler concept? – Because it wouldn't interest us. – But what does that mean? Is it the correct answer?

Should I say: Our concepts are determined by our interest, and therefore by our way of living? (*LWPP* II § §43–4e)

Although it is true that many concepts do not *need* to change, there is an even stronger reply to be made with respect to the philosophical topics of Wittgenstein's concern, those that tend to generate philosophical confusions. With respect to such matters, there is no possibility of conceptual revision because they cannot be fully conceptually framed. Here there is no question of revision. With respect to the most fundamental issues, those of meaning, mind and logic, the very issues that Papineau identifies as live targets for naturalist treatment, change is not an option. To change our 'minds' or our 'logic' would not be merely a conceptual alteration, not even one with many drastic ramifications; it would be nothing short of a complete change of our form of life. Hence, Wittgenstein holds:

> Sometimes it happens that we later introduce a new concept that is more practical for us. – But that will only be in very definite and small areas, and it presupposes that most concepts remain unaltered.
>   Could a legislator abolish the concept of pain?
>   The basic concepts are interwoven so closely with what is most fundamental in our way of living that they are therefore unassailable.   (*LWPP II*, § §43–4e)

Given their nature, our fundamental concerns cannot be addressed by empirical investigations. As we have seen, there is no justification when we hit the bedrock that forms the very foundation of our practices. At this point, we encounter what is fundamental – indeed, what cannot be completely understood in conceptual terms. Philosophical puzzlement with respect to these matters cannot *be dealt with* by the replacement of one set of concepts with another. This is why philosophical problems are nothing like genuine empirical problems. At best, we can try better to understand such topics. However this crucially requires the breaking free of certain explanatory tendencies that engender confusions about them. To understand them is not to offer up new hypotheses. For:

> A reform for particular practical purposes, an improvement in our terminology designed to prevent misunderstandings in practice is perfectly possible. But these are not the cases we have to do with. The confusions which occupy us arise when language is like an engine idling, not when it is doing work.   (*PI* §132)

It is not as if each philosopher is entitled to a free first move in developing their theories, for example, stating some primary assumption, and only then charged with the task of ensuring that any future moves remain consistent with the initial one. To think this makes it appear as if the naturalists and Wittgenstein are on an equal footing to begin with; one leading with the *assumption* that we must start where we stand already and the other *assuming* first and foremost that science is sacrosanct. But clearly this too is to have a picture of what it is to do philosophy – one with heavy realist overtones. It is an illusion that what we think about these issues is up for grabs in this way. We have no option but start just where we are already – we must start by seeking to understand rather than explain the nature of logic, mind and meaning. As I have shown in earlier chapters, these topics cannot be addressed by developing better *theories* about them. This is why Wittgenstein is adamant that, 'It is the business of philosophy, not to resolve a contradiction by means of a . . . discovery, but to make it possible for us to get a clear view of the state of [the matter] that troubles us' (*PI* §125). For this reason, 'One might also give the name "philosophy" to what is possible before all new discoveries and inventions' (*PI* §126). Although Wittgenstein is quite aware that some of our concepts change and develop, he denies that properly 'philosophical' problems can be resolved by such activity (they cannot even be 'removed' by it). The crux of the matter is that those who see philosophy as progressive fail to recognise these important limits.

In contrast, scientific naturalism has nothing to offer but the empty promises of the future explanation of fundamental issues such as the 'nature of mental states', or 'rules' (in both cases these are attempts at explicating the foundations of our practices).[32] Yet, in all such cases scientific naturalists must presuppose something they cannot explain. Thus, if one is unrelenting in this ambition one must be prepared to cure philosophical diseases by killing the patients, as are the eliminativists.

Certain phenomena lie at the very epicentre of our practices. That is why the best line of reply for the traditional philosopher is to argue that certain concepts, such as 'person', 'knowledge', 'meaning', 'consciousness', and so on, are so central to our lives that they must be unchanging (see Miller 2000, p. 237; Brown 1999, p. 56). Although Wittgenstein acknowledges something similar, he is not interested in *defining* the concepts associated with these phenomena but rather better at understanding their nature and their place in our lives. In this he is not silent about them, as we have seen, but his observations are neither theoretical nor are they attempts at definition.

Wittgenstein does not deny that there are legitimate scientific questions. What he denies is that fundamental questions in philosophy are of this sort. For with respect to these, the only possible task for philosophy is to see the situation aright. It is for this reason, he writes:

> I may find scientific questions interesting, but they never really grip me. Only conceptual and aesthetic questions do that. At bottom I am indifferent to the solution of scientific problems; but not the other sort. (*C&V*, p. 79e)

Contemplation, therapy or clarification

Phillips holds that Wittgenstein's philosophy is thoroughly contemplative because he was primarily concerned with fundamental matters, such as understanding how meaning, judgement and inquiry are possible at all. He says, 'Wittgenstein's conception of philosophy is contemplative in that its aim is to bring us to an understanding of what it is to have a world picture' (Phillips 1999, p. 54; cf. also p. 107). Accordingly, Wittgenstein's awareness of the limits of philosophy lies behind his remark that philosophy must involve 'description alone' and can 'in no way interfere with the use of language'. This realisation is achieved, as we have seen, by a working out of problems relating to the conditions of the possibility of discourse. In this respect philosophy is not 'for anything' (Phillips 1999, p. 63).

> By their very nature philosophical *problems* don't have solutions but resolutions. If one doesn't want to SOLVE philosophical problems – why doesn't one give up dealing with them. For solving them means changing one's point of view, the old way of thinking. And if you don't want that, then you should consider the problems unsolvable.
>
> (*LWPP II*, p. 84e)

Echoing Wittgenstein's own sentiments, Phillips blames our inability to rest easy with this conclusion on the sort of desires that characterise our 'technological' age. For example, in a bid to mark recent progress in philosophy at the end of the twentieth century, *The New York Times* reported that Quine's dissolution of the analytic–synthetic distinction was a milestone of philosophical progress. It is interesting to compare this claim with Wittgenstein's response to a similar, if more disparaging, remark:

> I read: 'philosophers are no nearer the meaning of "Reality" than Plato got'. What a strange situation. How extraordinary that Plato could have got even as far as he did! Or that we could not get any further!   (*C&V*, p. 15e; cf. also, pp. 7, 8e)

Phillips does not deny that philosophy can produce goods that will be of use in other explanatory endeavours. As he notes, 'philosophical distinctions may be made in the service of [other] interests. I have also emphasized that this is quite different from a contemplative conception of philosophy, in which the interests themselves come from the fundamental questions of philosophy' (Phillips 1999, p. 102). There is something quite right about what Phillips' is advocating. As I have argued, gripped by the need to supply explanations of fundamental phenomena, many philosophers will fail to recognise the nonsense they generate. They crave to solve philosophical problems rather than coming to see matters in the right light, as I hoped to have illustrated in Chapter 4. In pursuing these ends they promote a vision of philosophy that wrongly insists it must have an active and progressive role, adding to an ever-growing compendium of knowledge. Nevertheless, I want to resist the attendant thought that Wittgenstein's approach eschews anything constructive in the sense of positive. Thus I object to Phillips' emphasis on the utterly passive aspects of the notion of contemplation, which he sees as ultimately hailing from the pre-Socratics and as having quasi-religious overtones (Phillips 1999, p. 61).

Certainly, Wittgenstein is not constructing theories, but Phillips goes too far in suggesting that philosophy 'does nothing at all'. For example, he is critical of certain other philosophers, such as Cavell, precisely because they view philosophy as having the role of a reappraiser. Phillips completely rejects the therapeutic understanding, seeing it as yet another product of our forlorn desire to make philosophy 'do something'. For example, he rails against Conant's reading, claiming that it 'seriously underestimates the independence of philosophy and the depth of its questions – for example, the questions that exercised Wittgenstein . . . in philosophical logic. These are not preliminary to anything' (Phillips 1999, p. 59). But if philosophy is an *activity* that aims to clarify our thinking on certain fundamental matters, it is bound to produce some results. Wittgenstein is explicit in several places about what we might call, for want of a better word, its therapeutic benefits. He tells us:

> The results of philosophy are the uncovering of one or another piece of plain nonsense and of bumps that the understanding has got by running its head up against the limits of language. (*PI* §119)

We must also bear in mind that Wittgenstein described his work on these fundamental issues as 'working on oneself' (*C&V*, p. 16). He thought of his writings as 'conversations with himself', but we can make sense of their wider value in that he also tells us that 'I ought be no more than a mirror, in which my reader can see his own thinking with all its de-formities so that helped in this way, he can put it right' (*C&V*, p. 18). Thus, he stressed that his work was not meant to spare his readers from thinking and would only have the appropriate effect on those who had had the same or similar thoughts themselves: those who approached his writings in the correct spirit (*PI*, p. viii; *TLP*, p. 3; *C&V*, p. 7e). Of course, the results of philosophical investigations and reflections, although decisive, do not add to our existing stock of knowledge in the way science does. Their effects are necessarily individual and case by case. One result of philosophical work is the change it brings about in the individuals engaged in it. This contrast enables us to understand the following remark:

> Philosophy hasn't made any progress? – If somebody scratches the spot where he has an itch, do we have to see some progress? Isn't it genuine scratching otherwise, or genuine itching? And can't this reaction to an irritation continue in the same way for a long time before a cure for the itching is discovered? (*C&V*, p. 86e)

Nevertheless, it would be wrong to infer from this that therapeutic activity is the legitimate end for philosophy. Philosophy is good for more than freeing us from false pictures and breaking our bad habits of thought. Wittgenstein's reminders have this effect, but they are primarily assembled for the purpose of removing confusions about what troubles us to enable us to get a clear view of the matter. His investigations, in both periods, were always prosecuted with the aim of clarifying the issues in question (*TLP* 4.0031; *PI* § §122–7). Of course, clarity is only achieved when intellectual obstacles that prevent us from seeing things aright are removed (*CV*, p. 44e; *PI* §109). It is with this in mind that we can understand the claim that:

> Philosophy unties knots in our thinking; hence its result must be simple, but philosophizing has to be as complicated as the knots it unties. (*Z* §452)

Seen in this light its procedure, *but not its aim*, is therapeutic. Indeed, it becomes clear that these activities cannot be prised apart precisely because they are not in competition. Hence, it is fruitless to argue which was Wittgenstein's real 'aim' in terms of an imagined contrast between elucidation and therapy, or to debate which of these held priority for him. Their relation is not that of two distinct ends, but rather that of means to end:

> It is rather, of the essence of our investigation that we do not seek to learn anything new by it. We want to *understand* something in plain view. For *this* is what we seem in some sense not to understand. (*PI* §89)

> We feel as if we had to *penetrate* phenomena: our investigation, however, is directed not towards phenomena, but, as one might say, towards the '*possibilities*' of phenomena. We remind ourselves of the *kind of statement* that we make about phenomena . . . Our investigation is therefore a grammatical one. Such an investigation sheds light on our problem by clearing misunderstandings away. (*PI* §90)

In so clarifying fundamental matters he is no quietist. Having untied these knots he does not advocate silence on important matters.[33]

These considerations also impact on our conception of our philosophical task with respect to non-fundamental matters, when philosophers are not simply serving as under-labourers. For in ridding ourselves of the confusion that our task is to test theories and determine *the* truth about certain issues, we will be better able to focus on our real needs. Getting free of misleading pictures about the philosophical enterprise enables us to understand that in many cases we are faced with decid-

ing on a range of 'possibilities'. For example, in exploring ethical possibilities we will need to assess the kinds of lives they will engender if
adopted and what sorts of people we wish to become, rather than imagining that we are simply neutrally assessing the truth or otherwise of
theories. Asking, for example, 'What is justice?' is not a question about
essences but a prelude to change.[34] Indeed, we might think getting us
to focus on our responsibilities in this way was the purpose of the Tractarian stress on ethics, aesthetics and religion, that were identified by
Wittgenstein as being at the very heart of the work. As he famously
writes in an undated letter to von Ficker:

> The point of the book is ethical. I once wanted to give a few words
> in the foreword which now actually are not in it, which, however,
> I'll write to you now because they might be a key to you: I wanted
> to write that my work consists of two parts: of the one which is here,
> and of everything which I have not written. And precisely this
> second part is the important one.
>
> (cited in Luckhardt 1996, pp. 94–5)

It is precisely because these possibilities are not 'chosen' in any simple
sense that they require serious examination and consideration. And,
although philosophers are not in a privileged position to judge the final
value of such potential developments, they can help in the business of
articulating, exploring and criticising them as participants. They are able
to contribute to debate and discussion, but only alongside the many
and those with experience. This will require more than a modicum of
practical wisdom and the ability to 'distinguish between the important
and the trivial' (Miller 2000, p. 346). For the exploration of such possibilities will not be a purely intellectual exercise.[35] As Wittgenstein
remarks:

> An important fact here is that we learn certain things through long
> experience not from a course in school. How, for instance, does one
> develop the eye of a connoisseur?   (*LWPP I*, §925)

Conclusion

I hope to have shown, throughout this book, that Wittgenstein's end
was always to clarify certain important philosophical issues and that his
approach was dictated by his recognition of certain genuine limits to

philosophy. It was not chosen on the basis of quirks of temperament, laziness or the desire to avoid serious issues, but rather a realisation of what is required for a rigorous working through and facing up to the deepest of philosophical problems. Although it is too much to think that Wittgenstein could have solved all of these, as he once claimed in the Preface to the *Tractatus*, he did put us on the right and only road to approaching certain types of legitimate philosophical concern.

Notes

Chapter 1

1. As Allison notes, the very activity of judging and understanding 'consists in the unification or synthesis of representations, and this unification occurs *in certain determinate ways* which can be called "forms" or "functions" of unity' (Allison 1983, p. 123; emphasis mine; see also p. 117).

2. Pippin observes, 'For Kant, the whole difference between a merely formal, or general logic, and a transcendental logic depends on the use of pure intuitions to distinguish "real possibility" from merely logical possibility, to distinguish, that is, conditions necessary for the representation of an object from conditions necessary for a thought just to be a possible thought or representation' (Pippin 1989, p. 24).

3. Hanna neatly captures the main features of Kant's position in a succinct summary: 'On Kant's account, the formal condition of the possibility of all cognitions is supplied by the categories or meta-concepts, together with the laws of pure general logic; and the material condition of the possibility of all cognitions is supplied by the factor of objective validity. But the pure general logic pre-supposes the original synthetic unity of apperception, and objective validity presupposes the pure *a priori* forms of human sensibility, (the representations of) space and time. Now both pure apperception and the pure forms of sensibility are transcendentally ideal – they are generatively/productively innate and mind-dependent. Therefore Kant's theory of objective mental representation of meaning is grounded on the doctrine of transcendental idealism' (Hanna 2001, p. 95).

4. Indeed, because of this, it has been 'convincingly shown that Kant can be read as a philosophical psychologist' (Hanna 2001, p. 16; see also 18–19, 22).

5. For a full account of the reasons and warrant for Kant's positing of 'the-thing-in-itself', see Allison's discussion (1983, ch. 11).

6. Pippin sets out his case in great detail in the second chapter of his *Hegel's Idealism* (Pippin 1989, ch. 2).

7. As he writes, 'Only thus, by demonstration of the *a priori* validity of the categories in respect of all objects of our sense, will the purpose of the deduction be fully attained' (*CPR* B 144–5).

8. The basic problem, as he notes, is that, 'unless we can do this – explain the possibility of claiming to know something about "whatever may present themselves to the senses" (and not just whatever may conform to our conditions of representability) – then "there could be no explaining why everything that can be presented to our senses must be subject to laws which have their origin *a priori* in the understanding alone" (B160)' (Pippin 1989, p. 28).

9. As Pippin explains, it is precisely in this territory that, 'a "speculative" identity between Concept and intuited Particular looms on the horizon' (Pippin 1989, p. 30).

10. Thus we should resist Guyer's claim to this effect which he based on the fact

that, 'Hegel does not engage in internal criticism in his response to Kant's theoretical philosophy . . . He does not examine Kant's own reasons for his subjectivism, and thus neither shows why Kant's subjective scruples are invalid nor how his own view can transcend them' (Guyer 1993, pp. 171–2). Although Hegel's exposition may show him to be unfair in his assessment of Kant, it is possible to 'reconstruct' his main argument against Kant as Pippin has attempted. In this way we see the real merit in Hegel's objections (see also Houlgate 2000, pp. 246–9). This is consistent with recognising that, 'Hegel nowhere provides adequate justification for his numerous critical remarks about Kant's *Critique of Pure Reason*' (Pippin 1989, p. 11).

11. For example, Kant not only held that, 'since Aristotle . . . logic has not be able to advance a single step, and is thus to all appearance a closed and complete body of doctrine' (*CPR* B viii), he rather too boldly claimed the former's logic allowed, 'an exhaustive exposition and strict proof of the formal rules of all thought' (*CPR* B ix). For a more detailed discussion of Hegel's criticisms of Kant on this front, see Guyer (1993, p. 187).

12. Brandom understands this 'unpacking' of *the* concept to be 'the gradual unfolding into greater explicitness of commitments that can be seen retrospectively as always already having been implicit in it' (Brandom 2000, p. 75; cf. Houlgate 2000, p. 248). This purification requires that the 'heirs to such a conceptual tradition must ensure that it is a rational tradition – that the distinctions it embodies and enforces between correct and incorrect applications of a concept can be justified, that applying it in one case and withholding application in another is something for which we can give reasons' (Brandom 2000, p. 75).

13. My current concerns allow me to sidestep the controversies over whether or not Moore and Russell were in any way genuinely responsible for the founding of analytic philosophy. For some, like Bell, doubt that its origins can be properly traced to Cambridge at the turn of the century (Bell 1999). Other scholars have sought to reverse the Dummettian emphasis on its alleged continental wellspring precisely by restoring 'Russell's role in the development of analytical philosophy' (cf. Dummett 1993; Monk and Palmer 1996, p. vii). Yet, despite disputing its genetic origins, both camps are agreed that 'the rejection of certain idealist doctrines was a necessary condition of the subsequent adoption of a number of distinctively analytic theories and methods' (Bell 1999, p. 195).

14. As Hylton says, 'mathematics thus functions as a counterexample to a claim which is a necessary part of any form of idealism' (Hylton 1991, p. 180). Of course, if Sainsbury is right, there was a still deeper motivation for Russell's pursuit of his logicist project. He relates that at age eleven Russell demanded to know what grounds there were for accepting Euclid's axioms, and received the unsatisfactory reply, ' "If you don't accept them, we cannot go on" ' from his brother (Sainsbury 1979, p. 1). Of course, if mathematics could be grounded in logic then there would be no worry that its axioms were, in effect, arbitrary and unproven. But it is quite plausible that Russell had more than one reason for chasing this dream.

15. It should be obvious that taking this line makes it difficult to account adequately for false propositions. The paradox was that the false proposition was supposed to be a real entity of our acquaintance while, at the same time,

it was supposed to be an essentially non-existent state of affairs. Put simply, the problem was that if a proposition was false then it was made up of nothing: no things.

16. That Russell should go this way ought not to surprise us, given his claim, in the preface to the *Principles of Mathematics*, to have 'derived the chief features' of his realistic atomism from Moore. Baldwin gives clear and succinct insight into Moore's thinking on these matters. He writes, 'I think it is helpful to regard Moore's position as the result of combining realism about meanings with the theory that an actual state of affairs just is a true proposition . . . For if reality is identical with true propositions, and these are constituted of concepts, then reality is constituted from these concepts . . . It is difficult to overestimate the importance of this identity theory in Moore's early philosophy' (Baldwin 1990, p. 43). Thus, in comparing Moore's views on this topic with those of Frege, he also writes, 'Moore's propositions, by contrast, are not intentional: they are possible states of affairs, and when true, actual ones' (Baldwin 1990, p. 44).

17. In this context, Russell explains, 'We can now understand why the constants in mathematics are to be restricted to the logical constants in the sense defined above. The process of transforming constants in a proposition into variables leads to what is called generalization, and gives us, as it were, the formal essence of a proposition' (POM §8). As Hylton writes, in 'the work of Russell from September 1900 on, the metaphysics of Platonic Atomism became interwoven with mathematics and mathematical logic' (Hylton 1991, p. 167). What was so important was that 'this interweaving . . . was to have a decisive influence on the development of analytic philosophy, a conception according to which the technical is not separable from the philosophical, and mathematical logic provides the crucial method for philosophy' (Hylton 1991, p. 167).

18. Again, not only are senses or thoughts independently true or false, they are so eternally. That he held this is in line with his interest in mathematics and logic, which do not have temporal subject matters. But he held it equally for more ordinary thoughts. For this reason he insisted that, 'Only a sentence with the time-specification filled out, a sentence complete in every respect, expresses a thought' (*T*, p. 53). For if we think of our statements as, in effect, having date-stamps then it is possible to regard them as timelessly true. Likewise, and for similar reasons, he held that indexical references such as 'this' and 'now', locked a thought to its context. Thus, for the statement 'This is the biggest thing I have ever seen' to be meaningful it would have to pick out its object unambiguously, be it Mount Everest or my coffee table, and so determining its truth or falsity on the occasion of use not only absolutely but once and for all. We are told, 'Truth does not admit of more or less' (*T*, p. 35). Thus, he held that, 'knowledge of certain conditions accompanying the utterance . . . is needed to grasp the thought correctly' (*T*, p. 40).

19. As is well known, the major advantage of this functional approach over its predecessor is that it provides the right degree of flexibility required for sophisticated logical analysis. In particular, the new logic allowed for the presence of an indefinite number of open variables in any given expression, as in: $x^2 + y$. Furthermore, functions could serve as arguments within func-

tions. This allowed for higher-level functions, making possible an adequate systematic treatment of quantifiers for the first time, which is Frege's most celebrated achievement.

20. The main attraction of seeing him in this light is that, 'If Frege is a metaphysical Platonist, it is easy to see that his position involves a semantics that is both truth-conditional and compositional' (Reck 1997, p. 130).

21. As Reck stresses in most cases those who support this reading of Frege present, 'the picture . . . as an explanation . . . In particular, certain semantic notions, namely "existence", "object", and "reference" are supposed to allow for an explanation of other such notions, namely "meaning", "truth", and "objectivity"' (Reck 1997, p. 129). He goes on to point out that, 'In this explanation the "building blocks", i.e., the words and what they stand for, are prior to the whole with respect to explanation; that is the construction is bottom up' (Reck 1997, p. 130).

22. We can better understand the source of Frege's 'realism' if we concentrate on the fact that, 'His is, for the most part, the relaxed Platonism of a mathematician who simply assumes that there are numbers, functions and so on, and who regards these as an abstract subject matter which can be accepted without special philosophical explanation' (Burge 1997, p. 4). In this regard, Peregrin recently speaks of 'Frege's down-to-earthness' and reminds us that 'his primary goal was relatively humble and modest, namely to contribute to the possibility of articulating mathematical proofs with such precision and clarity that no doubts about their validity could arise' (Peregrin 2000, p. 558).

23. Carl notes, 'That logic is a theory of thought and that thought is intimately connected with scientific knowledge were the main topics of the discussion of the relationship between logic and psychology conducted in the 1870s' (Carl 1994, p. 12).

24. As Conant puts it, 'They are laws in a descriptive sense insofar as they represent true statements about the physical world; they are prescriptive insofar as they prescribe how one ought to think about the physical world (if one wishes to think in accordance with the truth)' (Conant 1991, p. 138).

25. Burge says, 'Frege repeatedly inveighs against seeing logic (or mathematics) as embedded in language in the way grammar is. He thought logical objects, and logical functions bore no such essential dependence relation to the actual practice of thinking or language use . . . even when that practice accords with the laws of truth' (Burge 1997, p. 11).

26. Or as Friedlander puts it, 'Whereas a mistaken theory of physics would still be a theory of physics, a mistaken logical theory is simply inconceivable. But this just means that logic is not a theoretical domain' (Friedlander 2001, p. 90).

27. See Peterson and McGuinness for fuller discussion of the central place of this idea in his thinking (Peterson 1990, p. 48; McGuinness 1976, pp. 49–50).

28. Friedlander has recently argued, to good effect, that this distinction needs to be carefully observed (see Friedlander 2001, esp. chs. 1–6).

29. Pears tells us that Wittgenstein's understanding of pictures gave him 'a platform to criticise Russell's Platonic Theory of logic. The platform is Aristotelian in this sense: it brings down sentential forms from Russell's transcendent world and treats them as immanent in this world' (Pears 1987, p. 29).

30. 'The fact that the operation can be canceled shows most clearly that it is not a component expression of the sense. Insofar as these operations do not in themselves transform the space of signification, they can be repeated or applied repeatedly' (Friedlander 2001, p. 86).
31. As Coffa notes, to the extent that Wittgenstein's attack is directed against Frege it is off-target. For, 'Frege's work was aimed at providing a logical foundation for arithmetic. There is no indication that he ever seriously worried about the foundations of logic itself . . . [Therefore] Wittgenstein was wrong in assuming Frege intended the rule to play a justificatory role' (Coffa 1991, p. 123).
32. Brandom's 'expressive theory of logic' repeats the Tractarian thought that logic is contentless and formal in the properly Aristotelian sense of being embedded in the world and language, as merged in our practices.
33. Anscombe illustrates this very point when she writes, 'I once bought toffees with the names of the flavours. "Treacle", "Devon cream" and so on printed on the papers and was momentarily startled to find one labelled "fruit or nut". It cannot be "fruit or nut", I said. It's fruit or it's nut. Any attempt to say what the truth-functional constants like 'or' mean must fail: we can only shew it' (Anscombe 1959, p. 164).

Chapter 2

1. Thus Pears claims that 'The theory advanced in the *Tractatus* belongs to a type that has had a long vogue. The general mark of the type is the idea that the world imposes a fixed structure on our thought' (Pears 1988, p. 206).
2. He makes clear where he stands on the above debate by adding immediately that, 'In his late writings he jettisons that tradition' (Goldstein 1999, p. 26).
3. The source of this similarity resides in the fact that much of Russell's later thinking was based on his own limited understanding of Wittgenstein's ideas during a time when the First World War separated them. We can see evidence of this in the passage that prefaces his lectures on the *Philosophy of Logical Atomism* in which he says, 'The following of a course of eight lectures delivered in London, in the first months of 1918, are very largely concerned with explaining certain ideas which I learnt from my friend and former pupil Ludwig Wittgenstein. I have had no opportunity of knowing his views since August 1914, and I do not even know whether he is alive or dead. He has therefore no responsibility for what is said in these lectures beyond that of having originally supplied many of the theories contained in them' (*PLA*, p. 177).
4. Friedlander describes this procedure in terms of operations on proto-pictures (see Friedlander 2001, pp. 86–7).
5. Not only should we be suspicious of the idea that the *Tractatus* advances a *theory* of language, we should also be careful in saying it advanced an *argument*. Despite their strange appearance, to the extent that they function properly at all the remarks of the *Tractatus* are neither argued for nor defended in the usual fashion. We must not simply accept such common claims as, 'The basic argument of the *Tractatus* is a transcendental one: given that language is essentially representational, what do language and the world

have to be like for the former to represent the latter' (Koethe 1996, p. 21; cf. also pp. 30, 40).

6. He gave other related reasons for holding this. For example, he insists that simples must exist because it is possible to form new propositions using old components. He writes, 'It belongs to the essence of a proposition that it should be able to communicate a new sense to us' (*TLP* 4.027). If it is true that we can form novel propositions (and to do so we must understand the parts of these propositions) then it is natural to suppose that such propositions are wholly composed of simple components which we already understand and which need no definition. If this were not the case then we would not have been able to understand our very first propositions.

7. Lynette Reid makes this very point when she writes, 'One of the anti-metaphysical strands of the *Tractatus* is that logic cannot judge in advance what the internal articulation of fully analysed propositions will be: contrary to Frege and Russell, who think it essential to the nature of representation that a proposition segment into subject and predicate of some sort, the *Tractatus* denies that there is any point in discussing in advance whether elementary propositions will consist of names and concept-expressions, or n-termed relation-expressions, or anything else' (Reid 1998, p. 122).

8. This is not to deny other similarities that may exist between them. For example, several exegetes regard Frege's 'context principle' as directly influencing Wittgenstein's approach. For example, Reck claims that their, 'basic outlooks have something crucial in common; and ... that this is a result of the positive influence Frege had on Wittgenstein' (Reck 1997, pp. 124, 143). Likewise, Diamond holds that, 'In Frege we can see the beginnings of something which is fully developed in the *Tractatus*: what thought is made clear is not so much in sentences about thought but in the clear expression of thoughts in a concept-script' (Diamond 1995, p. 118).

9. Perhaps the laws of physics hold 'most generally', even in all possible worlds. Even so, they are not the same as 'laws of logic', which in describing what is formally necessary, say nothing at all.

Chapter 3

1. Elsewhere, he claims that Wittgenstein 'had argued that there are indeed metaphysical truths about the nature of the world. What he claimed, however, was that they are essentially ineffable, that they are shown (and must be shown) by the depth structure (which will be revealed by analysis) of any possible language' (Hacker 1996, p. 44).

2. She is openly hostile to standard readings because 'the attempt to take the *Tractatus* as metaphysical in a straightforward sense (as in Norman Malcolm's *Nothing is Hidden*) yields plain nonsense or plain self-contradictions' (Diamond 1995, p. 19).

3. Conant stands opposed to those who maintain that, 'for the *Tractatus* the propositions of ethics and religion – as well as either all or only the most important propositions of the *Tractatus* itself – are both nonsensical and deeply significant' (Conant 1989, pp. 244, 247, 1995, 252).

4. The description of such readings as 'full-fledged' comes from Read and Crary,

who hold that although some readings recognise a therapeutic aim in his early work they fall 'short of delivering a full-fledged reading of the work. What is at issue has to do with the most notoriously perplexing feature of the *Tractatus* – namely, its closing claim that its sentences are nonsense and that as readers we should treat them as rungs of the ladder which we have now ascended' (Read and Crary 2000, p. 11).

5. Conant remarks on the impossibility of there being different types of non-sense (cf. Conant 1989, pp. 252, 253, 261). Diamond, for her part, says, 'for Wittgenstein there is no kind of nonsense which is nonsense on account of what the terms composing it, mean – there is as it were no positive non-sense' (Diamond 1995, pp. 106, 112). She goes on, 'I should claim that [this] view of nonsense . . . was consistently held to by Wittgenstein throughout his writings, from the period before the *Tractatus* was written and onwards' (Diamond 1995, p. 107).

6. Koethe notes, 'On [Diamond's] account, the *Tractatus* does not attempt to articulate a metaphysical and semantic theory of the nature of language . . . Wittgenstein's aim is to subject the notions figuring in that ostensible articu-lation – states of affairs, objects, logical form, and so on – to "a destabliza-tion from the inside" in a effort to demonstrate their literal incoherence' (Koethe 1996, p. 37).

7. Koethe makes the same complaint, but allies it to a theoretical reading to which I object. He writes, 'it is important to remember that the kinds of claims the *Tractatus* construes as nonsensical are not confined to those involving metaphysical notions such as object, fact, and states of affairs but include semantic claims about propositions, names, and meaning, as well as mentalistic claims like "A believes that p" and "A has the thought that p", which Wittgenstein declares to have the form of the (nonsensical) sentence "'p' says p"' (*TLP*, 5.542). It is not difficult to reconstruct arguments *based on the picture theory* for the unintelligiblity of such claims' (Koethe, 1996, pp. 38–9; emphasis mine).

8. This period is of great interest precisely because, as Finch notes, 'Judging from the posthumously published *Philosophical Remarks* and *Philosophical Grammar*, Wittgenstein moved with almost agonizing slowness to the new position that language makes sense only as it is altogether intertwined with different kinds of activities' (Finch 1977, p. 4).

9. Mayer convincingly argues against the view that the numbering was meant to be in the style of a musical score or an intuitive rhythm. Indeed, she employs evidence from the *Prototractatus* to reveal that the sub-propositions of the *Tractatus* are for the most part, just as Wittgenstein claimed, meant as elaborations or comments upon earlier remarks. Thus, she likens the work to 'an architectonic construction' and claims that its numbering system 'reflects primarily a method of construction' (Mayer 1993, p. 112).

10. Friedlander tries to accommodate this by stressing the 'movement' of the book, suggesting that the image of the ladder should be replaced with that of the circle. Although it reminds us that we must be silent, the tension inherent in the book drives one back again to the beginning, as do all good paradoxes. The tension could be regarded as pointing to some profound insight, although unsatisfying to the critical intellect.

11. Nor was it the immediate catalyst for his later change of view.

12. It is common to misread the nature of this change; to see it in terms of his interests shifting in a more psychologistic direction. Some see his rejection of the name–object view as carrying an implicit critique of his own earlier lack of concern with seemingly important questions about how words actually get 'linked to the world', how meanings are socially established, etc. Hence, a recognition that 'Words, however, never refer or describe, people do so by means of words. And these are inevitably psychological' (Burbridge 1993, p. 88). By such lights, it becomes hard to understand his seemingly new openness to some kind of 'naturalism' yet his resistance to theorising. It is a puzzle that Wittgenstein should have only moved partially in the direction of naturalism, but still resisted treating his concerns as a form of 'natural history'. However, from a different angle, it is easy to see that his concerns never moved in a more 'empirical' direction at all.

13. If they did, ethical statements could not be absolute (cf. Wittgenstein 'A Lecture on Ethics' 1929, p. 39).

14. He claims that Wittgenstein's preface to the *Tractatus* misleads on the issue of nonsense by suggesting a fourfold schema, when it should describe a sixfold one (cf. Peterson 1990, p. 7, and especially p. 8). A similar account of the various senses of nonsense in the *Tractatus* can be found in Cyril Barrett's discussion (see Barrett 1991, esp. pp. 24–5).

15. In considering to what extent Wittgenstein ought to be thought of as a transcendental philosopher, Meredith Williams usefully compares and contrasts his philosophical approach with that of Kant's. The similarities are clear. Both are concerned with issues concerning the bounds of sense such that it makes it look as if Wittgenstein's grammar could be a substitute for Kantian *synthetic a priori* categories. But one key difference between them is that even in his early philosophy, logical form, which says nothing, does not constrain in the way that the Kantian categories are meant to, if these are regarded as defining an articulable limit to the bounds of sense. In this sense Wittgenstein might be thought to invert, 'the Kantian order of priority' (Williams 1998, pp. 76, 177). Yet, he tells us that 'The limit of language is shown by its being impossible to describe a fact which corresponds to (is the translation of) a sentence without simply repeating the sentence (This has to do with the Kantian solution to the problem of philosophy)' (*C&V* 1931, p. 10e).

16. Dilman hits the nail on the head when he writes, 'There is, of course, a dimension of reality with which animals and pre-linguistic children engage and which we share with them. That dimension of reality similarly cannot be prized apart from those pre-linguistic engagements and the instinctive reactions and behaviour in which those engagements take place. It is this behaviour which, as Wittgenstein argues, our language extends and transforms and therein expands the world of the pre-linguistic child' (Dilman 2002, p. 117; see also Hutto 1999 ch. 4, 5, sec. 2, 2000, chs. 1, 2).

17. 'I think that much of the controversy surrounding the question of a constructive element in Wittgenstein's later thought is due to the unclarity of the notions of philosophical theses and theories themselves' (Koethe 1996, pp. 61–2). Nor is this surprising given that he also believes that, 'Kripke is broadly correct in taking Wittgenstein to offer a kind of constructive response to the failure to locate a suitable basis for semantic claims' (Koethe, 1996, p. 61).

Chapter 4

1. In this he is carrying through a project the origins of which can be traced to his first published work (Dennett 1969). For a detailed and critical examination of that early project, see Bricke (1984 and 1985).

2. The rest of the passage reads: 'When I was an undergraduate he was my hero, so I went to Oxford, where he seemed to be everybody's hero. When I saw how most of my fellow graduate students were (by my lights) missing the point, I gave up trying to "be" a Wittgensteinian, and just took what I thought I had learned from the *Investigations* and tried to put it to work' (Dennett 1991a, p. 463).

3. In fact, many see the essential problem with this 'tradition', as Searle has taken to calling it, as being that 'the only real choices available [are] between some form of materialism and some form of dualism' (Searle 1992, p. 2). However, although Searle is aware of this problem, he does less well at finding a new vocabulary to employ. Hence, we find him writing such confusing things as: 'what I really mean is consciousness *qua* consciousness, *qua* mental, *qua* subjective, *qua* qualitative, is physical and physical because mental' (Searle 1992, p. 15).

4. As Wittgenstein remarked: 'We talk of processes and states and leave their nature undecided. Sometime perhaps we shall know more about them – we think. But that is just what commits us to particular way of looking at the matter' (*PI* §308).

5. It is important to note that Dennett classifies all materialists who foolishly, by his lights, mix their austere metaphysics with 'the imagery of the Cartesian Theatre' under this heading (Dennett, 1991a, p. 107; see also Kirk 1993, p. 335). That is to say, even those materialists who take consciousness to be 'indiscreetly' spread across the brain, rather than easily locatable, will be branded as Cartesians so long as they subscribe to the model of the mind as an inner theatre (cf. Seager 1993, p. 117). For a fuller discussion of the character of this manoeuvre see Malcolm (1986, ch. 10).

6. This is why he tells us: ' "Mental" for me is not a metaphysical, but a logical, epithet' (*LWPP II*, p. 63e).

7. He tells us: 'The reader of a novel lets the text constitute a (fictional) world, a world determined by fiat by the text' (Dennett 1991a, p. 81).

8. As Dennett puts it, 'We might classify the Multiple Drafts model . . . as first-person operationalism for it brusquely denies the possibility of consciousness of a stimulus in the absence of the subject's belief in that stimulus' (Dennett 1991, p. 132). Michael Tye has attacked this aspect of Dennett's account (Tye 1993, pp. 895–6).

9. His definition of a virtual machine is as follows, 'a virtual machine is a temporary set of highly structured regularities imposed on the underlying hardware by a programme: a structured recipe of hundreds of thousands of instructions that give the hardware a huge, interlocking set of habits or dispositions to react' (Dennett 1991a, p. 216). Dennett is able to help himself to this kind of account, for even though Joycean texts are serial in nature and the brain's architecture is parallel (and not serial) in character, there is no reason why, in principle, a parallel architecture cannot generate a virtual machine which makes use of serial operations. This latter point is supported

by the fact that serial virtual machines can be generated by existing parallel hardware.

10. As Bricke says, 'His intentionalist theory is best viewed as a successor of the folk psychology of consciousness' (Bricke 1985, p. 248).

11. In describing this criterion Bricke uses the adjectives, 'austere, regimented, coherent' (cf. Bricke 1985, p. 249).

12. As Dennett has happily admitted, 'I choose to take what may well be a more radical stand than Wittgenstein's' (Dennett 1990, p. 524).

13. This is related to Wittgenstein's views on lying about our psychological situation. 'If I lie to him and he guesses it from my face and tells me so – do I still have the feeling that what is in me is in no way accessible to him and hidden? Don't I feel rather that he sees right through me?' (*LWPP II*, p. 33e). 'It is as if he became *transparent* to us through a human facial expression' (*LWPP II*, p. 67e). 'When my gesture and circumstances are unambiguous then the inner seems to be the outer' (*LWPP II*, p. 63e).

14. This is, of course, McDowell's turn of phrase (see McDowell 1988, p. 221).

15. 'Our first answers reveal naïve and apparently irresistible ideas about assertion and meaning' (Ebbs 1997, p. 9, see also p. 30; McGinn 1984, p. 142).

16. As McDowell says, 'The picture of the "super-rigid" machine is a picture of the patterns as sets of rails' (McDowell 1998, p. 231).

17. Accordingly Pettit proposes that, 'We know that in picking up rules from examples, human beings develop inclinations of the kind which this proposal requires . . . The rule is that which, other things being equal, the standardized inclination would identify, instance by instance' (Pettit 1990, p. 14).

18. Similarly, Pettit notes that 'not only should a rule be normative over an indefinite variety of applications, it should be determinable or identifiable by a finite subject independently of any particular application: the prospective rule-follower should be in a position to identify the rule in such a manner that he can sensibly try to be faithful to it in any application' (Pettit 1990, p. 3). This is what drives him to say that rules must be both directly yet fallibly readable by those who follow them. Shogenji gets to the heart of the matter by stressing that, 'without epistemic access to the rule no decision-making agent can use it as a guide to her conduct – she must walk in the dark without consulting the rule, of which she has no knowledge' (Shogenji 2000, p. 513). Or as Forbes puts it, 'The problem is that the rules themselves have to be understood by the subject' (Forbes 2002, p. 17).

19. Despite acknowledging the importance of this epistemic dimension to our investigation of independent rules, Wright does not make the mistake of seeing the sceptical challenge as having a *distinct* epistemic side to it. Indeed, he criticises McGinn precisely for thinking that the ontological and epistemological aspects can be treated separately (see Wright 2002, p. 109).

20. Wright gives the following assessment, 'The principal philosophical issues to do with rule-following impinge on every normatively constrained area of human thought and activity: on every institution where there is right or wrong opinion, correct or incorrect practice' (Wright 2001, p. 1). Or as Blackburn stresses, 'Our topic is the fact that terms of language are governed by rules that determine what constitutes correct and incorrect application of them . . . The topic is that there is such a thing as the correct and incorrect

application of a term, and to say that there is such a thing is no more than to say that there is truth and falsity' (Blackburn 2002, p. 29). Or again, in Boghossian's words, 'the passages on rule-following are concerned with some of the weightiest questions in the theory of meaning, questions – involving the reality, reducibility, and privacy of meaning – that occupy centre-stage in contemporary philosophy' (Boghossian 2002, p. 141).

21. This is true even of sophisticated writers such as Wright who credits Wittgenstein with 'essentially inventing' the problem and who also recognises that 'He did not intend it as something we should try to *solve*, beyond understanding its roots' (Wright 2001, p. 6). Yet, he goes on to say, 'Still, one could realise that this was not Wittgenstein's own intention without believing that his deflationary attitude to the concerns involved was right' (Wright 2001, p. 6).

22. Shogeni illustrates the point nicely: 'Suppose someone who used to bring a slab in response to hand-waving unexpectedly brings a beam instead. Suppose further that later investigations reveal she was tired when this happened. Some people may think that this discovery enables us to dismiss the incident as an error due to an unusual circumstance. However, it is conceivable that the person brought a beam not by an error, but in perfect accord with her rule – e.g. the rule of bringing a slab in response to hand-waving *except when she is tired*, in which case she is permitted to bring a beam!' (Shogenji 2000, p. 514).

23. McDowell reprimands Wright for a crime of which Bloor is equally guilty. He writes, 'Wright's claim that "for the community itself there is no authority, so no standard to meet" can be, at the very best, an attempt to say something that cannot be said but only shown. It may have some merit, conceived in that light; but attributing to Wittgenstein as a doctrine can yield only distortion' (McDowell 1998, p. 257).

24. As McDowell remarks if 'it is only going out of step with one's fellows that we make room for . . . [then] the notion of right and wrong that we have made room for is at best a thin surrogate for what would be required by the intuitive notion of objectivity' (McDowell 1998, p. 225).

25. McGinn does not leave matters here since he goes on to suggest other, ultimately not very promising reductive proposals.

26. For this reason, Ebbs is right to say, 'no primitive meaning facts can satisfy the requirements on meaning evoked by Kripke's skeptical challenge' (Ebbs 1997, p. 31).

27. Or as Stueber puts it, 'The absurdity of the sceptical paradox does not, therefore, show that meaning itself is an illusion but rather that *a certain model* in explaining meaning and understanding is wrong' (Stueber 1994, p. 20; emphasis mine).

28. In this respect, McDowell is quite right to make the focus of his concern a repudiation of 'the assimilation of understanding to interpretation' (McDowell 1998, p. 261).

29. Elsewhere, he writes: 'and now I have been told 'Go on like that': how do I *know* what I have to do next time? – Well, I do it with *certainty*, I shall also know how I defend what I do – that is, up to a certain point. If that does not count as a defence then there is none' (*RFM* VI: 29, emphasis mine; cf. also VI: 23–4, 38, 46–7). And, 'If someone is not a master of a language, I may bring him to mastery of it by training. Someone who is master of it, I

may remind of the kind of training, or I may describe it; for a particular purpose; thus already using the technique of language.

To what extent can the function of a rule be described? Someone who is master of none, *I can only train*. But how can I explain the nature of a rule to myself?

The difficult thing here is not, to dig down to the ground; no, it is to recognise the ground that lies before us as the ground' (*RFM* VI: 31; emphasis mine).

30. Elsewhere, he again recognises that 'Wittgenstein the principled theoretical quietist does not attempt to provide a theory of practices, nor would he endorse the project of doing so. The last thing he thinks we need is more philosophical theories. Nonetheless, one of the projects pursued in the rest of this work is to come up with an account of norms implicit in practices that will satisfy the criteria of adequacy Wittgenstein's arguments have established' (Brandom 1994, p. 29). For philosophers who believe theorising is the essential method in philosophy, it is natural to worry about the consequences of accepting 'quietism'. For example, when advocating non-reductionism Boghossian epitomises this sort of concern when he asks: 'What sort of room is left for theorizing about meaning' (Boghossian 2002, p. 186)? By way of reply, he proposes that one can at least still ask questions about the relation between language and thought, and chart the principles we deploy in interpreting others.

31. He denies that norms can exist outside of societies. As he says, 'norms are in an important sense in the eye of the beholder, so that one cannot address the question of what implicit norms are, independently of the question of what it is to acknowledge them in practice' (Brandom 1994, p. 25; see also p. 161). And elsewhere, 'The theory developed in this work can be thought of as an account of the stance of attributing original intentionality . . . The key to the account is that an interpretation of this sort must interpret community members as taking or treating each other *in practice* as adopting intentionally contentful commitments and other normative statuses . . . the intentional contentfulness of their states and performances is *the product of their own activity*, not that of the theorist interpreting that activity . . . their intentionality derives from each other, not from outside the community' (Brandom 1994, p. 61; emphases mine).

32. He tells us his idea is to construe 'the normative attitude of taking or treating something as correct or incorrect in practice in terms of the application of positive and negative *sanctions*' (Brandom 1994, p. 45).

33. This is why he holds that 'the normative attitude must be construed as somehow implicit in the practice of the assessor' (Brandom 1994, p. 33).

34. All the same, McDowell has raised some cogent concerns about the nature and direction of his overall project (see McDowell 1997).

35. As he notes, 'The pragmatist starts rather with a notion of norms implicit in practice and is obliged then to develop an account of what it would be for such things to become propositionally explicit, as claims or rules' (Brandom 1994, p. 26). This is why he also says, 'The normative house has many mansions. The particular norms of concern in this work are *discursive* normative statuses, the sort of commitment and entitlement that *the use of concepts involves*' (Brandom 1994, p. 55; emphasis mine).

36. Elsewhere he writes, 'My account of discursive practice makes sense of commitments to getting things right, and funds a sense of "right" that is attitude-transcendent in the sense of swinging free of the content of any and all actual or possible attitudes – though not the very possibility of contentful attitudes' (Brandom 1997, p. 201).
37. As McDowell observes, 'an opinion is something for which one may reasonably offer justification; whereas what is at issue here is below that level' (McDowell 1998, p. 240).
38. Meredith Williams notes that by stressing the social character of meaning and the importance of training, Wittgenstein produces, 'a dynamic rather than a static account of the rule-governed practice' (M. Williams 1998, p. 168).
39. Steuber suggests a similar role and understanding of the appeal to practices. He tells us, 'The knowledge of meaning, hence, is not to be thought of as knowledge of a special meaning-fact but as a capacity which *cannot be described again by rules* . . . The notion of practice is, one might say, the philosophical therapy for over-ambitious attempts which try to explicate meaning according to the scientific model' (Stueber 1994, p. 20). Of course, 'the scientific model' is one through which we expect to get explanations.
40. Not everyone understands how this can be. Thus, Boghossian remarks: 'Oddly, however, McDowell does not take this to commit him to a quietism about meaning, a position from which no substantive results about the conditions for the possibility of meaning can be gleaned' (Boghossian 2002, p. 181).
41. McDowell is notorious for using other such metaphors, in his *Mind and World*. For example, he speaks of us being answerable to the world and, 'The world [being] embraceable in thought' (McDowell 1994, p. 33).

Chapter 5

1. It is important to note that Williams was only ever offering a way of making sense of the later writings and not a definitive interpretation of those writings. As he wrote, 'We have here, in a vague sketch, the outline of a view . . . I am not going to claim anything as strong as that [Wittgenstein] held it . . . I offer this model and its implied connection with the earlier work as a way of looking at and assessing [the] later material' (Williams 1974, p. 85).
2. This reading fits nicely with Wright's description of the idealist as one who 'challenge[s] the whole idea that [discourse] is properly seen as geared to the expression of thoughts whose aim is to reflect an independent reality' (Wright 1993, p. 3).
3. Williams sums up his views on this matter in this passage: 'The fact that in this way everything can be expressed only *via* human interests and concerns, things which are expressions of mind, and which themselves cannot be explained in any further terms: that provides grounds, I suggest, for calling such a view a kind of idealism' (Williams 1974, p. 85).
4. Actually, Williams follows Hacker's lead and calls Wittgenstein a transcendental solipsist.

5. Williams stands in direct opposition to Hacker on this point. For as Hacker sees it: 'In 1929 Wittgenstein overthrew his earlier philosophical views on meaning and representation. With the collapse of the logical independence of elementary propositions, the bulk of the *Tractatus* went down like a row of dominoes. With them went the peculiar form of solipsism and the implicit transcendentalism that seemingly accompanied and supported it' (Hacker 1986, p. 106).

6. What makes Williams' interpretation so interesting is that it challenges more orthodox readings, like Hacker's, by seeing the later work as embodying a 'detailed refutation of solipsism and of idealism' (Hacker 1986, p. 81). In this light it is odd that Williams tells us that he is 'substantially in agreement with Mr. P.M.S. Hacker' (Williams 1974, p. 77).

7. As Williams puts it, 'the move from "I" to "we" was not unequivocally accompanied by an abandonment of the concerns of transcendental idealism' (Williams 1974, p. 79).

8. He writes: 'We can understand the use of the word "pain" of the imagined tribe, in the sense that we can describe it. I cannot see what Williams means in saying that our description is "non-trivially conditioned" by our own use to the world "pain" and our related form of life' (Malcolm 1982, p. 261).

9. Michael Root also reads Wittgenstein as allowing for the existence of 'people who are engaged in ritual actions that are so different from our own actions that we may not be able to understand them; [actions] that we cannot see . . . as resembling any of our own' (Root 1986, p. 304). Yet even though he seemingly agrees with Malcolm on this issue, he also makes it clear that, by his lights, 'Wittgenstein too discounts the idea of the radical other' (Root, 1986, p. 304).

10. The difference between their concepts and ours must not be too extreme. Wittgenstein seems to be aware of this. He writes: 'If someone were to draw a sharp boundary . . . [h]is concept can then be said to be not the same as mine, but akin to it' (*PI*, §76).

11. Needham recognises his methodological debt to Wittgenstein in his introduction (cf. Needham 1972, pp. 8–9).

12. This is not say that we do not have latitude to explore other perspectives. Even if we cannot step outside our form of life there are a range of possibilities within it and some of these are unexplored, as noted in Chapter three (see also *RFM I*, §§143–51). Lack of understanding of others, in many cases, is a matter of degree, complete agreement and complete incomprehensibility being the endpoints of this spectrum.

13. Malcolm makes reference to this remark from *Zettel*: 'Concepts other than though akin to ours might seem very queer to us: derivations from the usual in an unusual direction' (*Z*, §373; cf. Malcolm 1982, p. 258). Note, however, that even the judgement that they are 'unusual' comes unavoidably from 'our' stance.

14. Despite Malcolm's talk of adopting an objective stance on our proceedings, he recognises this point when he writes, 'we can describe the language-game of those other people. In this sense it is "accessible" to us. It is trivial to say that this description is formulated in our language. How else could we formulate it? But this does not imply that we may be failing to see their practice as it really is. The failure of understanding would be, as I said, not at

the level of description, but at the deeper level of instinctive action and reaction. We can describe this difference too. What makes those people incomprehensible to us is that we cannot imagine ourselves instinctively rejecting all pain-behaviour as expressive of pain if it is not accompanied by visible injury' (Malcolm 1982, p. 260).

15. He writes: 'In general, Wittgenstein's philosophy is limited by its lack of consideration of reflective activity' (Lear 1986, p. 280). And again: 'Because he ignores reflective practices Wittgenstein's own philosophical practice must be deficient in self-understanding' (Lear 1986, p. 283).

16. He even goes so far to claim that: 'Even a sympathetic reader of Wittgenstein's later philosophy must, I think, conclude that it represents an unfinished work' (Lear 1986, pp. 267, 283). He goes on to support this view by considering some of Wittgenstein's remarks in the preface of the *Investigations* concerning his inability to 'weld his thoughts together'.

17. With this in mind consider this remark of Putnam's: 'as soon as one tries to state relativism as a position it collapses into inconsistency or into solipsism (or perhaps solipsism with a "we" instead of an "I")' (Putnam 1993, p. 177).

18. Lear sees that the only way to avoid this quandary is to realise that 'the anthropological stance is not what it pretends to be. It is not genuinely an observational stance, it is rather an artefact of philosophical inquiry . . . We take up the anthropological stance not when we actually go out and observe other tribes, but when, in philosophical reflection, we construct various tribal practices and locate rule-following activity within them . . . we discover that the anthropological stance is not at war with transcendental inquiry, it is of a piece with it' (Lear 1986, p. 289). Because of this he says, 'What we are confronted with is not the limit of the world, but the limit of the anthropological stance' (Lear 1986, p. 292).

19. Lear is right to say, 'Perhaps . . . Wittgenstein should have distinguished between we and a form of life in much the same way Kant should have distinguished the "I:" from the "I think". "Form of life" is a predicate which may be predicated of various objects . . . We should eventually come to appreciate that when we talk philosophically about "our form of life" what we are trying to describe is not an object' (Lear 1986, p. 291).

20. Or as he puts it: 'in making manifest the large features of our language, we make manifest the large features of reality' (Davidson 1984, p. 199).

21. He writes, 'A community of minds is the basis of knowledge; it provides the measure of all things. It makes no sense to question that standard or to seek a more ultimate one' (Davidson 1991, p. 264).

22. He tells us: 'It would be good if we could say how language came into existence in the first place, or at least give an account of how an individual learns his first language, given that others in his environment are already linguistically accomplished. These matters are, however, beyond the bounds of reasonable philosophic speculation' (Davidson, 1991, p. 157). As Maker says, 'Our general ability to know and describe what there is – at this juncture – is taken for granted' (Maker 1991, p. 356).

23. It is for this reason that Davidson insists, 'causality plays an indispensable role in determining the content of what we say and believe' (Davidson 1986a, p. 317).

24. As Evnine says, 'Causation . . . is a non-holistic relation between a belief and

an object or event. If we hold that what a belief is about is determined by what causes it, we allow the possibility of a gap between what a belief is about, and what else is believed about that thing' (Evnine 1991, p. 150). Evnine sees Davidson's programme as threatening to endorse a causal variant of the scheme/content distinction, the third dogma of empiricism, which Davidson himself denounces.

25. Davidson tells us, 'Communication depends, then, on each communicant having, and correctly thinking the other has, the concept of a shared world. But the concept of an intersubjective world is the concept of an objective world, a world about which the communicant can have beliefs' (Davidson 1985, p. 480). As he also says, 'We have the idea of belief only from the role of belief in the interpretation of language, for as a private attitude it is not intelligible except as an adjustment to the public norm provided by language' (Davidson 1984, p. 170). Or, in Taylor's words, '[the] "transcendental" condition of our having a grasp on our own language [is] that we in some fashion confront it or relate it to the language of others ... the very confidence that we know what we mean, and hence our having our own original language depends on this relating ... We are induced into language by being brought to see things as our tutors do' (Taylor 1989, p. 38).

26. Davidson acknowledges Wittgenstein's influence on his thought on these matters: 'Someone who has a belief about the world – or anything else – must grasp the concept of objective truth, of what is the case independently of what he or she thinks. We must ask, therefore after the source of the concept of truth. I believe Wittgenstein put us on the track of the only possible answer to this question. The source of the concept of objective truth is interpersonal communication. Thought depends on communication. This follows at once if we suppose that language is essential to thought, and we agree with Wittgenstein that there cannot be a private language' (Davidson 1991, p. 157).

27. Davidson strongly cautions us in several places not to try to further explain truth. 'We should not say that truth is correspondence, coherence, warranted assertability, ideally justified assertability, what is accepted in the conversation of the right people, what science will end up maintaining, what explains convergence on single theories in science, or the success of our ordinary beliefs. To the extent that realism and antirealism depend on one or another of these views of truth we should refuse to endorse either' (Davidson 1990b, p. 309). Elsewhere he writes, '[T]ruth is as clear and as basic a concept we have. Tarski has given us an idea how to apply the general concept (or try to apply it) to particular languages on the assumption that we already understand it; but of course he didn't show how to define it in general (he proved, rather, that this couldn't be done). Any further attempt to explain, define, analyse or explicate the concept will be empty or wrong: correspondence theories, coherence theories, pragmatist theories, theories that identify truth with warranted assertability (perhaps under "ideal" or "optimum" conditions), theories that ask truth to explain the success of science or serve as the ultimate outcome of science or the conversations of some elite, all such theories either add nothing to our understanding of truth or have obvious counter-examples' (Davidson 1990a, pp. 135–6).

28. Lear makes this point well by saying: 'The Metaphysical Subject need not be

conceived, as Kant thought, as lying outside the world, nor, as the early Wittgenstein thought, as its limit: it is we who live in the world. What we are confronted with is not the limit of the world, but the limit of the anthropological stance' (Lear 1986, p. 292).

29. Davidson illustrates what he means here rather nicely: 'If I were bolted to the earth I would have no way of determining the distance from me of many objects. I would only know they were on some line drawn from me toward them. I might interact successful with objects, but I could have no way of giving content to the question where they were. Not being bolted down I am free to triangulate. Our sense of objectivity is the consequence of another sort of triangulation, one that requires two creatures. Each interacts with an object, but what gives each the concept of the way things are objectively is the base line formed between the creatures by language' (Davidson 1985, p. 480).

30. It is for this reason that Ramberg says of Davidson that he 'proclaims himself a realist because the only way to construct a semantic theory of truth, to give the truth conditions of sentences, is to postulate a relation between language and world. But this relation does not serve justificatory purposes of any kind' (Ramberg 1989, p. 47). In fact, he goes on to say, 'Davidson's realism is realistic only in the negative sense that his naturalist semantics leaves no room for idealism' (Ramberg 1989, p. 48).

31. He tells us, 'we no longer need to explain meaning on the basis of possible confrontation' (Davidson 1986a, p. 307). Instead, he has adopted the slogan 'correspondence without confrontation' (Davidson 1986a, p. 307). As he says, 'it is not the speaker who must perform the impossible feat of comparing his belief with reality [i.e., what caused it]; it is the interpreter who must take into account the causal interaction between the world and speaker to find out what the speaker means and hence what he believes' (Davidson 1986b, p. 332). 'My approach is . . . externalist: I suggest that interpretation depends (in the simplest and most basic situations) on the external objects and events salient to both the speaker and the interpreter, the very objects and events the speaker's words are then taken by the interpreter to have as a subject matter. It is the distal stimulus that matters to interpretation' (Davidson 1990b, p. 321).

32. As Rorty puts it, 'if one follows Davidson, one will not know what to make of the issues between realist and anti-realist. For one will feel in touch with reality all the time' (Rorty 1986, p. 145).

33. For example he tells us that, 'Every language-game is based on words "and objects" being recognised again' (*Z*, §455). He says such things as: 'Giving grounds, however, justifying the evidence, comes to an end; – but the end is not certain propositions' striking us immediately as true, i.e., it is not a kind of *seeing* on our part; it is our *acting*, which lies at the bottom of the language-game' (*OC*, §204; emphasis original). And also: 'I want to regard man here as an animal; as a primitive being to which one grants instinct but not ratiocination. As a creature in a primitive state. Any logic good enough for a primitive means of communication needs no apology from us. Language did not emerge from some kind of ratiocination' (*OC*, §475).

34. Smart provides us with an excellent comparison between these two thinkers on just this issue (cf. Smart 1986, pp. 98–100).

35. In the surrounds of this remark Wittgenstein is careful to distinguish between the common-sense man and the common-sense philosopher. As Hacker points out, this is because the commonsense philosopher is likely to be some kind of naive realist of a Johnsonian sort – and hence they will have no power to settle the debate since they are participants in it (cf. Hacker 1986, pp. 226–7). I believe this is connected with Wittgenstein's view that one cannot give a commonsense answer to a philosophical problem (*BBB*, pp. 58–9).

36. In the *Investigations* he makes this explicit by saying: 'the solipsist [does] not want any practical advantage when he advances his view' (*PI* §403; see also *BBB*, p. 59). This follows swift on the heels of remarks which echo points made in *The Blue Book*: '– when . . . we disapprove of the expressions of ordinary language (which are after all performing their office), we have got a picture in our heads which conflicts with the picture of our ordinary way of speaking. Whereas we are tempted to say that our way of speaking does not describe the facts as they really are . . . For this is what disputes between Idealists, Solipsists and Realists look like. The one party attack the normal form of expression as if they were attacking a statement; the others defend it, as if they were stating facts recognised by every reasonable human being' (*PI*, §402). This is why 'A philosophical problem has the form: "I don't know my way about"' (*PI*, §123).

37. Hacker's way of putting this is as follows: 'everything the realist wishes to say can be said; and nothing the transcendental solipsist (idealist) wishes to say can be spoken of. There will be no practical disagreement between them, nor will they quarrel over the truth-values of propositions of ordinary language' (Hacker 1986, p. 104).

38. According to Rorty, this idea was lost when the later Wittgenstein, 'became reconciled to the notion that there was nothing ineffable, and that philosophy, like language, was just a set of indefinitely expandable social practices, not a bounded whole whose periphery might be "shown"' (Rorty 1991, p. 57; emphasis mine). On the later view each move is always a move within language. A better metaphor would be to see language as simply moving forward rather than outward.

39. Rée vividly describes this kind of activity as 'a gorging on reality until one's mental gut [is] fit to burst' (Rée 1997, p. 19).

40. Rée recognises this when he says: 'It makes no sense to say either that subjectivity exists, or that the world exists: subjectivity and the world together create the environment in which questions of existence arise' (Rée 1997, p. 22). And again the reply to those who would cast Wittgenstein in idealist garb is identical to the reply that one could make on Davidson's behalf. It is that, 'Idealism as philosophically interesting and shocking presupposes the intelligibility of a radical, unbridgeable gulf between mind or language and the world in order then to deny it. It presupposes the intelligibility of the radical other inaccessible to language which Davidson has deconstructed' (Maker 1991, p. 360).

41. This is also expressed in Wittgenstein's *Notebooks* with direct reference to idealism: 'In this way idealism leads to realism if it is strictly thought out' (*NB*, p. 85).

42. As he writes: 'The point only becomes clear when one notices the topic

announced by the first words of the book: the *world*. "The world is all that is the case", according to the opening sentence; and as Wittgenstein develops the theme, it turns out that the world must also include possibilities – everything, that is to say, that might have been the case but happens not to be. It is only against the background of these unactualised possibilities that actual facts take shape. But if this is what the world is, then, unlike the facts of which it is the "totality" *the world cannot be pictured'* (Rée 1997, p. 22).

43. I have put the point in what Williams' describes as 'Hume's tone of voice' (Williams 1974, p. 77). Nevertheless, it can be recast easily to fit with what he takes to be Wittgenstein's by saying that it is wrongheaded to even think of looking for such 'things'.

44. He writes: 'The results of philosophy are the uncovering of one or another piece of plain nonsense and of bumps that the understanding has got by running its head up against the limit of language' (*PI*, §119).

45. It lends credence to this interpretation to note, as Hacker does, that the 'archetypal fly in the original flybottle was the solipsist' (Hacker 1986, p. 215). He provides this quotation of Wittgenstein's from his 'Notes for Lectures on "Private Experience" and "Sense Data"': 'The solipsist flutters and flutters in the flyglass, strikes against the walls, flutters further. How can he be brought to rest?' (*NFL*, p. 300). It would seem that when, even in doing philosophy, one does refrain from the use of 'super-concepts', the fly can escape his bottle and philosophy can find peace. We can escape our 'puzzlement' and 'mental discomfort' once we realise that what we are striving for isn't at odds with commonsense – what we crave is just a different way of looking at facts of which we are already quite well aware (cf. *BBB*, p. 59).

Chapter 6

1. As McDowell notes this attitude seems to have transferred to Dummett's one-time protégé. He writes, 'Wright cannot see how a quietistic hostility to constructive philosophy can be warranted: if Wittgenstein reveals tasks for philosophy, he cannot appeal to what now looks like an adventitiously negative view of philosophy's scope to justify not engaging with those tasks' (McDowell 1998, p. 277).

2. This is perhaps easier to see if we consider the following remark from *On Certainty*. He writes: 'Isn't what I am saying: an empirical proposition can be transformed into a postulate – and then becomes a norm of description. But I am suspicious even of this. The sentence is too general. One almost wants to say 'any empirical proposition can, theoretically, be transformed' but what does "theoretically" mean here? It all sounds too reminiscent of the *Tractatus'* (*OC* §321).

3. Indeed, Wittgenstein did not regard our use of concepts to be strictly defined by 'use' alone but also determined by the place of our concepts within the fabric of our lives more broadly (see Diamond 1989).

4. We might even come to suppose that 'the lack of reflection about itself that has characterized analytical philosophy . . . has allowed the old-fashioned and improper conception of its activity to endure, even after strong attacks' (Gomila 1991, p. 91).

5. As Gomila notes, thought experiments are meant to 'enable the explicit formulation of our intuitions by means of a resort to boundary situations' (Gomila 1992, p. 87).

6. Brown quotes from a paper by Graham and Hogan in which they similarly propose that 'we recast our understanding of conceptual analysis as a "broadly *empirical* enterprise" in which "our own introspectively accessible linguistic intuitions" provide *defeasible evidence* about our concepts' (Brown 1999, p. 36; second emphasis mine).

7. Noting this is important since 'Modern analytic philosophers often deny that they rely exclusively on intuitions, but in fact the vast majority of objections to proposed analyses do take the form of complaints that our intuitions show that the analysis fails to match the existing concept' (Miller 2000, p. 233).

8. Of course, as we have seen, philosophers such as Frege have tried to argue on other grounds that the presupposition that concepts have determinate content is justified. They claim this must be so, otherwise we will be left only with similarity and not the strict identity of contents; this would undermine the very possibility of inter-subjective communication, rational decision-making, reasoning and argument itself. I hope to have already cast doubt on this claim in Chapter 4. Yet, without this presumption in place, what warrants the claim that the modes of analysis that are appropriate in this domain should or could be applied to any other?

9. As Miller notes, 'the past forty years of philosophical argument demonstrate that reliance on intuitions will never yield the clarity we seek . . . The ordinary concepts that are of interest to philosophers, the concepts of person, justification, moral agency and so on, are simply too indistinct to function in the premises of serious arguments' (Miller 2000, p. 239).

10. This comparison is doubly pertinent since, 'while some Analytic philosophers appeal to intuitions, others provide arguments instead. But giving arguments in the context of Analytic philosophy rapidly involves disputes over intuitions. Arguments have premises and premises can be challenged. Philosophical arguments always have premises involving debatable philosophical concepts. These premises are typically challenged by putative counterexamples whose legitimacy must be secured. A "successful" counterexample is one that conflicts with the theory at issue and is backed by the "right" intuitions. Therefore the claim that Analytic philosophy can avoid intuitions by sticking to arguments falls flat' (Miller 2000, pp. 233–4).

11. Feyerabend associates this view of the power of proofs with the kind of essence seeking that he thinks gives philosophy a bad name. Specifically, his charge is bound up with its pursuit of essences, which get at 'the Real'. He holds that we live in a rich and varied world, which is 'abundant beyond our wildest imagination' (Feyerabend 1999, p. 3). But exploring, understanding and indeed recognising this richness is precluded by the philosopher's concern to sift 'reality' from 'appearance' and 'essence' from 'accident'. Once we begin to employ such simple dichotomies as these, instead of recognising and tolerantly respecting various genuine alternatives among those available for living, thinking about and engaging with things, we misrepresent the nature of the world and our relation to it. In the hope of developing a single, uniform account of things, we disregard all that will

not fit with it or reduce to it. Although this is often billed as progress towards the 'real', it is in fact nothing but a bias in favour of one way of seeing things over others.

12. Feyerabend concludes that 'Arguments about reality have an 'existential' component: we regard those things as real which play an important role in the kind of life we prefer' (Feyerabend 1999, p. 71).

13. He writes, 'I am sometimes asked – in a tone that suggests that the question is a major objection – why if conceptual analysis is concerned to elucidate what governs our ordinary classificatory practice, don't I advocate doing serious opinion polls on people's responses to various cases? My answer is that I do – when it is necessary. Everyone who presents the Gettier cases to a class of students is doing their own bit of fieldwork, and we all know the answer they get in the vast majority of cases' (Jackson 1998, pp. 36–7).

14. 'The extraordinary situations depicted surprise us, mobilize our intuitions, obliging us to clarify them, to bring to light our implicit knowledge of the concepts in virtue of which we think' (Gomila 1991, p. 88).

15. Brown gives a detailed discussion of the kind of serious disagreement that can break out in this regard by citing debates about causal relations, but he also points to other cases involving 'the analysis of such concepts as perception, truth, good, art and just about any concept to which philosophers have turned their minds' (Brown 1999, p. 39).

16. Few philosophers would hold that what we think before we philosophise is naturally correct. For example in his discussion of the nature of 'coming-to-be' in *On Generation and Corruption,* Aristotle has this to say, 'Coming to be *simpliciter* and perishing come out differently on the common view and on the correct view' (*On Generation and Corruption,* 318^b 27–8). The very idea that there is a correct view, at odds with the common view, indicates that even though we must respect what is 'universally said', we need not accept it as the final court of appeal on all matters. Quite to the contrary, philosophy seeks, *via* dialectic, to reach more secure first principles upon which to rest our understanding.

17. As Miller notes, one reason Strawson was driven to assume that our most basic concepts are 'changeless' is that 'Analysis presumes a stable target' (Miller 2000, p. 235). Or as Gomila remarks, 'if meanings were not fixed . . . then the whole analytical project would have to be abandoned' (Gomila 1991, p. 85).

18. He also writes, 'I am proposing that philosophical reflection on concepts should be recognised as a significantly more creative endeavor than it would appear to be on the usual accounts . . . I am urging that conceptual revision and innovation constitute a respectable and important part of philosophy' (Brown 1999, p. 51).

19. Brandom is clear that 'Concepts by themselves don't express commitments; they only determine what commitments would be undertaken if they were applied' (Brandom 2000, p. 80).

20. Brandom is not shy about advertising the Hegelian character of his thought. He tells us his conception of philosophy is based on 'acknowledging a distinction between things that have *natures* and things that have *histories.* Physical things such as electrons and aromatic compounds would be paradigmatic of the first class, while cultural formations such as English Roman-

tic poetry and Ponzi schemes would be paradigmatic of the second ... Physical, chemical, and biological *things* have histories, but what about the disciplines that define and study them? ... And from here it is a short step (though not, to be sure, an obligatory one) to the thought that natures themselves are the sort of thing that have a history; certainly the concepts "electron" and "aromatic compound" are that sort of thing. At this point the door is opened to a thoroughgoing historicism. It is often thought that this is the point to which Hegel – one of my particular heroes – brought us' (Brandom 2000, p. 74).

21. Houlgate makes this very comparison. He writes, 'Like Wittgenstein, therefore, Hegel wishes us to eschew abstract generalisations and to attend to forms of life in their particularity' (Houlgate 1991, p. 17).

22. As our concepts and practices are so tightly linked, it is correct to think that 'practices can be displaced as well as theories' (Churchland 1993, p. 218). The former are changed due to alterations in the latter and *vice versa*.

23. Brown cites one of my favourite examples in this regard. He writes, 'The recently discovered buckminsterfullerines are a previously unsuspected allotrope of carbon and led to the introduction of a new concept' (Brown 1999, p. 46). This case is interesting precisely because of the intense intellectual resistance there was to reception of this new concept and how it was eventually overcome.

24. Anscombe, for example, notes the important role Aristotle played in developing our concepts by drawing crucial distinctions. She writes, 'consider the concept of relation. Plato had distinguished between what was *per se* (*kath auto*) and what was to something else; Aristotle replaced "to something else" by the simple to "something", for, as we would now say, a thing may stand in relation to itself. Again, the concept of matter is one we owe to Aristotle: such a concept as is implicit in the reasonings of Lavoisier when he re-obtained mercury by heating *mercury calx* (as it was then called) in a closed vessel. The same matter but a change of chemical substance and an increase in how much matter in the vessel was air' (Anscombe 1991, p. 2).

25. For example, 'the development of new knowledge, particularly the development of science, involves the introduction of new ideas, and requires the invention of a new language that is not wholly specifiable in the vocabulary that we already have available' (Brown 1986, p. 295).

26. As Feyerabend notes, 'Absorbing the perception and moods of a new era [concepts] first become ambiguous and then dip over into new meanings' (Feyerabend 1999, p. 126).

27. In defending Sellars, Brown has convincingly argued that what makes it possible to learn 'new' concepts – and in particular new scientific concepts – is that 'the gap between the two languages can be bridged by analogies' (Brown 1986, p. 297).

28. As Feyerabend puts it, 'it was more a foreboding than a concept – but the foreboding engendered new linguistic habits and, eventually, a new linguistic stage with (relatively) clear new concepts (frozen concepts ... are the endpoints of this line of development)' (Feyerabend 1999, p. 124).

29. It is worth reminding ourselves that ' "Similarity", like its close cousin "analogy", is a pragmatic notion, and the comparisons we make will depend on our interests in a particular context' (Brown 1986, p. 302).

30. Because they cling to the idea that meaning is defined by its 'use' understood solely in terms of its appropriate inferential connections, 'Many philosophers find the suggestion that concepts undergo change to be virtually unintelligible, maintaining instead that it only makes sense to talk of concepts being replaced by different concepts' (Brown 1986, p. 302).

31. Wittgenstein asks of seeing and hearing, 'what kind of connexions and analogies exist?' (*Z* §475)? After some discussion, he concludes, 'I might also have said earlier: The tie-up between imaging and seeing is close; but there is no similarity. The language-games employing these concepts are radically different – but hang together' (*Z* §625).

32. I have tried to show this *in detail* in my previous work with respect to our understanding of intentionality and conceptual content in *The Presence of Mind* and consciousness in *Beyond Physicalism*.

33. Clarifications can be better or worse, more or less complete. For example, Frege's explication of logic is superior to that of Aristotle's. Yet although we can compare them, neither can be regarded as speculative proposals about some independent subject matter.

34. Review the merits of this proposal in light of Feyerabend's condemnation of a recent appeal made by prominent philosophers and scientists which asked, 'all parliaments and governments of the world to introduce, support, and underwrite with full force the study of philosophy and its history and the related history of the natural humane sciences' (Feyerabend 1999, p. 269). In particular, he is scathing about the way the authors of this document claim that such study is necessary for 'every genuine encounter between peoples and cultures' and for 'the creation of new categories to overcome existing contradictions', all of which will enable us to 'direct humanity on the path of goodness'. It is not just that Feyerabend is embarrassed by the bold rhetoric and hyperbole of these sorts of claims; he is much more sceptical of the fruits of philosophy in general. He writes, 'Philosophy is not a single Good Thing that is bound to enrich human existence; it is a witches' brew, containing some rather nasty ingredients' (Feyerabend 1999, p. 269). In his eyes, philosophy is not obviously a 'good' thing at all. He charges its pursuit with the stifling of the human situation as opposed to enriching it. He concludes his condemnation of the appeal by suggesting that philosophers should only concern themselves primarily with moral and political issues in order to show 'that philosophy is more than an autistic concern with empty generalities' (Feyerabend 1999, p. 273). He proposes they ought to concern themselves with certain important but rather 'obvious' ethical issues by asking governments to step in and do something about the serious problems of hunger, disease and environmental disasters. I find this suggestion about what philosophers ought to do unimaginative and disappointing. In many respects it amounts to nothing short of abdicating our responsibility in a different way. For surely to be effective such appeals would require us to first change the thinking and habits of those to whom we would make such an appeal. I suggest one important way that might happen is through the study of philosophy.

35. This connects, I believe, with Wittgenstein's claim that philosophical errors primarily involve the will, not the intellect (cf. Diamond, 1995, p. 21).

References

Allison, Henry E. *Kant's Transcendental Idealism: An Interpretation and Defense*. New Haven: Yale University Press, 1983.

Anscombe, Elizabeth. *An Introduction to Wittgenstein's Tractatus*. Philadelphia: University of Pennsylvania Press, 1959.

——'Wittgenstein: Whose Philosopher?' In *Wittgenstein Cententary Essays*, edited by P. Griffiths. Cambridge: Cambridge University Press, 1991.

Aquinas, Thomas. 'Five Proofs for the Existence of God'. In *Reason at Work*, edited by Stephen M. Cahn, Patricia Kitcher and George Sher. Orlando: Harcourt Brace Jovanovich, 1984.

Aristotle. *The Complete Works of Aristotle: The Revised Oxford Translation*. Edited by J. Barnes. Princeton, NJ: Princeton University Press, 1984.

Baldwin, Thomas. *G.E. Moore*. London: Routlege, 1990.

Barrett, Cyril. *Wittgenstein on Ethics and Religious Belief*. Oxford: Basil Blackwell, 1991.

Beaney, Michael. *Frege: Making Sense*. London: Duckworth, 1996.

——'Conceptions of Analysis in Early Analytic Philosophy'. *Acta Analytica* (2000): 15(25) 97–115.

Bell, David. 'The Revolution of Moore and Russell: A Very British Coup?' In *German Philosophy since Kant*, edited by Anthony O'Hear. Cambridge: Cambridge University Press, 1999.

Bencivenga, Ermanno. *Hegel's Dialectical Logic*. New York: Oxford University Press, 2000.

Bishop, Michael A. 'The Possibility of Conceptual Clarity in Philosophy'. *American Philosophical Quarterly* 29, no. 3 (1992): 267–77.

Blackburn, Simon. 'The Individual Strikes Back'. In *Rule-Following and Realism*, edited by Alexander Miller and Crispin Wright, 28–44. Chesham: Acumen, 2002.

Bloor, David. 'The Question of Linguistic Idealism Revisited'. In *The Cambridge Companion to Wittgenstein*, edited by Hans Sluga. Needham Heights: Cambridge, 1996.

——*Wittgenstein, Rules and Institutions*. London: Routledge, 1997.

Boghossian, Paul A. 'The Rule-Following Considerations'. In *Rule-Following and Meaning*, edited by Alexander Miller and Crispin Wright. Chesham: Acumen, 2002.

Bowie, Andrew. 'German Philosophy Today: Between Idealism, Romanticism and Pragmatism'. In *German Philosophy since Kant*, edited by A. O'Hear. Cambridge: Cambridge University Press, 1999.

Brandom, Robert. *Making It Explicit*. Cambridge, Mass: Harvard University Press, 1994.

——'Precis of Making it Explicit'. *Philosophy and Phenomenological Research* LVII, no. 1 (1997): 153–6.

——'Reason, Expression and the Philosophic Enterprise'. In *What Is Philosophy?*, edited by C.P. Ragland and Sarah Heidt. New Haven and London: Yale University Press, 2000.

Bricke, John. 'Consciousness and Dennett's Intentionalist Net'. *Philosophical Studies* 48 (1985).

Brockhaus, R. *Pulling up the Ladder. The Metaphysical Roots of Wittgenstein's Tractatus*. Chicago and La Salle: Open Court, 1991.

Brown, Harold I. 'Sellars, Concepts and Conceptual Change'. *Synthese* 68 (1986): 275–307.

——'Why Do Conceptual Analysts Disagree?' *Metaphilosophy* 30, no. 1–2 (1999): 33–59.

Burbidge, John. 'Hegel's Conception of Logic'. In *The Cambridge Companion to Hegel*, edited by Fredrick C. Besier. Cambridge: Cambridge University Press, 1993.

Burge, Tyler. 'Frege on Knowing the Third Realm'. In *Early Analytic Philosophy*, edited by W. Tait. Chicago and La Salle, Illnois: Open Court, 1997.

Carl, Wolfgang. *Frege's Theory of Sense and Reference: Its Origins and Scope*. Cambridge: Cambridge University Press, 1994.

Churchland, Paul M. 'Evaluating Our Self Conception'. *Mind and Language* (1993): 8(2) 211–22.

Coffa, J. Alberto. *The Semantic Tradition from Kant to Carnap: To the Vienna Station*. Cambridge: Cambridge University Press, 1991.

Conant, James. 'Must We Show What We Cannot Say?' In *The Senses of Stanely Cavell*, edited by R. Fleming and M. Payne. Lewisbury, PA: Bucknell University Press, 1989.

——'The Search for Logically Alien Thought: Descartes, Kant, Frege and the Tractatus'. *Philosophical Topics* 20 (1991): 115–80.

——'Kierkegaard, Wittgenstein and Nonsense'. In *The Anxieties of Reason. In Pursuits of Reason.*, edited by T. Cohen, P. Guyer and H. Putnam. Texas: Texas Tech University Press, 1993.

——'Putting Two and Two Together: Kierkegaard, Wittgenstein and the Point of View for Their Works as Authors'. In *Philosophy and the Grammar of Religious Belief*, edited by T. Tessin and M. von der Ruhr. Basingstoke: Macmillan, 1995.

——'Elucidation and Nonsense in Frege and Early Wittgenstein'. In *The New Wittgenstein*, edited by A. Crary and R. Read. London: Routledge, 2000.

Crary, A. and R. Read eds. *The New Wittgenstein*. London: Routledge, 2000.

Davidson, Donald. *Inquiries into Truth and Interpretation*. New York: Oxford University Press, 1984.

——'Rational Animals'. In *Actions and Events*, edited by Ernest Le Pore, 473–81. Oxford: Blackwell, 1985.

——'A Coherence Theory of Truth and Knowledge'. In *Truth and Interpretation: Perspectives on the Philosophy of Donald Davidson*. Cambridge: Blackwell, 1986a.

——'Empirical Content'. In *Truth and Interpretation: Perspectives on the Philosophy of Donald Davidson*. Cambridge: Blackwell, 1986b.

——'The Structure and Content of Truth'. *Journal of Philosophy* (1990a): 87(6) 279–328.

——'Afterthoughts, 1987'. In *Reading Rorty: Critical Responses to Philosophy and the Mirror of Nature (and Beyond)*, edited by E. Lepore. Oxford: Blackwell, 1990b.

——'Three Varieties of Knowledge'. In *A J Ayer Memorial Essays*, edited by Phillip Griffiths. New York: Cambridge University Press, 1991.

Dennett, Daniel C. 'Quining Qualia'. In *Mind and Cognition*, edited by William Lycan. Oxford: Blackwell, 1990.

———*Consciousness Explained*. London: Penguin Books, 1991a.

———'Granny's Campaign for Safe Science'. In *Meaning in Mind: Fodor and His Critics*, edited by Barry Loewer. Cambridge: Blackwell, 1991b.

———'Living on the Edge'. *Inquiry* (1993): 36(1–2) 135–59.

Diamond, Cora. 'Rules: Looking in the Right Place'. In *Wittgenstein: Attention to Particulars*, edited by D.Z. Phillips and P. Winch, 12–34, 1989.

———'Ethics, Imagination and the Method of Wittgenstein's *Tractatus*'. In *Bilder Der Philosophie*, edited by R. Heinrich and H. Vetter, 55–90. Vienna and Munich: Oldenburg, 1991.

———*The Realistic Spirit: Wittgenstein, Philosophy and the Mind*. Cambridge, MA: MIT Press, 1995.

Dummett, Michael. *Truth and Other Enigmas*. London: Duckworth, 1978.

———*Origins of Analytical Philosophy*. London: Duckworth, 1993.

Ebbs, Gary. *Rule-Following and Realism*. Cambridge, Mass: Harvard University Press, 1997.

Evnine, Simon. *Donald Davidson*. Cambridge: Polity Press, 1991.

Fellows, R. and A. O'Hear. 'Consciousness Avoided'. *Inquiry* 36 (1993).

Feyerabend, Paul. *The Conquest of Abundance*. Chicago: University of Chicago Press, 1999.

Fine Arthur. 'The Natural Ontological Attitude'. In *Scientific Realism*, edited by J. Leplin. Berketey: University of California Press, 1984.

Finch, Henry. *Wittgenstein: The Later Philosophy: An Exposition of the 'Philosophical Invesitigations'*. New Jersey: Humanities Press, 1977.

Fodor, Jerry A. *A Theory of Content and Other Essays*. Cambridge, Mass: MIT Press, 1990.

Fodor, Jerry A. and E. Lepore. *Holism: A Shopper's Guide*. Oxford: Blackwell, 1992.

Fogelin, Robert. *Pyrrhonian Reflections on Knowledge and Justification*. Oxford: Oxford University Press, 1994.

Forbes, Graham. 'Skepticism and Semantic Knowledge'. In *Rule-Following and Meaning*, edited by Alexander Miller and Crispin Wright, 16–27. Chesham: Acumen, 2002.

Frege, Gottlob. *The Basic Laws of Arithmetic: Exposition of the System*. Translated by Montgomery Furth. Berkeley: University of California Press, 1964.

———*Posthumous Writings*. Translated by Peter Long and Roger White. Edited by Hans Hermes and Friedrich Kaulbach. Oxford: Blackwell, 1979.

———*Foundations of Arithmetic: A Logico-Mathematical Inquiry into the Concept of Number*. Translated by J.L. Austin. Oxford: Blackwell, 1980.

———*Collected Papers on Mathematics, Logic & Philosophy*. Translated by B. McGuinness. Oxford: Blackwell, 1984.

———'The Thought: A Logical Inquiry'. In *Propositions and Attitudes*, edited by N. Salmon and S. Soames. Oxford: Oxford University Press, 1988 [1918–19].

Friedlander, Eli. *Signs of Sense: Reading Wittgenstein's Tractatus*. Cambridge, Mass: Harvard University Press, 2001.

Gadamer, Hans-Georg. 'The Nature of Things and the Language of Things'. In *Philosophical Hermeneutics*, Berkeley: University of California Press, 1976.

Gefwert, Christoffer. *Wittgenstein's on Thought, Language and Philosophy*. Aldershot: Ashgate, 2000.

Genova, Judith. *Wittgenstein: A Way of Seeing*. London: Routledge, 1995.

Gert, Heather J. 'Wittgenstein on Description'. *Philosophical Studies* (1997): 88(3) 221–43.

Goldfarb, Warren. 'Wittgenstein on the Fixity of Meaning'. In *Early Analytic Philosophy*, edited by W. Tait, 75–90. Chicago and La Salle: Open Court, 1997.

——'Kripke on Wittgenstein on Rules'. In *Rule-Following and Meaning*, edited by Alexander Miller and Crispin Wright, 92–107. Chesham: Acumen, 2002.

Goldstein, Laurence. *Clear and Queer Thinking: Wittgenstein's Development and His Relevance to Modern Thought*. London: Duckworth, 1999.

Gomila, Antoni. 'What is a Thought Experiment?' *Metaphilosophy* (1991): 84–92.

Griffin, Nicholas. 'Denoting Concepts in the Principles of Mathematics'. In *Bertrand Russell and the Origins of Analytical Philosophy*, edited by Ray Monk and Anthony Palmer. Bristol: Thoemmes Press, 1996.

Guyer, Paul. 'Thought and Being: Hegel's Critique of Kant's Theoretical Philosophy'. In *The Cambridge Companion to Hegel*, edited by Frederick C. Beiser. Cambridge: Cambridge University Press, 1993.

Hacker, P.M.S. *Insight and Illusion*. Oxford: Oxford University Press, 1986.

——'Was He Trying to Whistle It?' In *The New Wittgenstein*, edited by A. Crary and R. Read. London: Routledge, 2000.

Hamlyn, D.W. *Metaphysics*. Oxford: Blackwell, 1984.

Hanna, Robert. *Kant and the Foundations of Analytic Philosophy*. Oxford: Oxford University Press, 2001.

Hegel, G.W.F. *The Encyclopaedia Logic*. Translated by T.F. Geraets, W.A. Suchting and H.S. Harris. Indianapolis: Hackett, 1770–1831.

——*Science of Logic*. Translated by W.H. Johnston and L.G. Struthers. London: George Allen and Unwin, 1929.

Heidegger, Martin. *Being and Time*. Translated by Macquarrie and Robinson. New York: Harper & Row, 1962.

Houlgate, Stephen. *Freedom, Truth and History*. London: Routledge, 1991.

——'Substance, Causality, and the Question of Method in Hegel's "Science of Logic"'. In *The Reception of Kant's Critical Philosophy: Fichte, Schelling, and Hegel*, edited by Sally Sedgwick. Cambridge: Cambridge University Press, 2000.

Hutto, Daniel D. *The Presence of Mind*. Amsterdam and Philadelphia: John Benjamins, 1999.

——*Beyond Physicalism*. Amsterdam and Philadelphia: John Benjamins, 2000.

Hylton, Peter. *Russell, Idealism and the Emergence of Analytic Philosophy*. Oxford: Clarendon Press, 1990.

——'Functions, Operations and Sense in Wittgenstein's *Tractatus*'. In *Early Analytic Philosophy*, edited by W. Tait, 91–105. Chicago: Open Court, 1997.

Jackson, Frank. *From Metaphysics to Ethics: A Defence of Conceptual Analysis*. Oxford: Oxford University Press, 1998.

Jaquette, Dale. 'Wittgenstein and the Colour Incompatibility Problem'. *History of Philosophy Quarterly* 7, no. 3 (1990): 353–65.

Johnson, Paul. *Wittgenstein: Rethinking the Inner*. London: Routledge, 1993.

Joseph, Marc A. 'Mental Representation and the Metaphysics of Meaning in Wittgenstein's *Tractatus*'. *Philosophical Investigations* 23, no. 2 (2000): 122–46.

Kant, Immanuel. *Critique of Pure Reason*. Translated by Paul Guyer and Allen Wood. Cambridge: Cambridge University Press, 1998.

Kindi, Vassiliki. 'Is Wittgenstein's Resort to Ordinary Language an Appeal to Empirical Facts?' *Metaphilosophy* 29, no. 4 (1998): 298–305.

Kirk, Robert. ' "The Best Set of Tools?" Dennett's Metaphors and the Mind-Body Problem'. *The Philosophical Quarterly* 43, no. 172 (1993).

Klagge, James C. 'Wittgenstein and Neuroscience'. *Synthese* 78, no. 3 (1989): 319–43.

Koethe, John. *The Continuity of Wittgenstein's Thought*. Ithaca, NY: Cornell University Press, 1996.

Kripke, Saul A. *Wittgenstein on Rules and Private Language*. Oxford: Blackwell, 1982.

Langton, Rae. *Kantian Humility: Our Ignorance of Things in Themselves*. Oxford: Oxford University Press, 1998.

Lear, Jonathan. 'Transcendental Anthropology'. In *Subject, Thought and Context*, edited by P. Pettitand and J. McDowell. Oxford: Clarendon Press, 1986.

Locke, John. *An Essay Concerning Human Understanding*. London: William Tegg, 1689.

Lockwood, Michael. 'Dennett's Mind'. *Inquiry* 36 (1993).

Luckhardt, C.G. ed. *Wittgenstein: Sources and Perspectives*. Bristol: Thoemmes Press, 1996.

Maddy, Penelope. 'A Naturalistic Look at Logic'. *Proceedings and Addresses of the American Philosophical Association* 76, no. 2 (2002): 61–90.

Maker, William. 'Davidson's Transcendental Arguments'. *Philosophy and Phenomenological Research* LI, no. 2 (1991).

Malcolm, Norman. 'Wittgenstein and Idealism'. In *Idealism: Past and Present*, edited by Vesey. Cambridge: Cambridge University Press, 1982.

———*Nothing is Hidden*. Oxford: Blackwell, 1986.

Mayer, Verena. 'The Numbering System in the *Tractatus*'. *Ratio* 6., no. 2 (1993): 108–20.

McCulloch, Gregory. *The Game of the Name*. Oxford: Oxford University Press, 1989.

McDonough, Richard. 'A Note on Frege's and Russell's Influence on Wittgenstein's *Tractatus*'. *Russell* 14, no. 3 (1994): 39–46.

McDowell, John. *Mind and World*. Cambridge, MA: Harvard University Press, 1994.

———'Brandom on Representation and Inference'. *Philosophy and Phenomenological Research* LVII, no. 1 (1997): 157–62.

———'Wittgenstein on Following a Rule'. In *Mind, Value and Reality*. Cambridge, MA: Harvard University Press, 1998.

McGinn, Colin. *Wittgenstein on Meaning*. Oxford: Blackwell, 1984.

McGinn, Marie. *Wittgenstein and the Philosophical Investigations*. London: Routledge, 1997.

———'Between Elucidation and Therapy'. *Philosophical Quarterly* (1999).

McGuinness, Brian. 'The Grundgedanke of the *Tractatus*'. In *Understanding Wittgenstein, Royal Institute of Philosophy Lectures*. London: Macmillan, 1976.

Medina, Jose. *The Unity of Wittgenstein's Philosophy*. Albany, NY: SUNY Press, 2002.

Miller, Richard B. 'Without Intuitions'. *Metaphilosophy* (2000): 31(3) 231–50.

Minar, Edward H. 'Wittgenstein and the "Contingency" of Community'. *Pacific Philosophical Quarterly* (1991): 72(3) 203–34.

Monk, Ray and Anthony Palmer, eds. *Bertrand Russell and the Origins of Analytical Philosophy*. Bristol: Thoemmes Press, 1996.

Moore, G.E. 'Refutation of Idealism'. In *Philosophical Studies*. London: Routlege & Kegan Paul, 1922.

Moser, Paul K. *Philosophy after Objectivity: Making Sense in Perspective*. Oxford: Oxford Univerisity Press, 1993.

Mounce, H.O. *Wittgenstein's Tractatus*. Oxford: Blackwell, 1981.

Needham, Rodney. *Belief, Language and Experience*. Oxford: Blackwell, 1972.

Noonan, Harold. 'The "Gray's Elegy" Argument – and Others'. In *Bertrand Russell and the Origins of Analytical Philosophy*, edited by Ray Monk and Anthony Palmer. Bristol: Thoemmes Press, 1996.

Ostrow, Matthew B. *Wittgenstein's Tractatus: A Dialectical Interpretation*. Cambridge: Cambridge University Press, 2002.

Papineau, David. *Philosophical Naturalism*. Oxford: Blackwell, 1993.

Pears, David. *The False Prison: A Study of the Development of Wittgenstein's Philosophy:* Volume 1. Oxford: Clarendon Press, 1987.

——— *The False Prison: A Study of the Development of Wittgenstein's Philosophy*, Volume 2. New York: Clarendon Oxford, 1988.

Peregrin, Jaroslav. '"Fregean" Logic and "Russellian" Logic.' *Australasian Journal of Philosophy* (2000): 78(4) 557–74.

Peterson, Donald. *Wittgenstein's Early Philosophy: Three Sides of the Mirror*. Toronto: University of Toronto Press, 1990.

Pettit, Philip. 'The Reality of Rule Following'. *Mind*, no. 99 (1990): 1–21.

Phillips, D.Z. *Philosophy's Cool Place*. Ithaca and London: Cornell University Press, 1999.

Pippin, Robert. *Hegel's Idealism: The Satisfactions of Self-Consciousness*. Cambridge: Cambridge University Press, 1989.

Pleasants, Nigel. 'Winch and Wittgenstein on Understanding Ourselves Critically: Descriptive Not Metaphysical'. *Inquiry* 43 (2000): 289–318.

Putnam, Hilary. *Representation and Reality*. Cambridge, MA: MIT Press, 1987.

——— *Renewing Philosophy*. Cambridge, MA: Harvard University Press, 1993.

Quine, W.V. *The Ways of Paradox and Other Essays*. Cambridge, MA: Harvard Univerisity Press, 1966.

——— 'Two Dogmas in Retrospect'. *Canadian Journal of Philosophy* 21 (1991).

Ramberg, Bjorn T. *Donald Davidson's Philosophy of Language: An Introduction*. Oxford: Basil Blackwell, 1989.

Read, Rupert and Robert Deans. 'Nothing Is Shown'. *Philosophical Investigations* (forthcoming).

Reck, Erich. 'Frege's Influence on Wittgenstein: Reversing Metaphysics Via the Context Principle'. In *Early Analytic Philosophy*, edited by W. Tait. Chicago and La Salle: Open Court, 1997.

Rée Jonathan. 'Subjectivity in the Twentieth Century? In *Ethics and the Subject*, edited by Karl Summs. Amsterdam: Rodopi, 1997.

Reid, Lynette. 'Wittgenstein's Ladder: *The Tractatus* and Nonsense'. *Philosophical Investigations* 21 (1998): 97–151.

Root, Michael. 'Davidson and Social Science'. In *Truth and Interpretation: Perspectives on the Philosophy of Donald Davidson*, edited by Ernest Lepore. Oxford: Blackwell, 1986.

Rorty, Richard. 'Pragmatism, Davidson and Truth'. In *Objectivity, Relativism and Truth: Philosophical Papers I*. Cambridge: Cambridge University Press, 1986.

——— 'Wittgenstein, Heidegger and the Reification of Language'. In *Essays on*

Heidegger and Others: Philosophical Papers Ii. Cambridge: Cambridge University Press, 1991.

———*Truth and Progress.* Cambridge: Cambridge University Press, 1998.

Russell, Bertrand. *Principles of Mathematics.* London: Routledge, 1903.

———'On Denoting'. In *Logic and Knowledge,* edited by R.C. Marsh. London: Unwin Hyman, 1905.

———*The Problems of Philosophy.* Oxford: Oxford University Press, 1912.

———*Our Knowledge of the External World.* London: Routledge, 1914.

———'The Philosophy of Logical Atomism'. In *Logic and Knowledge,* edited by Robert C. Marsh. London: Unwin Hyman, 1918.

———'Logical Atomism'. In *Logic and Knowledge,* edited by Charles Robert Marsh. London: Unwin Hyman, 1924.

———*My Philosophical Development.* London: Routledge, 1959.

———*Autobiography.* London: George, Allen & Unwin, 1967.

———*Theory of Knowledge: The 1913 Manuscript.* London: Routledge, 1992.

Sainsbury, Mark. *Russell.* London: Routledge, 1979.

Schulte, Joachim. *Wittgenstein.* Albany, NY: SUNY Press, 1992.

———*Experience and Expression: Wittgenstein's Philosophy of Psychology.* Oxford: Oxford University Press, 1993.

Seager, William. 'Verificationism, Scepticism and Consciousness'. *Inquiry* 36 (1993).

Searle, John. *The Rediscovery of the Mind.* Cambridge, MA: MIT Press, 1992.

Shogenji, Tomoji. 'The Problem of the Criterion in Rule-Following'. *Philosophy and Phenomenological Research* LX, no. 3 (2000): 501–25.

Smart, J.C.C. 'How to Turn the *Tractatus* Wittgenstein into (Almost) Donald Davidson'. In *Truth and Interpretation: Perspectives on the Philosophy of Donald Davidson,* edited by E. Lepore. Oxford: Basil Blackwell, 1986.

Stroll, Avrum. *Moore and Wittgenstein on Certainty.* New York: Oxford University Press, 1994.

———*Sketches of Landscapes: Philosophy by Example.* Cambridge, MA: MIT Press, 1998.

———*Wittgenstein.* Oxford: One World Press, 2002.

Stueber, Karsten R. 'Practice, Indeterminacy and Private Language: Wittgenstein's Dissolution of Scepticism'. *Philosophical Investigations* (1994): 17(1) 14–36.

Taylor, Charles. *Sources of the Self.* Cambridge: Cambridge University Press, 1989.

Travis, Charles. *The Uses of Sense: Wittgenstein's Philosophy of Language.* Oxford: Oxford University Press, 1989.

Tye, Michael. 'Reflections on Dennett and Consciousness'. *Philosophy and Phenomenological Research* LIII, no. 4 (1993): 895–6.

Williams, Bernard. 'Wittgenstein and Idealism'. In *Understanding Wittgenstein.* Cambridge: Cambridge University Press, 1974.

Williams, Meredith. *Wittgenstein: Mind and Meaning: Toward a Social Conception of Mind.* London: Routledge, 1998.

Wittgenstein, Ludwig. *Tractatus Logico-Philosophicus.* Translated by D.F. Pears and B. McGuinness. London: Routledge, 1922.

———*Philosophical Investigations.* Translated by G.E.M. Anscombe. Oxford: Basil Blackwell, 1953.

———*The Blue and Brown Books: Preliminary Studies for the Philosophical Investigations.* Oxford: Blackwell, 1958.

Wittgenstein, Ludwig. *Zettel*. Translated by G.E.M. Anscombe. Edited by G.E.M
Anscombe and G.H. Von Wright. 2nd edition. Oxford: Basil Blackwell, 1967.
——'Notes for Lectures on Private Experience and Sense Data'. *Philosophical
Review* (1968): 77, 275–320.
——*Notebooks, 1914–1916*. Translated by G.E.M. Anscombe. Edited by G.H.
Von Wright and G.E.M. Anscombe. 2nd edition. Oxford: Blackwell, 1969.
——*On Certainty*. Translated by Paul Denis and G.E.M. Anscombe. Edited by
G.E.M. Anscombe and G.H. Von Wright. Oxford: Basil Blackwell, 1974.
——*Lectures on the Foundations of Mathematics*. Edited by Cora Diamond.
Chicago: Chicago Univerisity Press, 1975.
——*Wittgenstein and the Vienna Circle: Conversations Recorded by Fredrich
Waismann*. Translated by Joachim Schulte and Brian McGuinness. New York:
Barnes and Noble, 1979.
——*Culture and Value*. Translated by P. Winch. Edited by G.H. Von Wright.
Chicago: University of Chicago Press, 1980.
——*Remarks on the Philosophy of Psychology*, Volume 1. Edited by G.E.M.
Anscombe and G.H. Von Wright. Oxford: Basil Blackwell, 1980.
——*Remarks on the Philosophy of Psychology*, Volume 2. Edited by G.H. Von
Wright and Heikki Nyman. Oxford: Blackwell, 1980.
——*Last Writings on the Philosophy of Psychology:* Volume I. Oxford: Basil
Blackwell, 1982.
——*Remarks on the Foundations of Mathematics*. Translated by G.E.M.
Anscombe. Oxford: Blackwell, 1983.
——*Last Writings on the Philosophy of Psychology Volume 2: The Inner and the
Outer*. Edited by G.H. Von Wright and Heikki Nyman. Regardant ed.
Cambridge: Blackwell, 1992.
Wright, Crispin. *Truth and Objectivity*. Cambridge, MA: Harvard University Press,
1993.
——*Rails to Infinity: Essay on Themes from Wittgenstein's Philosophical Investiga-
tions*. Cambridge, MA: Harvard University Press, 2001.
——'Critical Notice of Mcginn's *Wittgenstein on Meaning*'. In *Rule-Following and
Meaning*, edited by Alexander Miller and Crispin Wright, 108–28. Chesham:
Acumen, 2002.

Index